Scenic Routes & Byways™

# CALIFORNIA'S
# PACIFIC COAST

## Help Us Keep This Guide Up to Date

We would love to hear from you concerning your experiences with this guide and how you feel it could be improved and kept up to date. Please send your comments and suggestions to:

editorial@GlobePequot.com

Thanks for your input, and happy travels!

SEVENTH EDITION

# Scenic Routes & Byways™
# CALIFORNIA'S PACIFIC COAST

## STEWART M. GREEN

gpp® travel

Guilford, Connecticut

To buy books in quantity for corporate use or incentives, call **(800) 962-0973** or e-mail **premiums@GlobePequot.com**.

Photography by Stewart M. Green
Photography on pages x, 19, 56, 93, 107, 111, 113, 120, 122, 123, 125, 127, 129, 136, 238 licensed by Shutterstock.com

Editor: Amy Lyons
Project Editor: Staci Zacharski
Layout: Casey Shain
Maps: Alena Joy Pearce © Morris Book Publishing, LLC

Library of Congress Cataloging-in-Publication data is available on file.

ISBN 978-0-7627-8105-8

Printed in the United States of America
10 9 8 7 6 5 4 3 2 1

*McWay Falls drops onto a lonely beach at Jules Pfeiffer Burns State Park.*

# CONTENTS

## The Scenic Routes & Byways

*Wildflowers cover bluffs at Pescadero State Beach.*

*Rock benches at Spooner's Cove at Montaña de Oro State Park
are perfect for tidepooling adventures.*

*Point Pinos Lighthouse at Pacific Grove was built in 1855.*

*Waves surge over coastal rocks and stacks at Glass Beach in Fort Bragg.*

*Cayucos Pier juts into Pacific surf at the beach town of Cayucos.*

*The Big Sur Coast is a lonely, remote, and rugged meeting of land and ocean.*

# Legend

| | | | |
|---|---|---|---|
| Interstate Highway/ Featured Interstate Highway | | | |
| US Highway/ Featured US Highway | | | |
| State Highway/ Featured State Highway | | | |
| County Road/ Featured County Road | | | |
| Local Road/ Featured Local Road | | | |
| Railroad | | | |
| Trail | | | |

| | | | |
|---|---|---|---|
| Airport | + | Lighthouse | |
| Bridge | | Museum | |
| Building or Structure | ■ | Picnic Area | |
| Capital | ⊛ | Point of Interest | ▫ |
| Campground | ▲ | Scenic Area/Overlook | |
| Cemetery | | Small State Park, Wilderness or Natural Area | |
| City | ◉ | Town | ○ |
| Cliff | | Trailhead | ⑩ |
| Dam | — | Visitor, Interpretive Center | ? |
| Gap/Pass | ) ( | Waterfall | |
| Historic Site | | | |

Mountain, Peak, or Butte ▲ Stony Man Mountain 4,010 ft.

River, Creek, or Drainage

Marsh

Body of Water

State Line  VIRGINIA

National/State Park Area

National/State Forest Area

Wilderness/Wildlife/Natural Area

Miscellaneous Area

# ABOUT THE AUTHOR

**Stewart M. Green,** a Colorado native, is a photographer and writer based in Colorado Springs, Colorado. He travels the US and the world working on projects for Globe Pequot Press and other publications. Stewart has written and photographed many books for FalconGuides and Globe Pequot Press, including *Rock Climbing Colorado, Rock Climbing Utah, Rock Climbing New England, Scenic Driving California, Scenic Driving Arizona, Rock Climbing Europe, Best Climbs Moab, Best Climbs Rocky Mountain National Park, KNACK Rock Climbing,* and *Scenic Routes & Byways New England.* He has over 35 years of experience as a photographer and is a leading climbing photographer. His work appears in many catalogs, advertisements, and national publications. Stewart is also the Guide to Climbing at About .com, climbing.about.com.

# ACKNOWLEDGMENTS

*Scenic Routes & Byways: California's Pacific Coast* details one of life's greatest adventures—driving the restless boundary between ocean and land on the western rim of North America. This book is partly based on my book *California Scenic Drives,* which Falcon Publishing originally published in 1993. The book was republished as *Scenic Driving California* in 1996. This new volume, packed with lots of information and stunning color photographs, explores the wild and scenic California coast from Santa Barbara north to the Oregon border.

Thanks to Globe Pequot Press for the opportunity to write about California, one of my favorite places to discover, especially its gorgeous coast. Also thanks to my editors on the two previous editions—Randall Green, Liz Taylor, and Cary Hull—for helpful comments and suggestions. Many thanks to Amy Lyons, Globe Pequot's Editorial Director for travel books, for suggesting I write this book and project editor Staci Zacharski who shepherded the book through the editorial process. Thanks also to fellow FalconGuide author Susan Joy Paul for editorial suggestions and comments. Editors make us writers better; I always appreciate their efforts and direction.

I'm grateful to many federal and state employees and rangers in California who generously dispensed information, answered questions, and reviewed portions of the manuscript for accuracy. Thanks to Martha Morris for help with my second edition and important map work. Thanks to friends in California who gave me suggestions about favorite places, particularly Cindy and John McCaffrey in Danville. Cindy, a world-class triathlete and fellow climber, was severely injured in a car accident while finishing a bike ride in May, 2013, and spent months in rehab before going home. I look forward to climbing with you again.

Lastly, thanks to my sons Ian and Brett Spencer-Green for driving up and down the California coast with me back in the early 1990s. We had lots of great adventures—climbing sea cliffs, swimming clear rivers, walking on wave-swept sand beaches, and watching a summer of sunsets. Now go and find your own great escape on the California coast.

# INTRODUCTION

The grandness of nature defines the 1,100-mile-long Pacific coast of California with a dramatic meeting of earth, sky, and sea. While the southern crescent-shaped coast bordering the great metropolises of Los Angeles, San Diego, and their sprawling suburbs is generally civilized with golden sand beaches and easy accessibility to the masses, the long stretch of ragged shoreline from Santa Barbara north to the Oregon border is spectacularly scenic and mostly unpopulated.

This is a wild coast of rocky headlands, wave-polished cliffs that collide with turbulent seas, pocket beaches scrubbed by emerald tides, crying seagulls and barking sea lions, offshore rocks and wind-beaten sea stacks, towering redwoods that scrape against the sky itself, and a twisting ribbon of asphalt that allows us a glimpse into eternity. This ancient dynamic landscape is split by the San Andreas Fault, one of California's major geographic features, and defined by coastal mountain ranges, broad bays, intimate coves, jutting peninsulas, and steep cliffs that hold back the relentless waves of the Pacific Ocean.

## A Coast of Contrasts

The California coast is the prized western edge of North America, a raw merging of ocean and land where millions make their homes in huge cities but where wild unruly nature still rules supreme. The coastline is a landscape of contrasts, a place of million-dollar beach houses, rustic adobe missions, and high-tech industries, as well as skies filled with migrating birds on the Pacific Flyway, migrating whales sailing offshore currents, gnarled cypress trees beaten by winds, the largest kelp forest in North America, redwood forests topped with the world's tallest trees, and desolate sand beaches battered by waves.

## Southern California Coast

Southern California and its balmy golden beaches dotted with tanned surfers and bikini-clad girls begins south of Point Concepcion, a rocky outcrop that juts out into the Pacific Ocean south of Morro Bay. Here the coast swings eastward, leaving the cold California current to flow southward away from land. This rocky

*The 115-foot-high Pigeon Point Lighthouse, one of the tallest in the United States, is a hostel north of Santa Cruz.*

block of land lessens the persistent northwest winds and choppy seas. Here the coast forms what geographers call the California Bight, a huge arcing bay that bends southeast to the Mexican border. Most of this coastal section is heavily developed and populated, having only small enclaves of pristine beach and wild mountains, so it is not included in this California coast driving guide.

## Coastal Climate

A bucolic Mediterranean climate, influenced and moderated by the Pacific Ocean, defines the California coast with warm, dry summers and cool, damp winters. Thick fogs and mists obscure the coast, particularly in summer, with the toll of buoy bells a reminder of offshore rocks. The redwood trees that characterize the northern coast thrive on morning fogs, deriving precious moisture via droplets rather than from heavy rainfall. The average daily temperatures along the coast are remarkably unvaried, usually fluctuating only 10°F to 15°F between summer and winter.

## The Coast Ranges

The Coast Ranges rise up from the Pacific coast, forming a high and often almost impenetrable barrier to travel. The ranges, divided into separate and distinct sub-ranges, stretch from Crescent City to San Luis Obispo, a maze of mountains that includes the famed redwood forests, the Napa wine country, and the Santa Cruz, Diablo, and Santa Lucia ranges above the Big Sur Coast. These ranges all lie along the heralded San Andreas Rift, an active fault zone that stretches some 650 miles from the Mexican border to Cape Mendocino. The Transverse Ranges, some of the only east-west trending mountain ranges in the US, lie north of the Los Angeles Basin, while the Peninsular Ranges march southward from the basin to the border with Baja California.

## Coastal Wildlife

The long California coast offers a huge diversity of geologic formations, plant communities, and habitats that provide refuge and home to a variety of mammals, birds, and fish. Vast flocks of migratory birds fly along the coast on the Pacific Flyway, part of the more than 550 bird species identified in California. Along the Big Sur Coast soars the majestic, endangered California condor which now survives only because of a successful captive breeding program. Plenty of mammals roam the coast too, including California gray whales, sea otters, sea lions, harbor seals, elephant seals, black bears, and Roosevelt elk.

# Overview

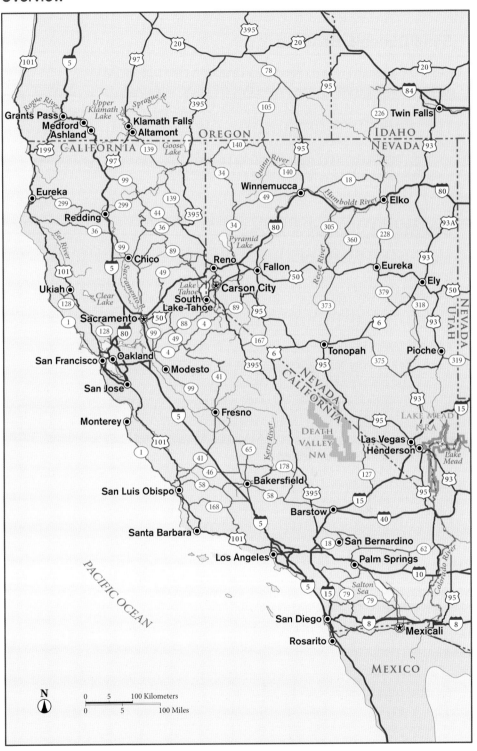

## Sand Dunes & Beaches

Along the coast are dynamic sand dunes and 27 dune fields, including the 40-square-mile Monterey Bay Dunes, that are often colonized by various grasses and other plants that anchor the sand, providing habitat for moths, butterflies, mice, voles, and lizards. Beaches are also sand features along the ever-changing shoreline. Some are pocket beaches tucked between cliffed ramparts while others are long stretches of wave-beaten sand and pebbles. Along this surf zone live mollusks like clams, crustaceans including crabs, and tube-building worms as well as various insects and shorebirds like gulls.

## Sea Stacks, Islands & Rocks

The California coast boasts over 20,000 sea stacks, jutting rocks, half-submerged reefs, and islands, all part of the California Coastal National Monument, that provide specialized habitats and isolated breeding areas for migrating birds and marine mammals. These sea-bound outcrops, including the Channel Islands and Farallon Islands, remain pristine and generally untouched by the human predators that plundered other more accessible sanctuaries for skins and seabird eggs. During the 19th century many species, including the elephant seal, fur seal, puffins, auklets, and murres were driven to the brink of extinction by trafficking and trade. These remote rock islands allowed many rare endemic species to evolve and others to survive the human onslaught and remain today as nature preserves.

## California Coastal Drives

*Scenic Routes and Byways: California's Pacific Coast* explores and discovers the rugged 1,100-mile-long coast that forms the western border of America's most populous state. The coast is divided into five distinct scenic driving routes, following US 101 and CA 1, from Santa Barbara to the Oregon border, which take from 1 day to 1 week to thoroughly cruise and enjoy. These drives showcase the wonders and mystery of California's fabled shoreline, sampling scenic wonders, hidden gems, and some of the state's most beautiful spots.

This reference book allows you to find a huge variety of activities and places, including beaches, hot springs, national and state parks, nature preserves, hiking trails, climbing areas, surfing waves, salt and freshwater fishing, campgrounds, historic sites, offbeat attractions, zoos, aquariums, wineries, and both large and small towns. Specific driving directions include GPS coordinates to parking areas as well as contact information for most sites.

The developed California coast south from Santa Barbara to Los Angeles, San Diego, and the Mexican border along with the San Francisco coastline is not described in this book. Lots of current information can be found in a wide variety of other books on these populated beaches and towns. *Scenic Routes and Byways: California's Pacific Coast* instead focuses on the state's wild and scenic coast—an expansive and stunning landscape where heaven meets earth and sea.

## Being Prepared

When you are driving California's coastal highways, be prepared for emergency situations and inclement weather. The highways often twist and curve across steep mountain slopes above the shoreline. Maintain a safe speed; use pullouts to allow faster traffic to pass when you are sightseeing; stay in your own lane; and watch for blind corners. When traveling the coast, especially after storms, call ahead to make sure that the highway is passable and the area you are going to is accessible. Heavy rain, storms, and mudslides can close sections of the highways in winter.

Coastal weather is often foggy or rainy, drastically altering driving conditions. Proceed carefully on rain-covered highways and turn your headlights on so other traffic can see you. Dense fog often creates visibility problems, especially on the North Coast. Slow down and stay alert. Watch for heavy traffic in urban areas and allow ample time to drive through cities. All of the drives feature frequent viewpoints and scenic pull-offs for sightseeing. Top off your gas tank in larger towns to ensure that you don't run low on fuel. Be sure that your vehicle is in proper working order, the windshield wipers are adequate, carry water and extra clothes.

Travelers are, unfortunately, potential crime victims. Stash all your valuables, including cameras, GPS units, removable sound systems, and luggage out of sight in your parked car, especially at remote parking lots near cities. Better yet, take them with you when you exit the vehicle. Always carry purses and wallets on your person rather than leaving them stowed away. Campers should also be wary of auto break-ins at popular campgrounds. Keep all valuables, including money, cameras, and video equipment with you in your tent at night.

The scenic drives and highways cross both public and private lands. Respect private property rights by not trespassing. Remember that federal laws protect both archaeological and historic sites, including Native American ruins and artifacts, petrified bone and fossils, and historic structures. Also camp only in designated sites and campgrounds to minimize impact, put out all campfires, and carry your trash out.

## How to Use This Book

*Scenic Routes and Byways: California's Pacific Coast* describes five of the best scenic coastal highway sections in the US. Each drive is complemented with detailed route maps, photographs of attractions and scenery, and trip planning information.

Each drive description is a compilation of points of interest, attractions, natural wonders, and recreational opportunities that follows the route from start to finish. The narrative text describes important and interesting sites, areas, and towns along the route, providing detailed travel information, interpretative information, miles and directions, descriptions of facilities, and phone numbers. Each drive is described in one direction; if you travel the route in the opposite direction, simply start at the end of the description.

Each map shows the drive's route, highway numbers and road names, campgrounds, points of interest, towns and cities along the way, recreation areas, national and state parks, national forests, and connecting roads.

Each trip planning section includes summaries of specific information for each drive. These self-explanatory sections allow quick access to relevant drive and trip details to help you make the most of your time.

- **General description** provides a brief summary of the length and scenic features of the drive.
- **Special attractions** are prominent points of interest, features, and activities found along the route.
- **Location** gives the area of California where the drive is set.
- **Drive route number** and name denotes the specific highway and road numbers and names that the drive travels.
- **Travel season** notes the best times of the year to make the drive and whether the route is closed by snow in winter. Remember that opening and closing times of roads are always approximate and depend on regional weather conditions. Always check local conditions before setting out on your drive.
- **Camping** includes listings of most National Park Service parks and monuments, state parks and recreation areas, USDA national forests, and BLM, regional, county, and city public campgrounds along the drive. Private campgrounds are generally not listed. Contact information for private campgrounds is easily obtained on the Internet. Consult the websites of specific governmental agencies for up-to-date information on making camping reservations.
- **Services** lists communities along the drive where you can obtain visitor services, including lodging, dining, groceries, telephone, medical services, and gasoline.
- **The appendices** at the end of the book provide names, telephone numbers, addresses, and websites of helpful organizations, including national parks and monuments, state parks, national forests, BLM public lands, chambers of commerce, and visitor bureaus. Before embarking on your scenic driving adventure, contact them for additional information and maps.

*Massive waves break across Hole-in-the-Wall Beach north of Santa Cruz.*

# 1
# NORTH CENTRAL COAST DRIVE

# Carmel to San Francisco

**General description:** CA 1 runs 107 miles along the north-central California coastline from Carmel to Pacifica just south of San Francisco.

**Location:** California coast between Carmel-by-the-Sea and Pacifica.

**Drive route number and name:** CA 1 (Cabrillo Highway).

**Travel season:** Year-round. Watch for fog along the drive in summer. Heavy rains in winter slicken the highway and may create landslides that close the highway.

**Camping:** Hundreds of campsites, including walk-in tent sites and RV sites, are in national forest, state park, and private campgrounds along the drive. Reservations, particularly in summer, are strongly recommended.

**Services:** All services in Carmel, Monterey, Santa Cruz, and Pacifica. Limited services are in other towns along the highway.

## The Route

The 107-mile-long Carmel to San Francisco scenic drive, following CA 1, the Cabrillo Highway, explores a diverse and beautiful section of California's Pacific shoreline. The picturesque and historic towns of Carmel-by-the-Sea, Pacific Grove, and Monterey anchor the drive's southern end, where you explore old missions, the famed Cannery Row and Monterey Bay Aquarium, old lighthouses, and a rocky coastline interrupted by glistening sand beaches.

The middle section encompasses scallop-shaped Monterey Bay and its rich marine environment. Offshore is Monterey Canyon, one of the world's deepest ocean canyons, wavering kelp forests, and marine mammals including gray and humpback whales, elephant seals, harbor seals, sea otters, and dolphins. A long stretch of beaches and sand dunes borders the bay from Monterey north to Santa Cruz.

The northern coast section, beginning at the eclectic city of Santa Cruz, is a cliff-lined coast with pocket beaches, crashing surf, grassy terraces carpeted with wildflowers, and towering inland stands of coast redwood trees.

This coastal drive, easily accessible from San Francisco, makes a wonderful day trip. Allow at least a full day to drive the highway and make a few stops. It's easy to spend 4 or 5 days puttering along the coast, sunning at wild beaches, visiting attractions, playing at the Santa Cruz Boardwalk, and enjoying some of California's best seaside scenery.

# Carmel to San Francisco

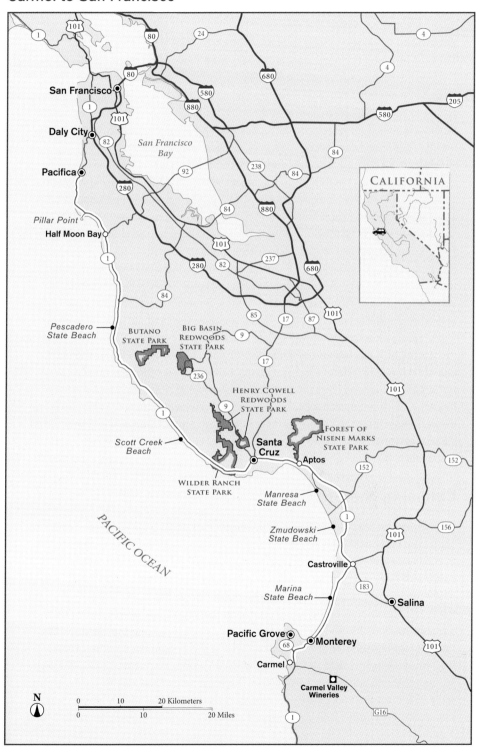

*Weather*

The climate along the north central coast is mild year-round. Around Monterey Bay on the drive's south end, the weather varies little between winter and summer. Only 10 degrees difference separates the mean temperatures for August and January, making the climate here one of the most uniform in the US. Summer brings thick fog banks that wrap the coast in gray shrouds. The fog usually burns off by midday, but temperatures are often cool. Bring a sweater for those days.

Inland temperatures on the mountains and valleys above the coast can be hot with daily highs reaching into the upper 90s. Thunderstorms are infrequent, although light showers may accompany the fog. The drive north of Santa Cruz and Monterey Bay is cooler and damper than the southern section.

September and October are among the best months for traveling the Carmel to Frisco coast. Expect lots of clear days with sunshine and warm temperatures; average daily highs are in the low 70s—just about perfect. Big winter storms pummel the coast from December through February, dropping heavy rains from sodden skies. About 18 inches of rain falls during those 3 months, so don't forget a raincoat. Springtime is lovely here, although March is rainy. April and May are often clear and breezy with scattered showers. clear and breezy with scattered showers.

Carmel-by-the-Sea and neighboring Monterey basks in a Mediterranean climate with damp winters and warm, dry summers. The temperatures here are remarkably even with the average winter high at 60°F and the average summer high at 72°F. Rainfall averages 19.5 inches annually, with most of that coming between November and April. January is rainiest with 4.2 inches while July is driest with a scant 0.09 inches of precipitation. It virtually never snows here, and only 2 days each year dip below a freezing 32°F.

## Carmel-by-the-Sea

Carmel-by-the-Sea, usually just called **Carmel,** lies on the southern side of the Monterey Peninsula. This resort town, with a population of 3,700 in 2010, is one of the most famous and picturesque towns on the California coast, with both a rich history and a beautiful seaside setting. Carmel is both quaint and ritzy, with fancy shops, expensive homes, over 100 art galleries (highest per capita in the US), manicured lawns and parks, and stunning scenery.

Although first home to Native American tribes, including the Ohlone, the Carmel region was later discovered and settled by the Spanish. Explorer Juan Rodriquez Cabrillo sailed past in 1542 but didn't stop. Sixty years later, Sebastian Vizcaino, a Spanish explorer and Carmelite friar, named the area in 1602 for Our Lady of Mount Carmel, patron saint of the Carmelites. The area, however, was not settled for another 168 years when Franciscan monks Junípero Serra and Juan

Crespí established a mission in nearby Monterey in 1770. That thriving port was the capital of Alta California until 1849 when the Americans took it over.

Carmel itself started out in 1888 as a resort town, ironic since it is often foggy here in summer. Developers wanted to build a Catholic retreat here and began selling lots. In 1902 the town post office opened, and in 1910 the Coastal Laboratory was established. Carmel-by-the-Sea incorporated in 1916.

With its beauty and quiet, Carmel quickly became a place for the well-heeled and the artistic crowd, who established an arts colony here after the 1906 San Francisco earthquake decimated that city. Artists bought lots for a $10 down payment. Some of those who took up residence included writers and novelists Jack London, Mary Austin, Ambrose Bierce, Upton Sinclair, and Sinclair Lewis. Photographer Arnold Genthe, who made many historic images after the '06 earthquake and was a color photography pioneer, also settled here.

In 1914 the great poet Robinson Jeffers moved to what he called his "inevitable place" at the dramatic interface of sea, shore, and sky. Here he built his famous Tor House and the nearby Hawk Tower out of local granite blocks on a rocky promontory overlooking the Pacific Ocean.

The great photographer Edward Weston moved to Carmel in 1929 and began a long love with Point Lobos. Weston's friend Ansel Adams moved here in 1962, living in his Carmel Highlands home until his death in 1984.

Carmel is still a colony for artists. The iconic **Carmel Bach Festival** (bachfestival.org), starting in 1935, offers a couple weeks that celebrate the music of Johann Sebastian Bach, attracting both music lovers and international musicians. The **Carmel Symphony Orchestra** (carmelsymphony.org) also offers an annual concert series, performing at the Sunset Cultural Center. In October, the **Carmel Art and Film Festival** (carmelartandfilm.com) is a veritable orgy of every kind of art plus 5 days packed with over 100 independent films, climaxing with the awarding of the Clint Eastwood Filmmaker's Award. Besides visual artists and writers, other Carmel residents now include actors like Eastwood, who also served as the town mayor back in the 1980s.

## Navigating Around Carmel

When navigating around Carmel, pay attention and plan to get lost sometimes since there are no street addresses. The town does not have home mail delivery so there are no house numbers. Addresses are given by street names and the nearest intersections, which makes night navigation a complete nightmare!

**Finding the town:** Carmel-by-the-Sea is on the south side of the Monterey Peninsula and west of CA 1, the Coast Highway, and about 50 miles south of Santa Cruz. The town lies 325 miles north of Los Angeles and 120 miles south of San Francisco. Nearby towns are Pacific Grove and Monterey, 5 miles to the north. The best streets to access the town center from CA 1 are Ocean Avenue on the north and Rio Road on the south.

**Carmel Chamber of Commerce** (San Carlos between 5th and 6th, PO Box 4444, Carmel, CA 93921; 800-550-4333; carmelcalifornia.com).

## Dog City USA

Carmel is considered one of the most dog-friendly towns in the US. Dogs are allowed almost everywhere. Clip a leash on Fido and stroll along Ocean Avenue, where you'll run into lots of other dogs and their owners. You can tie him up outside while you have lunch or you can find a cafe where your dog can sit beside you on the outdoor patio. Shopkeepers welcome you and your canine into the store, and some provide water bowls out front. There are also doggie-destination hotels where your pet is welcome. Then, of course, there is the Carmel City Beach where he can roam free, run wild, and sniff to his heart's content—as long as he's under voice command. Don't leave your pup locked in your car on hot days. The Carmel police are strict about canine abuse; they will bust him out, and you will get ticketed.

## Carmel-by-the-Sea Attractions

It's great fun to stop at Carmel-by-the-Sea and browse the shops and fill your stomach, but that quickly gets old when you realize that some of the California coast's most stunning natural attractions and recreational opportunities are right here. **Carmel City Beach** forms the town's west border, while **Carmel River State Beach** holds down the southwestern edge. The **Carmel Mission** on the south side of town is one of California's most beautiful 17th-century missions.

**Point Lobos State Natural Reserve,** just south of town off CA 1, is simply one of the prime scenic stops on the entire California shoreline. The rocky headland, jutting into the Pacific Ocean, offers a dramatic and primal meeting of earth and ocean, with waves crashing on rocks, seals and sea lions cavorting in the surf, and wind-twisted cypresses lining the cliff edge.

North of Carmel is the gorgeous **17-Mile Drive,** a meandering road that connects to **Pacific Grove** at the tip of **Monterey Peninsula.** Besides scenic views at every turn, the drive also passes by California's most famous and most beautiful golf course—**Pebble Beach Golf Links.** Every February a pro and celebrity golf tournament brings fans who watch their screen and sports idols take a few swings; the course also hosts major golf events like the US Open. If the $300+ tee fees for 18 holes are too pricey, there are other courses too, including **Spyglass Hill, Cypress Point, Poppy Hills Golf Course, The Links at Spanish Bay,** and **Monterey Country Club.**

## Carmel-by-the-Sea Shopping & Restaurants

Carmel-by-the-Sea is renowned for its diverse shops, boutiques, art galleries, and fine restaurants. What would you expect for a town that is like Beverly Hills North? Park your car and stroll around the compact downtown area, do some window-shopping and stop at whatever galleries strike your fancy to view paintings, watercolors, bronzes, and photographs. Galleries range in taste and price from rustic California to haute Europe with something for every palette.

Ditto for dining. Carmel offers culinary delights for every pocketbook and palate, including French, Italian, California, seafood, and Asian cuisines. Suggestions are **Katy's Place** for breakfast (Mission St., Carmel, CA 93921; 831-624-0199; katysplacecarmel.com); **La Bicyclette** for wood-fired pizza (29 Dolores St., Carmel, CA 93923; 831-622-9899; labicycletterestaurant.com); **Bruno's Market** (Junipero St., Carmel, CA 93921; 831-624-3821; brunosmarket.com) for take-out beach picnic fare; and **Marinus at the Bernardus Lodge** for California-style meals (415 W. Carmel Valley Rd., Carmel Valley, CA 93924; 831-658-3595; bernardus.com/lodge/restaurants).

## Carmel Mission

The Carmel Mission, properly called **Mission San Carlos Borroméo del Río Carmelo,** is a classic California Catholic mission that was established in 1770 by Father Junípero Serra (1713–1784) in Monterey before being moved to Carmel in 1771 to avoid the corrupting influence of the army garrison. The Basilica Mission, listed as a National Historic Landmark, is a must-see stop for anyone interested in California history and the missions. The mission with its 5-foot-thick walls and collection of Spanish Colonial church art is one of the most beautiful of the California missions.

Besides being an active church, the Carmel Mission also tells the story of California's Spanish heritage through five museums—the **Basilica Church;** the **Harry Downie Museum,** which tells of Downie's restoration efforts; the **Munras Family Heritage Museum** with keepsakes of a prominent area family; the **Jo Mora Chapel Gallery** and its **Serra Memorial Cenotaph;** and the **Convento Museum,** with the room where Padre Serra lived until his death in 1784. Serra was interred in a nearby chapel.

The mission is a place to wander around quiet hallways, peeking into spartan monk cells, looking at one of California's first libraries with its leather-bound books, remembering Serra and his contributions at his tomb, and wandering about the exquisite and colorful gardens on winding paths past fountains. Come on a weekday for peace and solitude. An entrance fee is charged.

**Finding the mission:** To find the mission from CA 1/Cabrillo Highway, turn west on Rio Road and follow it for about a half-mile to the mission on the

*The Carmel Mission, established in 1770, tells the story of California's early history in 5 separate museums.*

left. A large parking lot on Rio Road is conveniently in front of the mission (GPS: 36.542976 N / -121.919164 W). 3080 Rio Rd., Carmel, CA 93923; (831) 624-1271; carmelmission.org.

## Tor House

Robinson Jeffers (1887–1962), one of the best American poets in the first half of the 20th century, was greatly influenced by the rugged California coast in Carmel where he lived and penned verse for 40 years after moving there in 1914. The lonely sea and the sky became his poetic inspiration, and to find that, Jeffers had the **Tor House,** a small stone house, built on a rocky bluff a stone's throw away from the coast in south Carmel in 1919. Jeffers learned stonework from the mason and then constructed a stone tower, modeled after ancient Irish towers, over 4 years, starting in 1920, as a refuge for his wife Una. He named it **Hawk Tower** for a bird that regularly visited while he laid the stones, but disappeared upon its completion. Jeffers wrote poetry in the morning during those years and worked on the tower in the afternoon.

Now you can make a pilgrimage to the master poet's home and see firsthand the earth elements that influenced his physical verse. Tor House, owned by the Robinson Jeffers Tor House Foundation, preserves it much as it was during his lifetime. You will have to call or e-mail ahead for a reservation to see the house and tower; tours are limited to six people but are conducted hourly 10 a.m. to 3 p.m. every Fri and Sat. A fee is charged. No children under age 12 allowed.

**Finding the house:** Tor House is accessed from CA 1/Cabrillo Highway via Rio Road to Santa Lucia Avenue to Scenic Road. Turn left on Stewart Way and drive 1 block to Ocean View Avenue. Turn left to the house. 26304 Ocean View Ave., Carmel-by-the-Sea CA 93923; (831) 624-1813; thf@torhouse.org.

## Carmel River State Beach

The 297-acre **Carmel River State Beach** includes a mile-long beach (the southern section is Monastery Beach) and a bird-sanctuary lagoon formed by the Carmel River, which empties into the ocean here. The beach is popular for sea kayaking and scuba diving, but swimming is not recommended because of dangerous currents. The area is especially popular with birders in fall and winter. Spanish explorer Sebastian Vizcaino landed here in 1602.

**Finding the beach:** On the south side of Carmel, turn west from CA 1 on Rio Road; follow Rio to Santa Lucia Avenue and turn left. Follow Santa Lucia to Carmelo Street, turn left and follow to a parking area next to the beach (GPS: 36.5389 W / -121.927793 W). (831) 649-2836.

## Carmel City Beach

**Carmel City Beach** stretches along the coastline a half-mile west of downtown Carmel at the end of Ocean Avenue. It's a gorgeous beach of fine white sand edged by cypress trees. It's beautiful and popular so avoid weekends when the parking lot on Ocean Avenue fills up. The area offers great walking on the beach and on a 0.75-mile trail along the bluff above between 8th Avenue and Martin Way. Swimming is discouraged because of strong undertows. Just north of the beach is the famed Pebble Beach golf course.

**Finding the beach:** From CA 1/Cabrillo Highway in Carmel, go west on Ocean Avenue to a parking lot at its end (GPS: 36.555088 N / -121.929247 W). Other parking is along Scenic Road south of the main lot. (831) 620-2000.

## Pebble Beach Beaches

The beach scene at Pebble Beach is limited and restricted. **Stillwater Cove,** just north of Carmel City Beach, lies alongside Pebble Beach Golf Links and is accessed by the private Beach and Tennis Club. It's a great place for sea kayaking and diving, which is limited to 10 people per day. Call (831) 625-8507 for reservations.

**Spanish Bay** on the far northern edge of Pebble Beach next to Pacific Grove offers a big half-mile sweep of sand that is great for surfing on the big waves rolling in from the northwest. Best waves are September to March. Also check out the

cairns or stacks of rocks along the beach that are erected as impromptu sculptures. The beach is shared with Asilomar to the north, where dogs must be leashed. Here they can romp wild.

**Finding the beach:** Access from Spanish Bay Road on the coast. There is a small parking lot on the south, roadside parking along the road, and a large parking lot on the north (GPS: 36.609648 N / -121.948111 W).

## Carmel Valley Wineries

The broad Carmel Valley, lying east of the village of Carmel, slices through the coastal Santa Lucia Range. The picturesque valley boasts several excellent wineries, making it ideal for a romantic day of wine-tasting and vineyard tours. The valley's orientation makes it somewhat immune from the cool and foggy days common along the coast in summer, allowing grapes to mature under the hot afternoon summer in well-drained, gravelly soils. The valley is well-known for its superb cabernet sauvignon and merlot varietals, which make up 70 percent of the local wine.

For a wine-tasting tour, start with the cabernets at **Galante Vineyards** tasting room on Dolores Street in Carmel itself, then drive east from Carmel-by-the-Sea on CA 1 and Carmel Valley Road for 11.5 miles to Carmel Valley Village. Along the way are several wineries, including, at 6 miles, **Chateau Julien** in a French-style chateau on the south side of the road; this is the only winery and tasting room in the valley itself.

In **Carmel Valley Village** are several tasting rooms, including **Bernardus Winery, Boekenoogen, Chateau Sinnet Joyce, Heller Estate, Georis Winery, Joullian Vinyards, Parsonage,** and **Robert Talbott Vineyards.** Georis Winery, farther up the valley, makes small amounts of excellent merlot. Bernardus offers great estate wines; Heller has a nice tasting room for its 100 percent certified organic wines; Joullian is known for its unique chardonnays; and Talbott specializes in chardonnay and pinot noir varietals.

## 17-Mile Drive

The famed **17-Mile Drive** is exactly that—a 17-mile-long scenic route hugging the west coast of the **Monterey Peninsula** between **Carmel** and **Pacific Grove.** The twisting road passes crescent-shaped sand beaches, rocky headlands pounded by Pacific surf, twisted Monterey cypress trees, as well as lavish mansions and some

*Carmel River State Beach is a perfect spot for sand lounging, sea kayaking, and bird watching on summer afternoons.*

of America's most renowned and exclusive golf clubs. A toll is charged per car to drive the road, most of which is owned by the Pebble Beach Corporation, so some folks prefer not to take this route and help the rich get richer while others revel in the drive's stunning scenic beauty.

**Finding the drive:** It's easy to start the scenic drive from either Carmel or Pacific Grove; just follow signs to it. From CA 1, it's easy to get on it. Take the exit just north of Carmel for CA 68 and at the north side of the overpass, follow signs to the drive. The drive route is marked with a dashed red line down the center of the road to keep you on course as it zigzags through neighborhoods.

The drive runs north from Carmel past the famed **Pebble Beach Golf Links** and **Stillwater Cove.** It continues twisting along the ragged coastline. Stop at numerous pullouts to walk down to pocket beaches or along cliffed headlands to viewpoints which are perfect for watching the sunset.

One of the most famous scenic attractions is the famed **Lone Cypress** tree, a solitary Monterey cypress perched atop a rocky outcrop that is an iconic living symbol of the California coast. There are a roadside parking lot (GPS: 36.569555 N / -121.965615 W) and a short trail to a viewing area. Another good stop for seeing the sun dip into the golden ocean is **Sunset Point.** Take a short spur road left to a spacious parking lot (GPS: 36.577164 N / -121.974785 W) and an overlook. Farther north is **Cypress Point Lookout** (parking lot GPS: 36.583215 N / -121.971797 W) with a small pocket beach and a wonderful view of the rocky coast.

Farther along check out **Bird Rock** and you will not only see pelicans, gulls, and cormorants perched on the white-stained islet but also lounging sea lions, harbor seals, and sometimes sea otters frolicking in the surf. Keep an eye offshore from November to January for gray whales during their 10,000-mile-long migration along the coast from Alaska to Mexico, the longest migration of any mammal. Turn left off the drive to a short loop road to a large parking area (GPS: 36.59141 N / -121.964345 W) and overlooks.

The drive bends inland just before Pacific Grove at **Spanish Bay,** which makes a good stop to stroll along its half-mile-long broad sand beach or have a picnic. The drive ends at Sunset Road (CA 68) in Pacific Grove. Go right to get back to CA 1.

The 17-Mile Drive toll road has a fee charged at five entry gates. Allow 3 hours to drive the route, with stops along the way. Spring and fall offer the best weather with clear skies. Summer days can be foggy; come in afternoon for the best views. Weekdays are less crowded than weekends; although you will want to avoid it if there is a major golf tournament. If you spend more than $25 at a Pebble Beach Company restaurant on the road, they will deduct the entrance fee from your bill. Bring a camera, binoculars, and warm clothes, even in summer.

# The Lone Cypress

The Lone Cypress, perched on a rocky headland on the west coast of Monterey Peninsula, is a California landmark that's as famous as the Golden Gate Bridge and the Hollywood sign. The tree, estimated at 250 years old, has been depicted by painters; photographers including Edward Weston, Ansel Adams, and David Muench: and countless tourist snapshots. If you want an oil painting of it, venture down to a Carmel gallery and you'll find any number for sale.

The tree was first noted on January 19, 1889 by R. Fitch, who wrote: "Rounding a short curve on the beach, we approach Cypress Point, the boldest headland on the peninsula of Monterey. Down almost to the water grows the cypress, and on the extreme point a solitary tree has sunk its roots in the crevices of the wave-washed rock, and defies the battle of the elements that rage about it during the storms of winter."

*The iconic Lone Cypress has stood through storm and surf for over 250 years.*

The elegant 25-foot-high tree still defies the elements, although now the base of the two-trunked tree has been reinforced to keep it from eroding away. It also appears to have defied the wishes of the Pebble Beach Company, which has used the tree as its logo since 1919, to curtail the use of the Lone Cypress's image by commercial photographers. The company claimed in 1990 that use of photographs of the tree would cause confusion with the general public over the Pebble Beach logo if an image of it was used on something not associated with the company and that their trademark not only protected their logo but the tree itself.

Outrage, of course, ensued over Cypressgate and numerous trademark attorneys weighed in on the debate, with most of them agreeing that photographing and using images of the tree by either tourists or photographers for publication and exhibition would not cause confusion over Pebble Beach's logo or sponsorship.

## Pacific Grove Museum of Natural History

This small museum makes a good stop coupled with the Monarch Grove Sanctuary. It has a bunch of permanent exhibits detailing the area's natural history, geology, and Native Americans. The exhibits about the monarch butterfly are, of course, interesting in winter. Allow an hour or so to roam around the free museum, which is close to downtown, on Forest Avenue off Lighthouse. Look for the life-size sculpture of an adult female gray whale out front. Kids are usually climbing on it. Open 10 a.m. to 5 p.m. Tues to Sun.

**Finding the museum:** The museum is in downtown Pacific Grove on Forest Avenue between Lighthouse Avenue and Central Avenue. Lots of free parking on Forest and Central Avenues. 165 Forest Ave., Pacific Grove, CA 93950; (831) 648-5716; pgmuseum.org.

## Asilomar State Beach

**Asilomar State Beach,** on the west side of Pacific Grove, is a 36-acre beach with tide pools, rocky areas, sand beach, and dunes. The area is unsafe for swimming with riptide currents. Nearby is a conference center, designated a National Historic Landmark in 1987, in a pine and oak woodland and stabilized dunes. Asilomar means "refuge by the sea," a name given when the site became conference grounds for the Young Women's Christian Association (YWCA) in 1897. The park also offers a dune boardwalk and a 1-mile coastal trail through sand dunes and over headlands.

**Finding the beach:** The park and beach are by Sunset Drive and Asilomar Avenue. From CA 1, take exit 399 and go west on CA 68. Go left on Sunset Drive and follow to Asilomar Avenue and then go right to the park's main entrance (GPS: 36.619255 N / -121.935832 W). (831) 372-8016.

## Lovers Point Park & Beach

**Lovers Point Park and Beach** is a bluff-top area on a rocky hook that juts into Monterey Bay on the east side of Pacific Grove next to Monterey. Lovers Point, a well-manicured 4.4-acre park, offers spectacular views of the bay and is one of the rare places on the Pacific coast where you can watch the sun rise over the ocean. The area offers three small protected beaches and is sometimes crowded. The area is popular for photography, swimming (lots of kelp), surfing, scuba diving in the kelp forest, and picnicking (watch for cheeky seagulls). No dogs on beach.

**Finding the beach:** The park and beach are on the east side of Pacific Grove and the peninsula. Follow Ocean View Boulevard, which follows the coast, to a parking area (GPS: 36.626451 N / -121.916764 W) and roadside parking next to the park.

# Monterey

**Monterey,** with a population of 28,810 (2010 census), is considered the birthplace of California. Juan Rodriguez Cabrillo, a Portuguese sailor exploring for Spain, discovered Monterey Bay in 1542. CA 1 is called the Cabrillo Highway in honor of California's first European explorer. In 1602 Sebastian Vizcaino celebrated mass under Monterey's own "Plymouth Rock," an old spreading oak tree.

Almost 2 centuries later, explorer Gaspar de Portolà and Father Junípero Serra established a presidio and mission—Mission San Carlos Borroméo del Río Carmelo—on the fertile south shore of crescent-shaped Monterey Bay; and the town, called Monterey, grew into a lively port and the provincial capital of Alta California from 1777 to 1849 under the flags of Spain and Mexico. On July 7, 1849 after the Battle of Monterey during the Mexican-American War, Monterey fell to the Americans when Commodore John D. Sloat raised the Stars and Stripes over the Monterey Custom House and declared California to be American territory.

Monterey later became a major fishing port and fish cannery, immortalized in John Steinbeck's classic 1945 novel *Cannery Row* as "a poem, a stink, a grating noise, a quality of light, a tune, a habit, a nostalgia, a dream." Today, the Sardine Capital of the World attracts tourists who stroll along its charming streets and piers, and visit its historic attractions.

**Finding the town:** Monterey is on the Monterey Peninsula on CA 1 (Cabrillo Highway) 43 miles south of Santa Cruz; 95 miles south of Half Moon Bay; 32 miles north of Big Sur; and 99 miles north of San Simeon. Nearby towns include Carmel-by-the-Sea and Pacific Grove.

## Monterey Shopping & Restaurants

Monterey and nearby Pacific Grove offer lots of stores, shops, and galleries that are scattered throughout the downtown areas but concentrated in plazas, malls, and shopping centers, as well as in such places as **Cannery Row** and **Fisherman's Wharf.**

## Monterey Attractions

Monterey retains its old California historic flavor with more 18th- and 19th-century buildings than any other California town. The self-guided **"Path of History"** winds 2.7 miles through the downtown past whitewashed adobe buildings topped with red-tile roofs. Other popular attractions include Steinbeck's **Cannery Row,** touristy **Fisherman's Wharf, Monterey State Historic Park,** and the spectacular **Monterey Bay Aquarium.** The aquarium explores 60-mile-long Monterey Bay's diverse habitats and its 10,000-foot-deep canyons, kelp beds, and tidal flats through numerous exhibits.

## Monterey Bay Aquarium

The celebrated **Monterey Bay Aquarium** (MBA), on the west end of Cannery Row alongside Monterey Bay at the site of an old sardine cannery, is simply one of the California coast's great attractions. The huge aquarium, founded in 1984, displays thousands of aquatic animals and plants and over 600 species with a mission "to inspire conservation of the oceans." The MBA offers a glimpse into the wonders of nearby **Monterey Bay National Marine Sanctuary** and the Pacific Ocean. Indeed, the aquarium's seashore location allows aquarium scientists to study the ocean, including offshore Monterey Canyon, the deepest and largest underwater canyon off North America's Pacific coast.

The 2-story aquarium offers over 100 glass tanks filled with all kinds of denizens of the deep from starfish, sea horses, and sea otters to penguins, tunas, and great white sharks. About 2,000 gallons of Monterey Bay water is pumped through the tanks every minute, making the MBA a living part of the bay's ecosystem. The water is filtered by day to allow better viewing, but unfiltered at night to flood plankton and other micro-creatures into the tanks.

Some of the must-see exhibits are the **Kelp Forest,** housed in a 3-story tank; the **Open Sea Gallery,** which displays great white sharks, which are usually caught and kept for display and then released back into the ocean as well as other shark species, bluefin tuna, sunfish, and sea turtles; the sea otter exhibit is always popular with these playful mammals that live along California's coastline; and puffin, penguin, jellyfish, and sea horse exhibits. Look also for shallow tanks filled with tide pool critters.

It's best to allot a whole day for exploring the aquarium's exhibits. Plan your day on arrival by checking the feeding schedule. At midday you can leave for lunch or eat at a full-service restaurant or self-serve cafe on-site. The MBA is very busy in summer and on weekends and holidays. Buy advance tickets by phone or website to avoid long lines. Street parking is limited; look instead for nearby parking lots and garages. It's open year-round; admission fees are charged.

**Finding the aquarium:** The aquarium is at the junction of David Avenue and Cannery Row northeast of Lighthouse Avenue along Monterey Bay. Park in lots or garages. 886 Cannery Row, Monterey, CA;93940 montereybayaquarium.org; (831) 648-4888; tickets (866) 963-9645.

*A bust of writer John Steinbeck on Cannery Row commemorates California's most beloved writer who was born and lived along Monetery Bay.*

# Cannery Row

**Cannery Row,** once Ocean View Avenue, is a waterfront street on the northwest side of Monterey. The bustling street, lined with restaurants, boutiques, arts and crafts shops, hotels, and bars, was the site of numerous sardine canning factories in the first half of the twentieth century.

Monterey Bay's rich sardine population, one of the world's richest at that time, propelled the fishing and canning industry until it collapsed due to overfishing in the mid-1950s but not before Cannery Row became ingrained in the American consciousness with John Steinbeck's novels *Cannery Row* (1945) and *Sweet Thursday* (1954). The street was renamed Cannery Row in 1958 to honor both Steinbeck and the fishing industry.

It's worthwhile to stroll down Cannery Row, at once a historic district and the central coast's ultimate tourist trap. Allow a couple hours to explore the street. The northwest end of Cannery Row is anchored by the famed Monterey Bay Aquarium, which was once the Hoyden Cannery. It canned squid after the sardines ran out until it closed in 1973.

Down the street from the aquarium are historic buildings as well as sites in Steinbeck's novels. These include ocean biologist Ed Rickett's lab (Rickett famously replied "They're in cans!" to the question "Where did all the sardines go?"); worker houses where cannery laborers once lived; McAbee Beach; Reduction Plant, which once reduced all the sardine parts to chicken feed; San Xavier Cannery, featured in the Marilyn Monroe film *Clash by Night;* Factory Crossover, a flyway over the road that is the only one of the original 16 left; and San Carlos Beach, a popular scuba site. From here, reverse tracks back to the aquarium or follow the Monterey Bay Coastal Trail alongside and catch a free trolley back to the aquarium from the wharf.

**Finding the street:** Cannery Row is not only a district but also a street that parallels the Monterey Bay coast. Access it from exit 402 on CA 1/Cabrillo Highway by following Del Monte Avenue to Lighthouse Avenue.

# Fisherman's Wharf

**Fisherman's Wharf,** also called Old Fisherman's Wharf, juts into Monterey Bay at the east end of Cannery Row. The wharf, laden with restaurants, shops, and docks for fishing junkets and whale-watching boats, was a fish market until the 1960s when the commercial fishing industry tanked. The wharf was originally built in 1870 by the Pacific Coast Steamship Company to unload both passengers and goods that sailed around South America to California. Later it was used to unload fishing boats laden with sardines bound for Cannery Row. The current commercial fishing wharf, Municipal Wharf #2, was built in 1926. After the collapse of the sardine industry, Fisherman's Wharf became a tourist attraction.

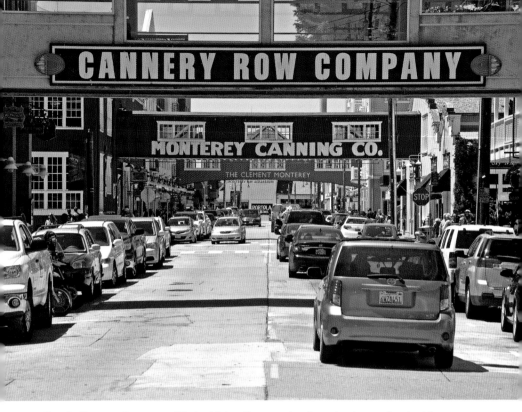

*Historic Cannery Row, once filled with bustling canning factories, is now lined with galleries, restaurants, boutiques, bars, and hotels.*

The wharf, basically a pedestrian mall, is thought by locals to be an overgrown tourist trap, but for visitors it offers fun and good food. There are lots of good restaurants that serve seafood, fresh crab, bowls of steaming chowder, and a raw seafood bar. Touts offer passersby samples of their chowder to entice them to come inside. Some have outdoor seaside eating where you catch watch sea lions lounging on rocks, sea otters frolicking in the surf, and tide pools that reflect sky. It's also a great place to buy coastal souvenirs at gift shops, art galleries, and jewelry stores.

You can also book a whale-watching tour with **Princess Monterey Whale Watching,** glass-bottom boat tours, or a private fishing trip on the bay. **Monterey Bay Sailing** offers shoreline cruises, passing Cannery Row to the open water beyond.

The wharf is crowded on weekends and holidays. Parking is scarce nearby on busy days. Look for metered spots or hourly lots.

**Finding the wharf:** Fisherman's Wharf is between Municipal Wharf #3 and Coast Guard Wharf. Access it from exit 402 on CA 1/Cabrillo Highway by driving west on Del Monte Avenue to Lighthouse Avenue, which goes belowground by the wharf. Look for parking in the area and walk to the wharf.

# Monterey State Historic Park

Monterey is old California, a place that has flown under three flags—Spanish, Mexican, and since 1846, American. Spanish explorers landed here in 1602 and established it as a colonial town and mission. Later it served as California's first capital. The architectural remains of Old Monterey are preserved and interpreted in **Monterey State Historic Park,** a collection of protected historic buildings and houses scattered through Monterey. The **Monterey Walking Path of History,** marked with yellow tiles, ties them all together along a 2-mile trail with 55 historic places in the federally designated **Monterey Old Town Historic District.**

The significant buildings in the state park include:

- **Custom House.** Built in 1821, it's the oldest government building in California.
- **Cooper-Molera Adobe Complex.** Built in 1823 in a Spanish adobe style with New England architectural flairs.
- **Larkin House.** Built in 1834 and used as headquarters for Lieutenant William Tecumseh Sherman, later of Civil War fame, in 1847.
- **First Brick House.** California's first brick house, built in 1847.
- **Colton Hall.** The 1849 site of California's constitutional convention.
- **Old Whaling Station.** Built in 1855 as the headquarters of the Monterey Whaling Company. Check out its unique whalebone sidewalk.
- **Stevenson House.** Formerly the French Hotel where writer Robert Louis Stevenson lodged while wooing his wife Fanny Osbourne. Great gardens behind the house.
- **First Theater.** California's first theater built in 1847 as lodging for sailors and converted to a theater in 1850.
- **Pacific House Museum.** An adobe built in 1847 that now exhibits the colorful history of Monterey and houses the Monterey Museum of the American Indian.
- **Casa del Oro.** Built in 1849 as an army barracks, general store, saloon, and then gold exchange for miners.
- **Casa Soberanes.** A 1840s adobe house, named for its blue gate, which overlooks the bay.

The park also has an **Interpretative Center** (20 Custom House Plaza; 831-649-7118) that offers educational tours, usually from spring through autumn, when the houses are open to the public. A good visit is in December when the homes are decorated for Christmas and staffed with volunteers dressed in period clothes. It's also well worth strolling the gardens at the various houses.

# Monterey Mural

Check out the **Monterey Mural** when you are strolling around downtown Monterey. The huge tile mural, created in 1984, adorns the Monterey Conference Center near the corner of Pacific Street and Del Monte Avenue. The mural, made by Guillermo Wagner Granizo, depicts the history of Monterey Bay from Native Americans and Spanish colonists to Mexican farmers and today's Monterey residents.

**Finding the mural:** From exit 402 on CA 1/Cabrillo Highway, drive west on Del Monte Avenue to Pacific Street near Fisherman's Wharf. The mural is on the northeast corner of the intersection (GPS: 36.619255 N / -121.935832 W).

# Monterey Museum of Art

The **Monterey Museum of Art** (MMA) displays a superb collection of California art and regional artists from the last 200 years in two buildings located at 559 Pacific St. and 720 Via Mirada. The Pacific Street museum, on a bluff looking over Monterey Bay, offers eight galleries and houses the museum's administration and Buck Education Center. The **La Mirada** museum is on the historic La Mirada estate with not only galleries but also a large garden that's well worth visiting.

The MMA's permanent collection, with over 14,000 objects, includes diverse collections, which cover early California paintings, American art, contemporary art, photography, and Asian art. The collection has works by Pablo Picasso, Henri Matisse, William F. Ritschel, Armin Hansen, and Joan Miró, as well as by famed California photographers Ansel Adams and Edward Weston, who made many images in the Monterey area.

**Finding the museum:** From exit 402 on CA 1/Cabrillo Highway, drive west on Del Monte Avenue to Pacific Street. Turn left or south on Pacific and drive a few blocks to the museum on the left. Park on the street. 559 Pacific St. and 720 Via Mirada, Monterey, CA 93940; (831) 372-3689; montereyart.org.

## Monterey Beaches

The Monterey and Carmel coast offers lots of diverse ocean-side terrain from rocky shores to sandy beaches. Most are state beaches that are easily accessed from CA 1, while others are along the coast in the towns of Monterey, Pacific Grove, and Carmel. Monterey County has almost 100 miles of shoreline.

Many of the beaches along the Monterey coast have dangerous rip currents. Swimming is generally not recommended. Lifeguards are not stationed at most beaches. Don't leave valuables in your vehicle at isolated parking areas at the beaches. Car break-ins are a problem at some of the remote beaches.

## McAbee Beach

**McAbee Beach** in Monterey borders a sheltered cove off Cannery Row. The postage-size beach offers a fun stroll on the sandy shore at low tide, seals and shorebirds, some tide pools, and great Monterey Bay views. Perfect kid-stop on your way to the aquarium.

**Finding the beach:** McAbee Beach is at the junction of Hoffman Avenue and Cannery Row (GPS: 36.615269 N / -121.899246 W).

## San Carlos Beach Park

This small beach is right in Monterey next to Coast Guard Pier and near Cannery Row. The beach is extremely popular with scuba divers; **Monterey Bay Dive Charters** (831-383-9276) on Cannery Row offers rentals, scuba classes, and guided dives.

**Finding the beach:** San Carlos is at the junction of Reeside Avenue and Cannery Row next to the Coast Guard Pier (GPS: 36.610117 N / -121.896044 W). Several parking lots are here.

## Del Monte Beach

**Del Monte Beach,** on the southern Monterey Bay coast in Monterey State Beach Park, is a popular local spot for beachcombing, surfing, and sand strolls. The 11-acre beach is accessed from CA 1 on its namesake Del Monte Avenue, which runs west from CA 1 into Monterey. Turn onto Casa Verde Drive to beachside parking. Dog-friendly and bonfires are okay.

**Finding the beach:** From CA 1, take exit 402 and drive west on Del Monte Avenue for about a half-mile. Turn right (north) on Casa Verde Drive. Follow the road right; it becomes one-way and becomes Surf Way. Follow it 0.4 mile to Tide Avenue. Go left and park alongside the road (GPS: 36.604603 N / -121.868652 W) above the beach.

## Monterey State Beach

This long state beach stretches from Fisherman's Wharf to the town of **Seaside** on the east side of Monterey Bay. The popular and most accessible sections are by the wharf and Seaside. The beach offers walking, tide pools, sea kayaking, surf fishing, and scuba diving. Find it from either Fisherman's Wharf in Monterey or by taking the Seaside exit off CA 218, off CA 1.

**Finding the beach:** The beach stretches northeast from Wharf #3 in Monterey to Seaside. The beach can be accessed from Del Monte Avenue and CA 1

(Cabrillo Highway). There is plenty of free parking along Del Monte and also paid municipal lots (GPS: 36.600389 N / -121.887329 W). (831) 649-2836.

## Monterey To Santa Cruz

The 980-acre **Fort Ord Dunes State Park,** off CA 1 north of Monterey at a former US Army base, protects 4 miles of scenic coastline on the east side of **Monterey Bay.** The beach is never crowded and offers lots of solitude. A towering bluff backs the long sandy beach, which is reached by a short trail from a parking lot to the beach. A boardwalk heads out to a bluff-top viewing station with several interpretive signs. Dogs are not allowed on beach.

**Finding the beach:** The park is south of Marina. To access it from CA 1 north of Monterey, exit onto Lightfighter Drive and go east a few blocks to 2nd Avenue. Go left on 2nd and drive north to Divarty Street. Turn left on Divarty and follow west to 1st Avenue. Go right on 1st and drive about a mile to 8th Street. Go left over the highway and follow signs to a parking lot at the beach (GPS: 36.660496 N / -121.821036 W). (831) 649-2836.

## Marina State Beach

**Marina State Beach,** west of the town of Marina on the east side of **Monterey Bay,** is a 170-acre parkland with a long sand beach. Stiff winds here make the beach popular for flying kites and hang gliding from a launch area south of the parking. It's also great for beach strolls, surfing, bird watching, and enjoying the sunset. Hike the **Dunes Trail,** an interpretive nature trail crossing 80-foot-high sand dunes and a boardwalk to the beach and an observation deck. No dogs allowed. Access the beach on Reservation Road off CA 1.

**Finding the beach:** From Monterey, drive north on CA 1 to the Reservation Road exit #410. Go left or west on Reservation Road and drive until it ends at the beach. Park in a large paved lot (GPS: 36.698524 N / -121.808759 W). (831) 649-2836.

## Marina Dunes Preserve

The 40-square-mile **Marina Dunes Preserve,** stretching from **Seaside** to **Moss Landing,** is a protected area of sand dunes by Marina State Beach on the east side of Monterey Bay next to Marina. The area's dunes, highest on the Central Coast, were purchased in 1988 by the Monterey Peninsula Regional Park District, protecting them from development, sand mining, and damage caused by off-road vehicles. The sensitive dune environment has been restored and access is limited strictly to hikers on designated trails. No dogs.

*Marina State Beach is an ideal playground for sunning, beach walking, surf fishing, and flying kites in the stiff breeze.*

**Finding the area:** From Monterey, drive north on CA 1 to the Reservation Road exit #410. Go left or west on Reservation Road for a block to Dunes Drive. Turn right on Dunes Drive and head north past an RV park until it dead-ends. Park at the cul-de-sac (GPS: 36.703526 N / -121.802437 W). (831) 372-3196.

## Salinas River National Wildlife Refuge

The 367-acre **Salinas River National Wildlife Refuge**, part of the San Francisco Bay National Wildlife Refuge Complex, lies along the **Pacific Flyway** for migratory birds. Thousands of birds stop here for needed rest and food while migrating north and south in the spring and fall. The area, established in 1973, is one of the last wetlands on the central California coast, with numerous habitats including beaches, coastal dunes, salt marshlands, ponds, meadows, and riparian habitats. Several threatened and endangered species are found here, including the western snowy plover which nests near the beach and is susceptible to predators and disturbances. The wildlife refuge, 11 miles northeast of Monterey, has no visitor facilities except a parking area. The only recreational activity allowed is wildlife observation. Dogs, fires, and camping are not allowed. All hikers must stay on designated trails to avoid damaging habitat.

**Finding the area:** From Monterey, drive north on CA 1 for 11 miles to exit 412 for Del Monte Boulevard. Go left on Del Monte to the refuge parking lot (GPS: 36.734663 N / -121.793696 W). (510) 792-0222.

## Salinas River State Beach

**Salinas River State Beach,** south of Castroville and west of Moss Landing off CA 1/Cabrillo Highway, offers a long stretch of lonesome sand backed by a coastal dune ecosystem. The beach offers good hiking, nature study, whale-watching, and fishing. Swimming is not advised due to rip currents. Horses are allowed on the beach, but not dogs.

**Finding the beach:** To access the beach from CA 1 southwest of Castroville, take exit 414 and go northwest on Molera Road to Monterey Dunes Way. Turn left and drive straight to the beach and a parking lot (GPS: 36.77543 N / -121.79467 W). From CA 1 north of Castroville at Moss Landing, go left or west on Potrero Road to a beachside parking lot (GPS: 36.790746 N / -121.791735 W). (831) 649-2836.

## Moss Landing State Beach

**Moss Landing State Beach,** lying off CA 1 north of tidal Elkhorn Slough about 16 miles north of Monterey, is a popular and easily accessible parkland with a long sand beach flanked by dunes. The park is great for fishing, but swimming is not recommended because of powerful rip currents. It does, however, offer great surfing. Beginners should surf by the jetty. Moss Landing, coupled with **Moss Landing Wildlife Area** is also one of the best wildlife-watching spots along this coast section, especially for birds including pelicans, grebes, gulls, loons, and sea ducks. The endangered California sea otter and sea lions are often seen here, as well as occasional whales offshore. No dogs or fires.

**Finding the beach:** Reach the beach on CA 1 by driving north from Moss Landing over a broad estuary and past Elkhorn Yacht Club and a couple kayak rental places to Jetty Road. Follow the road west and south around Elkhorn Slough and along a long sand spit to a parking area near its end (GPS: 36.809807 N / -121.788474 W). (831) 649-2836.

## Zmudowski State Beach

**Zmudowski State Beach** (pronounced mud-OW-ski with a silent "z") is a wonderful isolated beach north of Moss Landing on the northwestern edge of Monterey County that seems to be used mostly by locals. The Pajaro River and its estuary split the beach into two halves, with Palm Beach north of the river. The

*A great egret hunts for fish in shallow water in Elkhorn Slough at Moss Landing State Beach.*

2-mile-long sandy beach is backed by a bluff of vegetation-anchored sand dunes. The park is good for horseback riding on the beach, bird watching along the freshwater estuary, and surf fishing. Swimming is not recommended since there are often big waves and a strong undertow. Access the beach from CA 1 on Struve Road to Giberson Road.

**Finding the beach:** Access the beach by driving north from Moss Landing to a left or north turn on Struve Road (GPS: 36.823442 N / -121.78006 W). Follow Struve to a left turn on Giberson Road, which jogs through farmland to a parking lot (GPS: 36.835939 N / -121.801525 W) at the south end of the beach. (831) 649-2836.

## Palm State Beach

**Palm State Beach,** a small but popular local beach, offers a long strip of sand flanked on the east by the tall Pajaro dunes, backed up by condos and houses. It's a perfect beach for walking and the farther south you go, the fewer folks you'll find. After a mile you reach a sand spit where the Pajaro River enters the bay. Don't bother looking for palms here—there are none.

**Finding the beach:** Access the beach from CA 1/Cabrillo Highway on the southwest side of Watsonville. Take exit 425 and go left or west on Riverside Drive, then right on Lee Road to West Beach Street/Beach Road. Follow it southwest to the beach and parking to the right (GPS: 36.867914 N / -121.818139 W). (831) 763-7062.

## Sunset State Beach

**Sunset State Beach,** 16 miles south of Santa Cruz and west of Watsonville and CA 1, is a 1.5-mile stretch of beach with a 90-site campground, picnic sites, and large dunes that is just north of Palm State Beach. Sites at the popular campground are close together. The beach, easily reached from the main parking lot, offers great sunbathing after the fog burns off and is a good spot to watch sunset. Swimming, as elsewhere along the coast here, is discouraged because of strong rip currents.

**Finding the beach:** Access the beach from CA 1/Cabrillo Highway on the southwest side of Watsonville. Take exit 425 and go left or west on Riverside Drive, then right on Lee Road to West Beach Street/Beach Road. After a couple miles, turn right or north on San Andreas Road and follow it to Sunset Beach Road. Turn left or west and drive to the beach and a parking area to the right (GPS: 36.896898 N / -121.837671 W). Go left on the road to the campground and farther south to another parking area (GPS: 36.881071 N / -121.82757 W). (831) 763-7063.

## Manresa State Beach

**Manresa State Beach,** about 15 minutes south of Santa Cruz, offers a nice stretch of sandy beach backed by dune bluffs. The park offers surf fishing, surfing, and other beach activities. There's also a 63-site campground with walk-in tent sites, water, and showers. Don't leave valuables in your car as there are break-ins here. Between Manresa Beach and CA 1 is **Ellicott Slough National Wildlife Refuge** and **Santa Cruz Long-Toed Salamander Ecological Reserve,** a 168-acre swamp that protects the endangered Santa Cruz long-toed salamander with two of its eight known breeding populations. The refuge is closed to visitation.

The area is reached from CA 1 via Buena Vista Drive to San Andreas Road, and then follow signs through a neighborhood to the park.

**Finding the beach:** The beach is west of Watsonville. To reach the beach from CA 1, take exit 427 and go west on Buena Vista Drive to San Andreas Road. Go right or north on San Andreas Road and drive northwest to Sand Dollar Drive. Follow signs through a neighborhood, following Sand Dollar Drive, then left on Manresa Beach Drive to the beach. There are beach access and parking on the right (GPS: 36.919907 N / -121.852573 W) and at the end of the road (GPS: 36.919907 N / -121.852573 W). To reach the northern beach access, continue north on San Andreas Road to a parking lot on the west (GPS: 36.919907 N / -121.852573 W). (831) 761-1795.

## Seacliff State Beach

**Seacliff State Beach,** a 2-mile-long strand on the northeast shore of Soquel Cove about 5 miles southeast of Santa Cruz off CA 1, forms the coastline of the suburb of Aptos. The wide beach backed by a sandy bluff, the "seacliff," is a popular local spot for sunbathing and beginner surfing. The park also has a picnic area and interpretative center. Anglers use the long pier which juts out in the cove; this is the only fishing area at the beach. It can get crowded and noisy so avoid weekends and holidays for quiet. Also offers RV camping. Dogs must be leashed.

Walk out to the pier's end to view the wreck of the ship **SS *Palo Alto*.** It was one of three ships built of concrete at the US Naval Shipyard in Oakland during World War I, but it was never commissioned. The ship sat docked in Oakland until 1929 when it was purchased and towed here, where it was sunk to form an amusement ship with a dance floor, cafe, and swimming pool. After 2 years, the company that owned it went bust, so the ship was stripped and has lain here since. The unsafe ship is closed except to local denizens including seagulls and pelicans, which perch on the deck.

**Finding the beach:** The beach is in the town of Aptos at 201 State Park Dr. To access the beach from CA 1/Cabrillo Highway, take exit 435 and go west on State Park Drive. Follow it to an entrance booth and a large parking area on the left (GPS: 36.972839 N / -121.912078 W). A long strip of close-in parking borders the beach. (831) 685-6442

## Forest of Nisene Marks State Park

The 10,233-acre **Forest of Nisene Marks State Park,** donated to the state in 1963, protects a swath of coastal mountain terrain north of Aptos and CA 1 just east of Santa Cruz. The area is covered with secondary forest that grew up after the old-growth forest was logged between 1883 and 1923. The park, rising 2,600 feet from sea level to the mountaintops, offers over 30 miles of excellent trails for hiking, trail running, and horseback riding that wind through eerie stands of

*Palm trees line a beachside trail along Soquel Cove at Seacliff State Beach in Aptos.*

redwoods. Mountain biking is limited to a few trails here, but bikes can be rented nearby. While hiking, look for clear creeks, banana slugs, and wildlife.

The most popular attractions are **Five Finger Falls,** reached on **Big Slide Trail,** and the spot that is the epicenter of the Loma Prieta earthquake on October 17, 1989, which damaged nearby Santa Cruz as well as San Francisco. When you enter the park, pick up a trail map with distances at the entrance station. The park also has picnic facilities. Dogs are not allowed on trails, only on leash at the picnic area and entrance road.

**Finding the park:** The park is east of CA 1 and Aptos. To access it from CA 1/Cabrillo Highway, take exit 435 and go right on State Park Drive and then right on Soquel Drive. Follow Soquel to Aptos Creek Road. Turn left and follow it about 4 miles to the park. (831) 763-7062.

## New Brighton State Beach

**New Brighton State Beach,** just east of Santa Cruz at the head of Soquel Cove, is a great state beach with a half-mile of sandy beach backed by bluffs forested with Monterey pine and cypress. The site was originally called China Beach because a Chinese fishing village was here in the 1870s and 1880s. The park has a campground close to the beach, with restrooms, showers, tables, grills, and a 10 p.m. noise curfew that is enforced. Campfire and Junior Ranger programs are offered in summer. There is also a visitor center with exhibits and educational programs.

**Finding the beach:** Access the beach from CA 1/Cabrillo Highway by taking exit 436 and going south on Park Avenue. Make the first left turn on McGregor Drive and follow it into the state beach. The main beach parking is a long lot on the west side of the park (GPS: 36.97943 N / -121.938195 W). (831) 464-6330.

## Santa Cruz

**Santa Cruz,** Spanish for "Holy Cross," is a picturesque and eclectic city spread along the northern shore of Monterey Bay. The small city presses up against the **Santa Cruz Mountains,** a low range of rounded hills clad in green forest, including groves of redwoods, along its northern boundary.

Santa Cruz, with a population of almost 60,000 in the 2010 census, has long been a magnet for travelers, who come to sample its numerous attractions, including the famed **Santa Cruz Beach Boardwalk,** its sandy pocket beaches surrounded by tall cliffs, and pleasant climate. It's also known for its liberal leanings and being a far-out groovy kind of place, as first a center for the Beat Generation in the 1950s and then the counterculture and hippies of the late 1960s. In 1992, Santa Cruz became one of the first American cities to approve the use of medical marijuana.

Among the redwood trees in the hills above the city lies the **University of California, Santa Cruz,** established in 1965 as one of the state's best public universities. The school, with a student body of almost 18,000, combines the smallness and intimacy of a liberal arts college with the creative bent of a research institution. It's known for its astronomy and space sciences programs and also offers a degree in computer game design. The school's mascot—the ubiquitous yellow banana slug— is equally eclectic and was named the best college mascot in 2004 by *Reader's Digest*. The costumed mascot is dubbed Sammy the Slug. These slugs, shell-less mollusks, inhabit the moist forest floor surrounding the university.

A few smaller towns lie within the greater Santa Cruz area, including **Capitola** and **Aptos** on the east side of Soquel Cove to the southeast. Each community, while feeling like a suburb of its larger neighbor, has its own downtown with shopping areas, restaurants, and beaches.

Santa Cruz is also considered one of the best **surfing** spots on the West Coast with 11 surf breaks. The area's long surfing history began when three Hawaiian princes surfed waves on redwood boards near the mouth of the San Lorenzo River in July, 1885. Check out the **Santa Cruz Surfing Museum** for more info. The area also offers lots of other recreational opportunities, including rock climbing, hiking, bicycling, skateboarding at the **Santa Cruz Skatepark,** and disc golf at the **Da Laveaga Disc Golf Course.**

**Finding the city:** Santa Cruz is on CA 1 at the northern end of Monterey Bay. The city is 70 miles south of San Francisco; 42 miles south of Half Moon Bay; and 43 miles north of Monterey. The downtown is easily accessed from CA 1, which runs through the south edge of the city along the coast.

## *Santa Cruz Climate & Weather*

Santa Cruz enjoys a Mediterranean-type of climate with warm, dry summers and cool, damp winters. Expect low clouds and fog at night and in the morning, especially in summer. The city receives an average of 31.5 inches of rainfall annually, with the majority falling between November and March. January, the rainiest month, averages 6.4 inches of rain on an average of 10.6 days. July is the driest month with only a scant 0.01 inches of rainfall.

## *Santa Cruz Shopping & Restaurants*

Downtown Santa Cruz, with spacious tree-lined streets and handsome buildings, many rebuilt after the big 1989 Loma Prieta earthquake (which destroyed most of the city's 19th-century buildings), is a great place to explore the city's diverse and interesting shops, boutiques, art galleries, and specialty stores, as well as sample different foods and flavors at lots of restaurants and cafes.

A few recommended restaurants are: **Shadowbrook** with great views in Capitola (1750 Wharf Rd., Capitola, CA 95010; 831-475-1511; shadowbrook-capitola

.com); **Shogun Japanese** for fresh sushi rolls (1123 Pacific Ave., Santa Cruz, CA 95060; 831-469-4477; facebook.com/ShogunSantaCruz); **Cafe Brasil** on Mission Street (410 Mission St., Santa Cruz, CA 95060; 831-429-1855; cafebrasil.us); and **Kelly's French Bakery** for breakfast and lunch (402 Ingalls St., Santa Cruz, CA 95060; 831-423-9059; kellysfrenchbakery.com). For Mexican fare, try **El Palomar** (336 Pacific Ave., Santa Cruz, CA 95060; 831-425-7575; elpalomarsantacruz.com) and **Tacos Moreno** (1053 Water St., Santa Cruz, CA 95062; 831-429-6095; tacos-moreno.com).

### Santa Cruz Attractions

Most visitors come to Santa Cruz to visit the **Beach Boardwalk,** simply the best seaside amusement park in California; roam around the downtown area sampling the diverse restaurants and shops; visit a handful of interesting museums, including one devoted to the local sport of surfing; plumb the oddities of the world at the famed **Mystery Spot** and the **Seymour Marine Discovery Center,** stroll among towering redwood trees at **Big Basin Redwoods** and **Henry Cowell Redwoods State Parks** and hike along cliff tops above the crashing Pacific surf along **West Cliff Drive.**

## Santa Cruz Beach Boardwalk

The **Santa Cruz Beach Boardwalk,** California's oldest amusement park, is a seaside attraction similar to the big East Coast amusement parks. The 24-acre park, built in 1907, is sandwiched between Beach Street and the beach next to the San Lorenzo River by downtown Santa Cruz. The **Giant Dipper** roller coaster (built 1924), one of the world's largest wooden roller coasters and a Santa Cruz landmark, towers over the boardwalk; supposedly over 50 million people have ridden it.

The park includes 34 other rides, including the 1911 **Looff Carousel;** the carousel and roller coaster are registered together as a National Historic Landmark, while the whole boardwalk is a California Historical Landmark. Other rides are Riptide, Cliffhanger, Haunted Castle, and Ghost Blasters.

The boardwalk is free and the beach is public, but you have to pay for rides and arcade games. Ticket options vary from single rides to daily and season passes. Check the website for current prices and hours. Summer, while very busy, is the best time to visit. Also come at night for cool temps and colorful lights.

**Finding the boardwalk:** The boardwalk is south of downtown Santa Cruz along the beach. It's easy to reach from CA1/Cabrillo Highway by going east on

*Over 50 million people have ridden the Giant Dipper roller coaster since 1924 at the Santa Cruz Beach Boardwalk.*

Mission Street to Front Street, then south on Front to Pacific Avenue to Beach Street. Go left or east on Beach (one-way) to the boardwalk. Parking is on the north side of the street in a large lot (GPS: 36.965217 N / -122.019026 W). (831) 423-5590.

## Santa Cruz Mission State Historic Park

The **Mission Santa Cruz,** with the oldest building in town, was erected between 1822 and 1824 as part of the 12th California Mission, although the mission was established in 1791 for conversion of the Ohlone and Yokut natives that lived here. The remaining mission building, constructed with adobe bricks (literally mud and straw), is not as glamorous as other bigger California missions, especially because the main church was destroyed in an 1857 earthquake, leaving only part of the complex intact.

The surviving building, housing the state park, was originally a dormitory for Indian acolytes. The Spanish Colonial-style building was added to the National Register of Historic Places in 1975 and the whole area was designated a National Historic District in 1976. On-site, however, is a replica half-size chapel built in the 1930s and the Gothic-style Holy Cross Church, built in 1889 on the spot of the original mission; it's an active Catholic parish and not part of the state historic park. The park, with free admission, offers historic exhibits and interpretative programs.

**Finding the mission:** The mission is in downtown Santa Cruz. Reach it from CA 1/Cabrillo Highway by driving east on Mission Street to the second left turn onto Emmett Street. Drive 1 block and turn right on School Street and drive 2 blocks to the mission on the right and a parking area (GPS: 36.9776 N / -122.027809 W). (831) 425-5849.

## Santa Cruz Museum of Art & History

This small museum, located downtown in the McPherson Center, is hard to find initially but worth the effort. It has historical displays about Santa Cruz as well as rotating art exhibitions and an outdoor sculpture garden.

**Finding the museum:** The museum is in downtown Santa Cruz at 705 Front St. south of CA 1. (831) 429-1964; santacruzmah.org.

## Santa Cruz Museum of Natural History

The **Santa Cruz Museum of Natural History,** one of California's oldest, is a great small museum with an affordable entrance fee and free admittance for those under 18. The museum, established in 1905, has a wonderful collection of wildlife dioramas, exhibits on local geology, an ocean area explaining local sea creatures including whales and a hands-on tide pool, and cultural exhibits about the Ohlone, the local Native Americans. They really live up to their mission statement: "Connect People with Nature."

**Finding the museum:** The museum (GPS: 36.964485 N / -122.009557 W) is at 1305 East Cliff Dr. by the beach. Parking is along nearby streets. (831) 420-6115; santacruzmuseums.org.

## Santa Cruz Surfing Museum

The **Santa Cruz Surfing Museum,** in the Mark Abbott Memorial Lighthouse at Lighthouse Point on West Cliff Drive, documents over 100 years of California surfing history. The small museum is jam-packed with boards, photos, and memorabilia. Be sure to check out the surfboard with a big shark-bite taken out of it. The free museum offers great views from white cliffs that jut into the ocean below Lighthouse Point. Most days you'll see surfers and seals skimming the waves below. Well worth an hour stop. Limited hours.

**Finding the museum:** The museum is on central Santa Cruz's coast at Lighthouse Point Park. There are several ways to access the museum from CA 1/ Cabrillo Highway. A couple easy ways are via Bay Street and Swift Street exits. Both streets lead to West Cliff Drive, which you follow to Lighthouse Point Park and Lighthouse Field State Beach. Park at a lot by the lighthouse and museum (GPS: 36.951777 N / -122.026772 W). (831) 420-6289; santacruzsurfingmuseum.org.

## Natural Bridges State Beach
## & Monarch Butterfly Natural Preserve

**Natural Bridges State Beach,** a 65-acre state beach on the west side of Santa Cruz, is simply one of the must-see natural places on this section of California coast. The pocket-size parkland offers not only a sweep of sandy beach enclosed by cliffs, but also an offshore rock bridge surrounded by pounding surf and a monarch butterfly preserve that protects over 150,000 monarchs every winter.

Once the park had three natural bridges on a peninsula that jutted into the water but one collapsed almost 100 years ago and the other in 1980. The remaining bridge, composed of a soft mudstone, is quickly eroding away. The

*A surfer catches a wave below Lighthouse Point in Santa Cruz, where surfing began in 1885.*

sandbox-size beach is good for sunbathing on warm days, building sand castles, flying a kite, and watching the sun sink into the Pacific. At low tide you can explore the right or north side of the cove and by the bridge to see excellent tide pools filled with ocean critters including sea stars, anemones, and crabs. It's easy to spend hours here so make sure you check the tide schedule at the visitor center so you don't get stuck at the pools by rising tide.

The **Monarch Butterfly Natural Preserve,** the only State Monarch Preserve in California, is the other part of Natural Bridges that draws visitors. The **Monarch Grove** of eucalyptus trees attracts colorful monarch butterflies, which winter over here from October until February after flying as many as 2,500 miles from Canada and the northern US. A wheelchair and stroller-accessible boardwalk accesses the Monarch Grove, ending at an observation platform. Another nearby winter home for monarchs is at Lighthouse Field to the south.

**Finding the park:** On the west side of Santa Cruz. From CA 1/Cabrillo Highway, turn south on Western Drive and drive 1 block to Mission Street. Turn right on Mission and drive a half-block to Natural Bridges Drive and turn left on it. Drive south to the parkland and the main parking lot on the right (GPS: 36.952011 N / -122.057529 W). Reach another parking area and overlook by continuing on the road. (831) 423-4609; parks.ca.gov.

## Seymour Marine Discovery Center

The **Seymour Marine Discovery Center,** at Long Marine Laboratory, part of University of California, Santa Cruz, sits above the cliffs along Monterey Bay next to Natural Bridges State Beach just north of Santa Cruz. The center, the educational arm of a working marine laboratory, is great for kids with an 87-foot blue whale skeleton and a smaller gray whale skeleton, guided tours, hands-on exhibits with live sea creatures to touch, a shark touch-tank, knowledgeable docents, and other exhibits.

The center is a worthwhile and cheaper alternative to going to the Monterey Bay Aquarium. After visiting, take a hike on the center's trails along the cliff top above the crashing surf.

**Finding the center:** On the west side of Santa Cruz. From CA 1/Cabrillo Highway, turn south on Western Drive and drive 1 block to Mission Street. Turn right on Mission and drive a half-block to Natural Bridges Drive and turn left on it. Drive south to Delaware Avenue and turn right. Follow Delaware west to Shafer Road where it turns into McAllister Way. Follow McAllister west and south to the center and parking (GPS: 36.949647 N / -122.065181 W). (831) 459-3800; seymourcenter.ucsc.edu.

## Mystery Spot

While driving along the Coast Highway, you've probably seen the enigmatic bumper stickers that say "Mystery Spot." In a redwood forest just north of Santa Cruz, you can visit the famous **Mystery Spot** and see what the fuss is about. The website for this kitschy tourist attraction calls it a "gravitational anomaly" that is about 150 feet in diameter and discovered by surveyors in 1939. Here the laws of physics and gravity are suspended and the world appears haywire.

At the Mystery Spot, balls roll uphill, chairs sit on walls rather than floors, and people lean so far over that they can't see their feet, yet they don't fall over. It's fun, popular, entertaining, and mind-boggling. A lot of visitors feel nauseous or dizzy at the Spot. To figure out the illusion, you're going to have to visit Mystery Spot yourself and take the tour.

It's best to make reservations online or by phone beforehand because tours fill up, especially in summer. Check online and try to book for tours that aren't completely filled up, you'll have more chances to try the demonstrations. Bring cash for parking too. Strollers and pets are not allowed. Remember to pick up your coveted free bumper sticker on the way out.

**Finding the place:** Mystery Spot is north of Santa Cruz at 465 Mystery Spot Rd. Reach the Spot from CA 1 by taking exit 441 and driving north on Market Street which becomes Branciforte Drive. Drive north to a left turn on Mystery Spot Road. Follow the narrow road to a parking area. (831) 423-8897; mysteryspot.com.

# Henry Cowell Redwoods State Park

The 4,623-acre **Henry Cowell Redwoods State Park,** just north of Santa Cruz off CA 9, protects a grove of coast redwoods as well as other old-growth forest including Douglas firs and ponderosa pines. The park's tallest tree is 285 feet tall and 16 feet in diameter, while the oldest trees are 1,800 years old. The park offers 20 miles of trails, some up steep terrain and no bridges at creek and river crossings. Fishing is popular in the San Lorenzo River during steelhead and salmon season (catch and release only) in winter. The park also has a campground and visitor center. Dogs must be leashed at all times and are not allowed on trails. The park is near Felton north of Santa Cruz off CA 9.

**Finding the park:** The park is on CA 9/Graham Hill Road north of Santa Cruz. To reach it, drive north on CA 17/Santa Cruz Highway to Mount Hermon Road. Go left on it and drive until it ends at Graham Hill Road in Felton. Turn right and drive to the next stop light at CA 9. Turn left on CA 9 and drive a half-mile to the park entrance on the left or east. The campground is on the right or west 2.5 miles south on CA 9. (831) 335-4598.

# Wilder Ranch State Park

**Wilder Ranch State Park,** a 7,000-acre area, lies along the cliff-lined Pacific coast and CA 1 a couple miles north of Santa Cruz and Natural Bridges State Park. The park, originally part of the Wilder dairy farm in the 19th century, offers 34 miles of hiking, biking, and equestrian trails along the cliff edge above the ocean and on the coastal terrace. The trails are generally relaxing, with no steep grades, making them perfect for a relaxing stroll or bike ride. The easy-to-follow trails go to secluded beaches with few people as well as to stunning overlooks above the crashing surf—great for watching the sunset. Keep an eye out for wildlife, including sea lions as well as lots of shorebirds. Besides the coastal area, the park extends east into the Santa Cruz Mountains almost to the town of Felton. Besides hiking, the park also has a cave called **Hell Hole,** with a 90-foot-deep pit entrance.

**Finding the park:** Park is west of Santa Cruz. Drive 1.5 miles from the junction of Western Drive and CA 1/Cabrillo Highway and make a left turn on Coast Road. Follow the road past the interpretive center to a large parking area on the left (GPS: 36.960197 N / -122.085775W). Trails lead from here to the center and shoreline. The Coast Road continues west back to CA 1. (831) 423-9703.

*A wave crashes on a rock beach at Four Mile Beach at Wilder State Park.*

## Big Basin Redwoods State Park

**Big Basin Redwoods State Park,** established in 1902, is California's oldest state park and a designated California Historical Landmark. The park harbors over 18,000 acres of coastal redwoods, the state's largest stand, which is mostly second-growth forest since the area was heavily logged.

The park also offers over 80 miles of trails, several great campgrounds, picnic areas, and a visitor center. The park has many gorgeous waterfalls, including **Sempervirens Falls** and **Berry Creek Falls.** An excellent hike is the 29.5-mile **Skyline to the Sea Trail,** which descends from the Santa Cruz Mountains to the Pacific Ocean, with most hikers taking a couple days to complete it.

Campsite reservations are essential much of the year; book online at reserveamerica.com. The park visitor center is northwest of Santa Cruz via CA 9 to CA 236. The park also has the **Rancho del Oso Visitor Center** off CA 1 and east of Waddell Creek Beach on Canyon Road. Park in a lot on the right (GPS: 37.097176 N / -122.27467 W).

**Waddell Creek Beach,** on the west side of CA 1 and the visitor center, is a good sand beach that's often windy, making it ideal for sailboarding. Park in a large lot (GPS: 37.097176 N / -122.27467 W) above the beach just past the bridge over Waddell Creek.

**Finding the park:** The park is 25 miles northwest of Santa Cruz. From CA 1/ Cabrillo Highway, go north on River Street/CA 9. Drive north on CA 9 through Felton to the junction of CA 9 and CA 236/Big Basin Highway in Boulder Creek. Go left on winding CA 236 and drive 9 miles to the park. Park in a lot on the left (GPS: 37.172107 N / -122.222369 W) across the highway from the visitor center. (831) 338-8860.

## Laguna Creek Beach

**Laguna Creek Beach,** a pocket beach hiding a half-mile south of Panther Beach, is a half-mile stretch of sand tucked into a pocket of cliffs west of CA 1. Laguna Creek, draining off the Santa Cruz Mountains, meanders across the south end of the beach. The narrow beach is popular with sunbathers and the north end of the beach, reached by walking across bedrock and tide pools at low tide, is a thin cliff-bound beach that's popular with nudists.

Lock your vehicle at the parking area and take all valuables with you. Glass fragments in the lot are a telltale sign of break-ins. Swimming is discouraged because of strong undertow currents.

**Finding the beach:** The beach is close to milepost 26.0 on CA 1. Park on the east or inland side of CA 1 in either a large lot by the highway (GPS: 36.987227 N / -122.155397 W) or on the north shoulder of Laguna Road. Cross the highway and look for a gap in bushes. Follow an old road down to railroad tracks and continue to the beach about 10 minutes away. Watch for poison oak along the trail.

## Panther & Hole in the Wall Beaches

**Panther Beach,** a small pocket beach tucked into tall cliffs, is a great sand beach that is popular with nudists. The secluded 300-foot-long beach is primarily used for sunbathing. Climbers also stop here to go bouldering on the sandstone cliffs, doing a variety of traverses and short problems before dropping onto the sand. The beaches are part of the Coast Diaries parkland. Don't bring glass or alcohol. Parking closes at 10 p.m. No camping. Swimming is not advised because of dangerous riptides.

**Hole in the Wall Beach** is a long sand beach, backed up by 30- to 50-foot cliffs, just south of Panther Beach that may be accessed at low tide by walking through the gap in the cliff at the south end of Panther. This was the site of the original Hole

*Hole in the Wall Beach is a spectacular sand beach washed*
*by emerald waves that break on sheer cliffs.*

*Pacific breakers roll against rocky headlands at Panther Beach.*

in the Wall arch, which collapsed. Go to the beach only at low tide. If you're there when the tide starts coming in, hightail it back to Panther so you aren't trapped.

**Finding the beach:** Panther Beach, also called Yellowbank Beach, is about 2 miles south of Davenport and a half-mile south of Bonny Doon Beach with the parking turnoff between *mile markers 26.86 and 26.40.* Turn off CA 1, no sign, and park in a dirt lot between CA 1 and the railroad tracks (GPS: 36.991412 N / -122.165175 W). It's hard to see the parking when driving south. Cross the railroad tracks and hike 5 minutes down a short steep path to the beach. Don't leave valuables in your vehicle.

## Bonny Doon Beach

**Bonny Doon Beach** is a wide peaceful sand beach tucked into a deep cove. Tall sandstone cliffs border the beach on the north and south, with steep grassy slopes on the east side below the highway. The cliffs on the north side create a windbreak so it usually feels warm beneath them—which is why it is used as the nude sector. The beach lies directly west of the junction of CA 1 and Bonny Doon Road about 1.5 miles south of Davenport.

Bonny Doon, now part of the California State Park system, has long been a popular nude beach for the Santa Cruz crowd, with even an annual New Year's Day nude event. The north part of the beach has traditionally been the clothing-optional beach, while the south is not.

Don't leave valuables in your car, and it's advised to depart the beach before dark since assaults have occurred here. Swimming is discouraged because of a strong undertow. No restrooms or water.

**Finding the beach:** The beach and parking are at milepost 27.6 at the junction where CA 1 intersects Bonny Doon Road. A long strip of paved parking parallels the highway on the west (GPS: 37.000955 N / -122.180546 W). The parking lot is closed 10 a.m. to 6 p.m. No parking along CA 1. Follow a trail from the north end of the park across the railroad tracks, then descend steeply down to the beach. Hiking time is 5 minutes.

## Shark Fin Cove

**Shark Fin Cove** is a beautiful pocket beach surrounded by cliffs just off CA 1 about 0.2 miles south of Davenport. The cove, popular with photographers, is dominated by the **Shark's Fin,** a blocky sea stack that resembles a shark's dorsal fin in profile. Swimming is not advisable since rogue waves can occur at any time, pushed up deep channels between the cliffs and the fin.

**Finding the beach:** Park in a large lot on the west side of the highway (GPS: 37.005603 N / -122.185484 W) and follow a steep path down to the sandy beach. Social trails follow the edge of the cliffs above the beach, offering more great views of this gorgeous spot.

## Davenport Beach

**Davenport Beach,** directly west of the historic town of Davenport, is a sand beach hemmed by cliffs at both ends and a sand bluff below the highway. It's a beautiful beach with a sea stack on the south end, tide pools, caves in the cliffs, lots of seclusion, free parking, amazing views, and is dog-friendly. It's a fine surfing spot too. There's good hiking on trails along the cliff top. Across the highway from the parking are convenient restaurants and shops. The beach is closed 10 p.m. to 6 a.m., and the local sheriff patrols it. No camping, fires, alcohol, or fireworks. Don't park on the Davenport streets after 10 p.m.; it is residents only.

**Finding the beach:** The beach is west of CA 1 and Davenport. Park in a large lot on the west side of the highway opposite shops and restaurants (GPS: 37.011112 N / -122.195408 W). Follow a trail along the railroad tracks before dropping steeply down to the beach. There's also a parking area along the highway to the south. (831) 454-7901.

*Boys explore a sea cave at Shark Fin Cove, a spectacular and hidden pocket beach.*

## Davenport Landing Beach

**Davenport Landing Beach,** at the original site of the town of Davenport, is a popular beach at the head of a protected cover just north of Davenport. The beach, like the others on this stretch of coast, is flanked by steep cliffs. The beach, a Santa Cruz County Park, is popular with locals but generally less busy than the beaches near Santa Cruz. It offers great surfing, windsurfing, walking, and has great tide pools for low tide exploration. There are also restrooms (no water) and picnic tables along the trail. The beach is handicapped accessible, one of the few on the coast that are. You can rent a beach wheelchair at Shared Adventures (831-459-7210) in Santa Cruz.

**Finding the beach:** Drive north from Davenport and make a left (west) turn on Davenport Landing Road. Follow the road to a designated parking along the sides of the road (GPS: 37.024958 N / -122.215565 W). Restrooms are here. Descend down on either the regular trail or a wheelchair-accessible trail to the beach. 831-454-7956.

*A giant wave sprays and splashes against a rock wall in Shark Fin Cove.*

# Scott Creek Beach

**Scott Creek Beach,** a couple miles north of Davenport, is a broad and long sandy beach flanked by soft stone cliffs that is next to the highway. It's popular for sunbathing and wading; swimming is discouraged because of strong undertows and cold water. The beach is big enough to get away from other visitors. The far north part, reached by hiking over a rocky section to a long sandy beach, is clothing-optional so avoid those sections if you bring kiddies. The north part of the beach also offers great surfing with big waves between October and May. Wear a wet suit since the water is cold. The bluffs above the beach offer a great seat for watching the sunset. Scott Creek divides the beach; do not attempt to wade the creek if it's running high as it can be deep and fast. Instead cross on the highway shoulder.

**Finding the beach:** Scott Creek Beach is just west of CA 1 about 2 miles north of Davenport near milepost 31.3. There is plenty of parking on both sides of the highway on wide paved shoulder lots (GPS: 37.039637 N / -122.22812 W). Be extremely cautious when crossing the highway since cars fly along this straight section.

# Greyhound Rock County Park & State Marine Conservation Area

**Greyhound Rock,** a Santa Cruz County Park, is named for a massive mound of gray rock, composed of Miocene-age mudstone, which sits just off the coast, forming the outside rim of a cove. The area is also protected as the **Greyhound Rock State Marine Conservation Area** to shelter its unique biodiversity, including more than 300 species of fish, invertebrates, marine mammals, and birds. The large kelp forests harbor lots of animals like sharks, whales, and dolphins. The area offers surf fishing, beachcombing, tide pools, sunbathing, and walking. Park facilities include paved parking, restrooms, picnic tables, benches, and a handicapped-accessible viewing platform. A good hike goes 2.8 miles up the beach to **Waddell Creek Beach** to the north. You can scramble up to the flat summit of Greyhound Rock at low tide.

**Finding the beach:** Drive 6.2 miles north from Davenport on CA 1 to the signed Greyhound Rock Park. Turn left (west) into a large paved parking lot GPS: (37.080029 N / -122.264786 S). Walk down a steep paved path to the beach. (831) 454-7956.

# Waddell Creek Beach & Rancho del Oso

**Waddell Creek Beach,** part of **Big Basin Redwoods State Park** is a long stretch of sandy beach that offers some of the best windsurfing on the California coast with its consistently strong northwest winds; because of strong winds and heavy surf, the park recommends it for experts only. The beach has a lot to recommend it with beachside parking just off the coast highway, lots of beach so you can get away from others, and just across the road is the **Rancho del Oso** entrance to Big Basin Redwoods. Over there, away from the beach, you can hike, mountain bike, and camp in the Santa Cruz Mountains. Besides stellar windsurfing, the beach offers boogie boarding, kite surfing, surfing, surf fishing, as well as birding at the **Theodore J. Hoover Natural Preserve** on the east side of CA 1. The beach has free parking, no admittance fee, and pit toilets.

**Finding the beach:** From Davenport, drive 7.6 miles north on CA 1 to Waddell Beach and Rancho del Oso or 17 miles north of Santa Cruz. Park in a large lot on the left (west) side of the highway next to the beach (GPS: 37.09694 N / -122.279723 W). (831) 427-2288.

# Año Nuevo State Park

**Año Nuevo State Park,** a 4,209-acre parkland on the coast 55 miles south of San Francisco, protects a rocky point that juts into the Pacific Ocean. The rocky point, swept by surf and flanked by lonely sand beaches, offers one of California's great wildlife spectacles.

The state park, including **Año Nuevo Island** just offshore, is the largest mainland breeding colony for the northern elephant seal. Come during the December to March breeding season and you'll see these huge seals, some 16 feet long and weighing 2.5 tons, with the bulls vying for breeding dominance and then the females giving birth and nursing pups which can grow to 300 pounds in a month. By mid-March most of the adults have left, with the pups remaining until they've learned to swim. The pups leave in late April and head northward for the summer off British Columbia. The elephant seals return to molt from May through August, so if you miss the winter mating season, you get a second chance to witness these magnificent marine mammals.

The park also preserves important habitats for other species including the rare San Francisco garter snake as well as an ancient Ohlone Indian habitation site. During the elephant seal season, December 15 to March 31, all access to the park is by guided hike only to avoid disturbing the seals. The hike out to the seal rookery takes about an hour each way. Advance reservations are recommended. Call the reservations number (800-444-4445) or book online at anonuevo

*Seals, seal lions, and elephant seals all thrive along the rocky shorelin at Año Nuevo State Park.*

.reserveamerica.com up to 56 days in advance. Also visit the park information center for more details.

**Finding the area:** The park is about 20 miles north of Santa Cruz off CA 1/ Cabrillo Highway. Turn west off the highway onto Año Nuevo State Park Road and follow it south a short distance to the visitor center and parking lot (GPS: 37.120342 N / -122.307326 W). Trails begin here to access the preserve. **(**650) 879-2025.

## Gazos Creek State Beach

**Gazos Creek** is a lovely and remote beach that is usually empty and quiet except for the crash of the surf. It's a clean sandy beach with lots of privacy, a locals beach, on a beautiful section of coast. It offers excellent surfing, windsurfing, and kite surfing, but only for the experienced. Watch out for sharks if you're out in the water. Walk north up the beach at low tide to check out some big sea stacks.

**Finding the beach:** Drive 14.7 miles north from Davenport to a left (west) turn, which leads to a large paved parking lot (GPS: 37.166469 N / -122.361545 W). Follow a mellow trail southwest to the beach.

# Butano State Park

**Butano State Park,** one of central California's lesser known scenic gems, is a 4,728-acre parkland that sprawls across a couple drainages on the western slope of the Santa Cruz Mountains. The area protects a lush redwood forest with mostly second- and third-growth trees although a few majestic uncut old-growth trees scatter along the creeks. The park offers lots of trails, which can be combined into great loop hikes, or venture into nearby Big Basin Redwoods and Año Nuevo parks. There's also spacious Ben Ries Campground with 21 drive-in campsites and 18 walk-in campsites, restrooms, drinking water, and, in summer, nature walks and campfire programs. Dogs are not allowed on trails and must be leashed in the campground.

**Finding the park:** Access the park by turning east from CA 1/Cabrillo Road about 4.5 miles south of Pescadero onto Gazos Creek Road. Drive a couple miles and turn left on Cloverdale Road. Continue a short distance to the park entrance on the right. This can also be reach from the north via Pescadero Road to Cloverdale. (650) 879-2040.

# Bean Hollow State Beach

**Bean Hollow State Beach,** originally named Arroyo de los Frijoles or Creek of Beans, is a fabulous state beach with both a sandy stretch as well as lots of rocky shoreline filled with tide pools and crashing surf. The sand beach forms a crescent-shaped cove with headlands on either side. The 44-acre area offers surf fishing, sunbathing, picnicking, and beachcombing. Swimming is not recommended because of heavy surf, cold water, dangerous riptides, and sharks. There's also **Arroyo de los Frijoles Trail,** a great 2-mile hike that explores the craggy shoreline, winding above cliffs and surf. It ends at the parking area for Pebble Beach. Dogs are allowed in the park but must be leashed at all times. Open 8 a.m. to sunset.

**Finding the beach:** Drive 17.5 miles south from Half Moon Bay on CA 1 to mile marker 12.0. Make a right (west) turn into a small parking lot just above the beach (GPS: 37.225561 N / -122.408651 W). (650) 726-8819.

# Pebble Beach

**Pebble Beach,** not to be confused with the other more famous Pebble Beaches in California, is a small pretty stretch of shore tucked into a cove among rocky headlands that is part of Bean Hollow State Beach. From the parking area, a stairway drops down to the beach, which is covered with polished pieces of quartz and rocks deposited thousands of years ago during the Pleistocene epoch as gravel on shoreline terraces. Also check out tafoni, the honeycomb weathering caused when the moist salty air attacks sandstone.

This is a good place to explore the tide pool life zone at low tide or to sit and watch the rolling surf break on the reefs and rocky shore. Don't swim—dangerous currents, cold water, and big waves wait for you. It's also called Bean Hollow Beach North.

**Finding the beach:** Drive 17.2 miles south from Half Moon Bay on CA 1 to mile marker 11.8. Make a right (west) turn into a small parking lot just above the beach (GPS: 37.236535 N / -122.415557W). (650) 726-8819.

## Pescadero State Beach

**Pescadero Beach** is a mile-long stretch of sand broken by rocky headlands that jut into the ocean. Steep bluffs of tan mudstone separate the beach from the highway above. The state beach divides into three separate areas, each with its own parking and character, with sandy beaches, pocket beaches, a lagoon, sand dunes, and tide pools.

**Finding the beach:** The south beach is directly opposite the junction of CA 1 and Pescadores Road. Park in a lot above the cliffs (GPS: 37.259625 N / -122.413576 W) and scramble down to the small stony beaches on either side of a headland.

The middle parking area (GPS: 37.265235 N / -122.412208 W) allows access to the **Pescadero Marsh Natural Preserve** farther up the highway. This is a good spot for bird watching, over 160 species have been sighted, along the edges of a big marshy lagoon east of the highway and where Pescadero Creek empties into the ocean.

The north parking area (GPS: 37.274279 N / -122.408928 W), about a quarter-mile north of Pescadero Road, gives access to a long stretch of beach backed by sandy bluffs.

Dogs and fires are prohibited on the beach and at the natural preserve. Day use only; open 8 a.m. to sunset. Located 15.2 miles south of Half Moon Bay. (650) 879-2170.

## Pomponio State Beach

**Pomponio State Beach,** named for a Miwok Indian who rebelled against Mexican rule in the early 1800s, is a broad sand beach flanked by a steep headland on the south and a long stretch of sandstone bluffs to the north. The popular beach offers sunbathing, beachcombing, as well as a lagoon that is popular for wading and warmer than the ocean. Swimming is discouraged due to dangerous rip currents. The narrow beach north of the main beach can be accessed at low tide; know the tide table times to avoid getting stranded below the cliffs. The beach is

*Wildflowers spill down a bluff to a rock-strewn beach at Pescadero State Beach.*

easily accessed from a large parking area with restrooms (no water) and has picnic tables and barbecue pits. No dogs and beach fires are allowed.

**Finding the beach:** Pomponio is 12 miles south of Half Moon Bay. Look for a spacious parking lot just west of CA 1 (GPS: 37.299887 N / -122.405317 W). Day use only, open 8 a.m. to sunset. (650) 879-2170.

## San Gregorio State Beach

**San Gregorio State Beach** is a broad pocket beach tucked into a shallow cove where San Gregorio Creek flows into a freshwater estuary or lagoon before seeping into the ocean. It's popular on weekends with the San Francisco crowd but generally quiet during the week. The beach offers tanning, beachcombing, walking, and great scenic views. Don't swim in the cold surf with its dangerous undertow or in the lagoon, which tends to be stagnant. There's also lots of driftwood tossed onto the shore, offering benches with a view. Some folks make driftwood sculptures and even fantastical buildings. Dogs are prohibited since the area is the nesting ground of the endangered western snowy plover. The area offers picnic tables, barbecue grills, and restrooms

The beach is also a California historic landmark since a Spanish explorer and his men camped here in 1769 en route to discovering San Francisco Bay. A nude beach with the same name is just north of the state beach. Access it from CA 1 and a paid parking area above the beach bluffs.

**Finding the beach:** San Gregorio is 10.5 miles south of Half Moon Bay west of the junction of CA 1 and CA 84. The large parking area, offering easy beach access, is off CA 1 (GPS: 37.323481 N / -122.401487 S). Day use only; open 8 a.m. to sunset. (650) 726-8819.

## Martin's Beach

**Martin's Beach** is a long stretch of sand and surf flanked by a towering pyramid-shaped rock on its north end. The popular beach, a privately owned cove and small community, has unfortunately had access problems after it was sold in 2008 for $39.5 million. This effectively shut off ingress to generations of Californians who had come to Martin's Beach to surf, beachcomb, sunbathe, fish, and hike; prior to the sale, visitors paid an entrance fee to use the beach area. Access to the beach is now complicated by California coastal law, which regulates beach access and coastal development as well as by the decades of public access which has created an easement through the private property to the beach. Stay tuned for future resolution.

**Finding the beach:** Martin's Beach is a few miles south of Half Moon Bay. Turn west from CA 1 onto Martin's Beach Road (GPS: 37.376501 N / -122.404057 W). Follow the road, which may not be open in the future, to the beach.

## Cowell Ranch State Beach

**Cowell Ranch State Beach** is a great off-the-beaten-track beach that is reached by a 0.6-mile dirt trail through an artichoke field to a scenic overlook above the beach. Wooden stairs descend 100 feet down to the crescent-shaped beach, which is isolated from the world above by a towering bluff. It's a great place to enjoy privacy, the ocean breeze, good hiking, and a harbor seal protection area, which lies south of the overlook at Seal Beach. Look for the seals below bobbing in the waves or sunning on the rocks. The seals can be seen February through May, with the pups in March and April. There is no public access to the seal area. Keep away from the soft cliff edge; it can break away unexpectedly. No dogs are allowed.

**Finding the beach:** Cowell Ranch State Beach is 3.3 miles south of Half Moon Bay off CA 1. Park in a lot on the west side of the highway (GPS: 37.422223 N / -122.426367 W). The overlook (GPS: 37.419936 N / -122.434752 W) above the seal area is at the end of a closed road-trail.

## Arroyo Cañada Verde Beach

This small crescent-shaped beach, flanked on the north by the Ritz-Carlton Hotel and on the south by a golf course, is on the south side of Half Moon Bay. The beach is easily accessed by a short trail that bisects the golf course above a wooded arroyo.

**Finding the beach:** Go west from CA 1 on Miramontes Point Road; where the road bends right, park in a small lot on the left (GPS: 37.43038 N/ -122.437179 S). Follow the trail to an overlook above the beach. Descend down the bluff to the beach.

## Redondo Beach

This lovely secluded beach, just north of the Ritz-Carlton Hotel and golf course, is a great local beach with wonderful ocean views from the top of the bluff. Descend to the beach by finding a steep path (no stairs). The south side of the beach has some tide pools in the bedrock. Nice to watch the surf crash on the rocks here. A scenic trail goes north along the cliff top to an arroyo, where you can also descend to the beach.

**Finding the beach:** Redondo Beach is a half-mile south of Half Moon Bay off CA 1. Turn west on Redondo Beach Road and follow it to a parking area at the end above the beach (GPS: 37.439114 N / -122.443024 W).

## Blufftop Coastal Park

**Blufftop Coastal Park** includes **Poplar Beach** on the south side of Half Moon Bay. It's very popular, especially with dog owners, who let Fido roam free, and horseback riders. Watch for road apples in the sand. There are several scenic overlooks along the **Half Moon Bay Coastal Trail** which follows the top of the bluff above the beach. Look for social trails that descend steeply to the golden sand. Dogs are allowed on leash.

**Finding the park:** Turn west from CA 1 on Poplar Street and drive to a parking area at its end above the beach (GPS: 37.455191 N / -122.443662 W). Parking is by credit/debit card.

## Half Moon Bay State Beach

This state park, stretching for about 4 miles along the central coast at **Half Moon Bay,** includes four beaches—**Roosevelt, Dunes, Venice, and Francis.** The long beachfront is great for sunbathing, walking, picnicking, and camping. Swimming is discouraged because the water is cold and there is a strong undertow. The park has a 50-site campground just north of the park visitor center off Kelly Avenue and next to Francis Beach. Reserve campsites well in advance because it is often full. The free visitor center is open Saturday and Sunday. Parking is by fee only (big complaint by visitors), and tickets are given if you're here past sunset. You can park nearby, including in town, for a cheaper price and walk to the beaches. Dogs are not allowed on the beach. Beaches are open 8 a.m. to sunset.

**Francis Beach** is the southernmost beach in the park. It borders both the visitor center and campground. Access it by turning west from CA 1 on the south side of Half Moon Bay and driving a half mile to the park entrance and the parking lot (GPS: 37.466722 N / -122.445298 W). A picnic area is between the parking and the beach.

**Venice Beach** is a popular sand beach that is easily accessed from the coast highway. Turn west from CA 1 on Venice Boulevard and drive a short distance to the park and a couple large parking lots (GPS: 37.479975 N / -122.44989 W).

**Dunes Beach** is the northern beach at the state park. Again, it's a long stretch of honey-colored sand. Reach the beach by turning west from CA 1 on Young Street. Park in a long parking lot with restrooms above the beach (GPS: 37.48373 N / -122.452438 W). Go right on a road just before the Dunes parking lot to reach **Roosevelt Beach,** a continuation of Dunes Beach, and its parking area (GPS: 37.487965 N / -122.454547 W) with restrooms. This beach isn't usually busy, but is popular for windsurfing and surfing.

**Coastside Trail** is a 3-mile-long trail for hikers and bikers that parallels the coast from the visitor center at Francis Beach north to Roosevelt Beach; if you walk out and back, it's a 6-mile hike. The trail offers lots of great ocean views from the tops of the bluffs and allows access to remoter beach sections. Because of its length, the park recommends riding a bicycle rather than walking.

For more state park information, contact **Half Moon Bay State Beach** (650-726-8819; campsite reservations 800-444-PARK (7275) or reserveamerica.com).

## Surfer's Beach

**Surfer's Beach** is exactly that—a popular beach for surfers. It has a lot going for it, including easy access and good waves. It's popular for beginning surfers with friendly waves as well as sea kayakers and windsurfers. If you want surf lessons, contact the **Jetty Betty Surf School** in Half Moon Bay (650-455-8141) and they will take you out to Surfer's Beach.

The beach is bordered by a long rock jetty that juts far out into the water. The jetty, built in the early 1960s to create a harbor, has caused much erosion on the Surfer's Beach side, causing much of the beach to wash away and leaving only a thin strip of sand.

**Finding the beach:** To access Surfer's Beach, park along the shoulder of CA 1 in Half Moon Bay where the highway runs alongside the water (GPS: 37.500919 N / -122.470525 W) or park at Pillar Point Harbor to the north. The crux of getting to the beach is crossing the busy highway—use extreme caution. Also look for safe places to scramble down rocks to the beach area.

## Pillar Point & Maverick's Beach

**Pillar Point** is a small peninsula that is just south on the west side of Pillar Point Harbor in Half Moon Bay. The fenced Pillar Point Air Force Station, an installation for tracking missiles, covers most of the pillar's hilltop.

The 0.6-mile-long **West Beach Trail** follows the east side of the point alongside the harbor to the end of Pillar Point. The trailhead (GPS: 37.501553 N / -122.496714 W) is at the south end of the parking area. Hike south on a flat dirt trail that edges alongside the west edge of the harbor below a bluff. After 0.5-mile, the trail ends at a breakwater. Walk right along sandy **Maverick's Beach** below bluffs until the beach ends at a rocky headland. It's possible to continue at low tide, but keep an eye on the rising tide so you don't get trapped.

The rugged western side of Pillar Point and the coastal section north to Moss Beach is the **Fitzgerald Marine Reserve,** a San Mateo County park that protects unique tide pool environments.

**Finding the beach:** Find Pillar Point and the trailhead from CA 1 north of Half Moon Bay by going west on Capistrano Road for 0.3 mile. Turn left on Prospect and drive 0.1 mile and turn left on Broadway then right on Princeton. Drive 0.4 mile and turn right on West Point Road and follow it for 0.6 miles to the parking area on the left (GPS: 37.501921 N / -122.49677 W).

## Maverick's Surf Area

**Maverick's surf area,** with waves breaking on an offshore reef a half-mile west of Pillar Point, is one of the California coast's most renowned surfing spots and attracts big-wave surfers from around the world. Here, because of the unique underwater geography, huge waves are created after winter storms with some reaching monster heights of 80 feet. Waves over 25 feet high are routinely surfed in winter.

**Finding the area:** The trailhead for West Beach Trail is the staging place for surfers to head out to Maverick's. From the parking area (GPS: 37.502045 N / -122.496767 W) on West Point Avenue, cross the road and pass a yellow gate at the entrance to a closed fire road. Walk up the paved road to several social trails that go west to the bluff top. Bring binoculars or a telescope to watch the surfers doing their thing a half-mile offshore. Pretty rad!

## Maverick's Surf Contest

The **Maverick's Surf Contest,** also called Maverick's Invitational and held every year depending on how high the waves run, is a world epicenter for big-wave surfing and surfers. In the autumn, invitations are extended to 24 elite surfers, and then they wait for the waves to arrive. Sometime between November and March, when giant swells begin rolling across the Pacific Ocean, the surfers get a phone call and have 24 hours to get to Half Moon Bay for the competition. As the contest website says, "the surfing community's bravest and most skillful souls assemble to confront the thundering mountain of salt water many consider to be the most dangerous wave Mother Nature has ever concocted."

The first contest was held in 1999, but no good waves led to cancellations in 2007, 2009, and 2012. The contest in 2010, won by Chris Bertish from South Africa, had the largest prize in US surfing history—a cool $150,000. As many as 10,000 spectators crowd the bluff opposite Maverick's to watch the surfers.

If you want to see the competition, you need to plan in advance like the surfers because you don't know when it's going to happen. Visit the comp website at mavericksinvitational.com for up-to-date details and to sign up for text alerts. You must buy tickets in advance for a parking pass and access to the festival. Shuttles bring you to the bluffs from area parking lots. Bring binoculars for a better view.

## Fitzgerald Marine Reserve

The **Fitzgerald Marine Reserve,** a 32-acre area managed by San Mateo County as a parkland, includes a 3-mile stretch of wild coast between Pillar Point on the south and Montara Lighthouse on the north. The area offers diverse marine and terrestrial ecosystems with great tide pools along with beaches, rocky headlands, towering bluffs, marshes, and woodlands.

It's best to visit the tide pools, one of the best tide pool habitats on the central California coast, which appear like seaside aquariums teeming with life including hermit crabs, sea urchins, anemones, red octopi, and sea stars. You can also see harbor seals and perhaps a whale swimming south in winter. The area's heavy visitation impacts the tide pools and their inhabitants. Follow the reserve's strict rules to preserve the animal life. These include not collecting anything, including shells, wood, and marine life; do not pick up or touch any marine life; be careful where and how you walk, footsteps damage tide pool life. Only step on bare rock surfaces.

Check the weather and tide tables before visiting. The reserve recommends a low tide of +1 or lower for the best viewing. You can find the tide table at the website fitzgeraldreserve.org/lowtides.

The reserve can be very busy on weekends. Try to come on weekdays for privacy. Dress warmly; it can be cool and foggy in summer. There is also free parking, a visitor center, and docent-led beach hikes.

**Finding the reserve:** Drive north from Half Moon Bay to the town of Moss Beach just north of the airport. Turn west on California Avenue (signed for the Reserve) and drive southwest until it dead-ends at Lake Street. The visitor center and parking are to the right (GPS: 37.524097 N / -122.516366 W). Several trails begin here that allow access to the reserve and along the top of the bluff above. (650) 728-3584.

## Point Montara Light Station

The **Point Montara Light Station** was established in 1875 with a foghorn to warn passing ships of hazards after several ran aground in the late 1860s. A light was added in 1900 to work in conjunction with the foghorn, enhancing the safety of ships sailing toward San Francisco Harbor. The cast-iron lighthouse was brought from Cape Cod in 1925. The property has been restored by Hostelling International along with California State Parks and the US Coast Guard.

Hostel guests can stay in shared or private rooms and can roam about the grounds or visit a secluded beach below. For reservations and rates to this **Point Montara Hostel,** call (650) 728-7177 or visit norcalhostels.org/montara.

**Finding the hostel:** The hostel and lighthouse is between the towns of Moss Beach and Montara. Look for a marked west turn off CA 1/Cabrillo Highway where 16th Street intersects it. Park in a lot on the left (GPS: 37.535838 N / -122.518373 W).

## Montara State Beach

**Montara State Beach,** 8 miles north of Half Moon Bay and 20 miles south of San Francisco, is a long expanse of clean sand with generally few people and dramatic views. Two access points allow easy ingress to the beach; both, however, require scrambling down a steep trail. Popular activities are walking, exploring tide pools, and surf fishing. Swimming is discouraged because of hazardous surf and a strong undertow. South of the beach is **Point Montara Light Station,** which offers accommodations through Hostelling International (650-728-7177).

**Finding the beach:** The beach is reached from two parking lots alongside CA 1 just north of the town of Montara as well as from roadside pullouts on the highway. Park at the south lot (GPS: 37.545475 N / -122.514349 W) opposite 2nd Street in Montara and next to a restaurant or at the north lot (GPS: 37.55168 N /

-122.512394 W) on the west side of the highway to the north. Follow steep trails down to the beach. The park is open daily 8 a.m. to sunset. Dogs are allowed but must be leashed. (650) 726-8819.

## Grey Whale Cove State Beach

This small intimate beach tucks into a deep cove flanked by cliffed headlands on the north and south. It's named for the great views from the cliff top of gray whales migrating along the coast; bring binoculars and sit on the grass above the beach if you're whale-spotting. The 600-foot-long sandy beach, sometimes called Devil's Slide Beach, has long been popular for nude sunbathing, so be advised before venturing down to the beach. The naturists are usually at the north end of the beach, leaving the south end for the modest and families. It is often cool and windy, and the water is, of course, cold. Hiking trails are also here. Busy on weekends.

**Finding the beach:** Drive 1.2 miles north from Montara or 18 miles south from San Francisco on CA 1. Park on the east side of the highway in a large lot (GPS: 37.563219 N / -122.512571 W). Crossing the highway to the beach side is dangerous. Follow an old road to a steep trail with almost 150 stairs that descends to the beach. The park is open from 8 a.m. to sunset. Dogs are prohibited. (650) 726-8819.

## Devil's Slide

The **Devil's Slide** area, one of the most treacherous sections of the Pacific Coast Highway, has long been one of its most spectacular sections with the highway edging shelf-like along the precipitous western slopes of bulky Montara Mountain, which drop directly below the asphalt into the surging surf. The road section from Montara to Pacifica just south of San Francisco, completed in 1937, has often been closed by landslides, leading to costly repairs. In early 2013, however, the famed highway section was closed, with traffic diverted through twin tunnels to avoid the curvy road. The **Tom Lantos Tunnels,** named after a late Congressman, cost $439 million, feature carbon monoxide sensors and exhaust fans, remote cameras, a 15-person safety staff, and 10 fireproof shelters.

In 2013, the closed highway was converted to a hike and bike trail called the **Devil's Slide Coastal Trail,** which winds for 7 miles from Grey Whale Cove State Beach to Pacifica Pier. The trail includes the spectacular 1.3-mile segment of CA 1 above the ocean as well as restrooms and other facilities.

# Pedro Point Headlands

**Pedro Point** is a rocky mountain that juts into the Pacific Ocean and forms the southern skyline of Pacifica above Linda Mar Beach just south of San Francisco. **San Pedro Rock,** a towering wave-washed rock of tilted strata, forms the tip of the steep headland. Pedro Point, lying northwest from CA 1 at the northern entrance to the tunnels, offers a handful of good trails that wind through scrubby woodlands and emerge at stunning scenic viewpoints above the ocean.

**Finding the trails:** Five trails access the headlands from the Green Gate Entrance on the north side of CA 1 just before the north tunnel entrance. It's easy to piece together the trails to form a great loop hike. A recommended hike is to follow **South Ridge Trail** out to overlooks above the ocean, then head north on **Bluff Trail** past **Judy Johnson Overlook** to an end point atop **Pedro Summit** overlooking the end of the promontory. Return to the trailhead via **Middle Ridge Trail** to **Arroyo Trail** for a 3- to 4-mile hike. Park at a small lot (GPS: 37.585416 N/ -122.505782 W) on the north side of the highway or look for other parking after the tunnels open.

# Pacifica State Beach

**Pacifica State Beach,** a mile-long beach also called **Linda Mar Beach,** is sheltered in a deep cove north of Pedro Point, a rocky promontory that juts into the ocean. The crescent-shaped beach, in downtown Pacifica off CA 1, is the most popular surfing spot near San Francisco. On busy weekends there are literally a hundred surfers plying the waves. It's popular because the cove is protected from big swells and the wind, making gentle beginner and intermediate waves—perfect for novices. Most surfers are not hard-core locals but rather day-trippers from the Bay Area. If you don't own a board and wet suit, you can rent from nearby businesses like **Nor-Cal Surf Shop** (650-738-9283) or **Sonlight Surf Shop** (650-359-0353) or get surf lessons at the **University of Surfing** (650-556-6515).

The beach is also popular for sunbathing and walking since it's close to Frisco. Linda Mar Beach often gets sun too because of geography; the San Pedro Valley to the southeast often warms up and wind blows down to keep the fog and chill at bay. Visitors also like the beachside Taco Bell between the two beach parking lots, as well as the restaurants and grocery store across the highway at **Linda Mar Shopping Center** (cityofpacifica.org), the nearby **Pacifica Beach Resort,** and the **Pacifica Skatepark** east of the beach.

If you're a fan of the 1970s cult classic film *Harold and Maude,* the startling scene where Harold drove his car off a cliff was filmed on the bluff north of the beach.

**Finding the beach:** Exit off CA 1 as it passes the beach onto San Pedro Avenue and turning into the south parking lot or turning west from CA 1 into the north parking lot. Dogs must be on a leash; owners must clean up after dogs. No alcohol, glass containers, or fires. Beach and parking are open 5 a.m. to 10:30 p.m. during Daylight Savings Time; otherwise 5 a.m. to 7 p.m. **Pacifica State Beach** (650-738-7381) or **City of Pacifica** (650-738-7381; cityofpacifica.org).

## Rockaway Beach

**Rockaway Beach** is a thin crescent-shaped beach encased by bluffs just north of Linda Mar Beach. The scenic beach, backed by hotels and buildings, has gotten smaller from increased erosion. The intimate beach is good for wave-watching if the surf's up or you can hike on the bluffs south of the beach. It's popular for surf fishing as well as surfers since the waves are usually bigger than at Linda Mar Beach.

**Finding the beach:** Exit west off CA 1 on Fassler Avenue. Go left on Old Country Road to the south parking lot (GPS: 37.60813 N / -122.497081 W) or right to the north parking lot (GPS: 37.61098 N / -122.496003 W).

## Pacifica Pier

**Pacifica Municipal Pier,** reaching 1,140 feet out into the ocean from **Sharp Park Beach** and Pacifica, is one of the best fishing piers on the central California coast. Anglers come to fish off the L-shaped pier, officially called the Reverend Herschell Harkins Memorial Pier, for Dungeness crab, red crab, rock crab, smelt, striped bass, ocean salmon, and shark. The salmon runs are particularly popular with hundreds of anglers lined up cheek to cheek on the pier. Crab season is also crazy. Check with the California Department of Fish & Wildlife for regulations, weight limits, and number of fish and shellfish that may be caught. Officers regularly check the pier for violations. No fishing license is required.

The pier is also great for watching migrating gray whales as well as sea lions, seals, pelicans, and seagulls. The pier was originally built in 1973 to carry sewage out for deposition in the ocean; a practice that ended in 2004. It's also popular because there is a restaurant by the beach, easy street parking, nearby bait shops, and there are restrooms.

The pier (GPS: 37.633459 N / -122.494398 W), managed by the City of Pacifica, is free and open 4 a.m. to 10 p.m. but may be closed for repairs or if the surf is high. No dogs, no alcohol, no bicycles, no smoking, and no overhead casting.

**Finding the pier:** Find the Pacifica Pier from CA 1 in Pacifica by exiting at the Paloma Avenue/Francisco Boulevard exit. Drive west on Paloma Avenue for 2 blocks to Beach Boulevard. Turn left and drive south to the pier. Park on the street.

# Carmel to San Luis Obispo

**General description:** The Big Sur Coast Drive follows CA 1 for 123 twisting miles along the scenic central California coastline from Carmel to Morro Bay.

**Location:** Western California between San Luis Obispo and Carmel-by-the-Sea.

**Drive route number and name:** CA 1 (Cabrillo Highway).

**Travel season:** Year-round. Watch for fog along the drive in summer. Heavy winter rains make the pavement slick and may create landslides that close the highway.

**Camping:** Hundreds of campsites, including walk-in tent sites and RV sites, are in national forest, state park, and private campgrounds along the drive. Reservations, particularly in summer, are strongly recommended.

**Services:** All services in Monterey, Carmel, Cambria, Morro Bay, and San Luis Obispo. Limited services in other towns along the drive.

## The Route

This 123-mile-long (198-kilometer) scenic drive follows CA 1, also called the Cabrillo Highway for an early Spanish explorer, and twists along the spectacular Big Sur Coast between Carmel and San Luis Obispo on central California's Pacific shoreline. The highway, designated an All-American Road for its gorgeous scenery, is simply one of the world's most breathtaking drives and a must-do adventure for any California traveler. The drive follows the Big Sur Coast Highway and the San Luis Obispo North Coast Byway. Allow a minimum of 5 hours to drive the route. More time is, of course, essential to really see the coast, to hike out to rocky points, to sit on golden sand beaches, and to visit redwood groves, wildlife refuges, museums, and state parks.

Along the highway, the steep ridges of the remote Santa Lucia Range plunge down to a rocky, wave-battered coast, making an abrupt and dramatic transition from high peaks to crashing surf. The roadway follows this transition zone, snaking along precipitous headlands, crossing grassy meadows above ragged coves, and traversing 33 bridges that span deep canyons and gorges. The central coast is a superb landscape that serves as a fitting boundary between North America and the Pacific Ocean.

### Weather

The climate along the Big Sur Coast is mild year-round. Around Monterey Bay on the drive's north end, the weather varies little between winter and summer. Only 10 degrees difference separates the mean temperatures for August and January,

# Carmel to San Luis Obispo

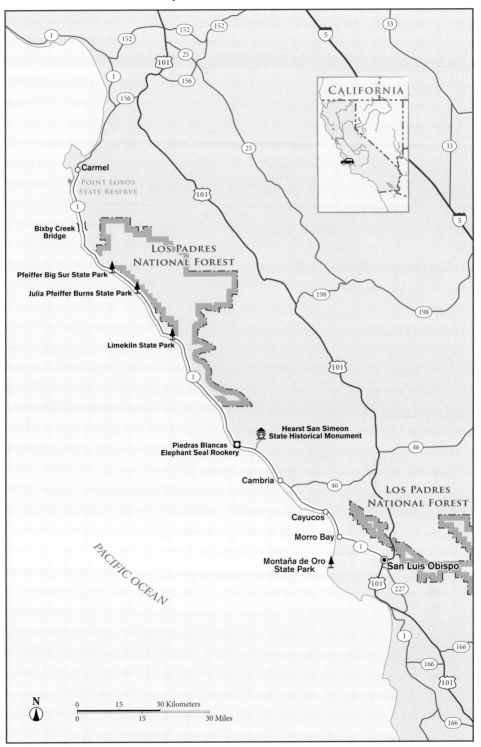

CALIFORNIA

1
152
152
152
101
25
5
33
1
156
156
25
33
Carmel
POINT LOBOS
STATE RESERVE
1
101
5
Bixby Creek
Bridge
LOS PADRES
NATIONAL FOREST
Pfeiffer Big Sur State Park
Julia Pfeiffer Burns State Park
198
198
Limekiln State Park
1
101
Hearst San Simeon
State Historical Monument
Piedras Blancas
Elephant Seal Rookery
46
Cambria
46
LOS PADRES
NATIONAL FOREST
Cayucos
Morro Bay
1
Montaña de Oro
State Park
San Luis Obispo
PACIFIC OCEAN
101
227
1
166
166
101
166

N

0    15    30 Kilometers
0    15    30 Miles

making the climate here one of the most uniform in the US. Summer brings thick fog banks that wrap the coast in gray shrouds. The fog usually burns off by midday, but temperatures are often cool. Bring a sweater for those days.

Inland temperatures on the mountains and valleys above the coast can be hot with daily highs reaching into the upper 90s. Thunderstorms are infrequent, although light showers may accompany the fog. The upper part of the drive between Big Sur and Carmel is cooler and damper than the southern section.

Autumn brings warm, clear days until winter storms sweep off the Pacific in December. Heavy rains lead to frequent landslides along the road. Forty-two landslides blocked the highway during the wet winter of 1982–83. One took over a year to clear away. The greenery in spring adorns the coastal meadows and forests, and the days are clear and breezy with occasional showers.

## Garrapata State Park

The first stop at Big Sur is 2,939-acre **Garrapata State Park** along the coast just north of Soberanes Point. This day-use parkland, named by the Spanish for the lowly wood tick, boasts gleaming white beaches flanked by rocky buttresses, arches, and grottoes. The park offers 2 miles of rugged coastline with **Soberanes Point** and beautiful **Garrapata Beach.** Garrapata is a wild park with no facilities, no camping, 19 numbered access points, and several trails that explore the coast as well as mountain slopes covered with chaparral and canyons, some with redwood groves.

Good trails lace the bluffs and foothills above the water and the coves offer fishing for greenling and surf perch. The best hike climbs east up the **Soberanes Canyon Trail** from the highway up Soberanes Creek for 1.5 miles to a verdant grove of redwoods nestled in the hills. A spur trail leads to the summit of 1,977-foot **Doud Peak.**

For the best coastal hike, park at a pullout on the west shoulder of CA 1 at stop 10. Follow a trail southwest past humped **Whale Peak** to **Soberanes Point,** a cliff-lined headland, then hike north along a cliff-top path before cutting back to the highway. Keep an eye out for playful sea otters in the surf below. The **California Sea Otter Game Refuge** includes the entire Big Sur Coast. Farther south is the mile-long **Garrapata Beach,** a wide sandy beach, one of Big Sur's best, but relatively unvisited. Park at two long pullouts on the west side of the highway (South parking GPS: 36.418997 N / -121.913263 W; mile marker 63.0) and follow trails down to the beach.

*Restless waves wash against the rocky shoreline*
*at Garrapata State Park south of Carmel.*

**Finding the park:** Garrapata State Park is 6.7 miles south of Carmel. Look for a small sign on the side of the road that marks the park boundary. Leashed dogs are only allowed on the beach. (831) 624-4909.

## Bixby Creek Bridge

The highway twists south from Garrapata State Park past Kaiser and Rocky Points to **Bixby Creek Bridge,** a dramatic concrete span that arches over deep Rainbow Canyon and Bixby Creek before it drains into the Pacific. The bridge, sometimes called Bixby Bridge, is an icon of the California coast. It was featured on a 2010 US Postal Service express mail stamp. The famed span, measuring 718 feet long and 279 feet above the creek, consumed 6,600 cubic yards of concrete poured into forms supported by a framework constructed from 300,000 board feet of Douglas fir.

The bridge, also called Rainbow Bridge, was completed in 1932. The highway through Big Sur was finished in 1937, hacked out of the remote coastline by convict laborers, who battled violent weather and tough engineering problems for 9 years. The road cost $199,861 in 1930s dollars or the equivalent of $10 million or $71,000 per mile today.

**Finding the bridge:** The bridge is 13 miles south of Carmel on CA 1. Pull off at turnouts at both the north and south end of the bridge for a look and a photo op. The best view is from the north pullout on the west side of the highway (GPS: 36.372524 N / -121.90295 W; mile marker: 59.8).

## Hurricane Point

From Bixby Creek Bridge, the highway hugs the coast and then climbs across grassy benches to a lofty viewpoint above **Hurricane Point** that is 1.5 miles south of the bridge. Expect breathtaking views of the ocean and the Big Sur Coast here. The view north includes abrupt cliffs that drop to the shoreline, isolated rock stacks bobbing on the ocean, and, of course, the graceful arch of Bixby Bridge. Look to the south to Point Sur, an isolated rock promontory that juts into the water. Old shipwrecks can sometimes be spotted below the point at low tide.

**Finding the point:** Hurricane Point is on the west side of the highway on a wide bend. Park in a paved lot lined with boulders along the west shoulder (GPS: 36.357386 N / -121.902792 W; mile marker: 58.3) or in another smaller roadside lot just south, which offers views south to Point Sur.

*The iconic Bixby Creek Bridge, completed in 1931, is one of the most popular viewpoints along the Big Sur coast.*

## Big Sur Highway History

The Big Sur Coast was one of California's least accessible regions at the end of the 19th century with the rocky coastline backed by the steep western slopes of the Santa Lucia Range, sometimes called the Big Sur Hills, which stretch from the Carmel Valley to the Cuyama River. In the 1890s, Monterey physician Dr. John Roberts often made house calls along the coast by riding horseback down a spiraling wagon track. During his journeys, Roberts gradually mapped and plotted a road course that ran from Monterey to San Luis Obispo. Roberts and state senator James Rigdon estimated the cost of building a road along the coast to be $50,000 and got legislation passed in 1919 to construct one.

In the late 1950s state engineers and land developers sought to modernize and straighten the road, turning it into an interstate-like highway. Big Sur's landowners, however, realized the folly of the plan and fought to preserve the coast. The highway, withdrawn from the state freeway system, was dedicated in 1966 by Lady Bird Johnson as California's first official scenic drive.

## Big Sur Village

**Big Sur Village** is a cluster of shops, restaurants, and a post office spread along the west side of the highway about a mile south of the Sycamore Road turn. There are also a couple hotels and a campground here as well as luxury second homes that are usually empty. It's a decent place to stop for a bite, a gasoline fill-up, or at a market or restaurant. Park on the west side of the highway near the Chamber of Commerce (GPS: 36.220751 N / -121.754145 W).

## Nepenthe

Past the turn to Pfieffer Beach, the coast highway rolls south and in 2 miles reaches **Nepenthe,** a restaurant on a tight highway bend with a big view of the Big Sur Coast and the azure Pacific Ocean. The scenic views here are stunning, especially if you have a drink or dine at the rail. This is a must-stop on your first drive up Big Sur for the views and ambience. Most folks, however, have strong opinions about the restaurant, so make up your own mind. It is a bit pricey, but what do you expect for five-star views and its remote location? Also be prepared for a bit of a wait for seating. Nearby are a gift shop, cafe, and gallery. Filmmaker Orson Welles, renowned for his classic film *Citizen Kane,* once owned a cabin near here. Nepenthe is open 11:30 a.m. to 10 p.m. every day except Christmas and Thanksgiving. (831) 667-2345.

## Henry Miller Memorial Library

The **Henry Miller Memorial Library,** a half-mile south of Nepenthe on the east side of CA 1, is an unassuming house among tall redwoods. This small library, a nonprofit bookstore and arts center, preserves rare copies of Miller's books, manuscripts, and paintings by iconic American writer Henry Miller (1891–1980), one of Big Sur's most famous bohemian residents. Miller, who lived at Big Sur from 1944 to 1962, willed his personal collection to longtime friend Emil White, who founded the library in 1981 in his house as a memorial to Miller.

Miller, an expat writer in 1930s Paris, was friends there with many great writers including Ernest Hemingway, Anais Nin, and Lawrence Durrell. He wrote a couple books—*Tropic of Cancer and Tropic of Capricorn*—in Paris before returning to the US during World War II. In 1957 Miller penned *Big Sur and the Oranges of Hieronymus Bosch* about the area.

Miller wrote of Big Sur: "At dawn, Big Sur's majesty is almost painful to behold. That same prehistoric look. The look of always. Nature smiling at herself in the mirror of eternity." He also said wisely, "One's destination is never a place,

## The Dark Watchers

Eerie spectral beings simply called the Dark Watchers are sometimes seen at twilight on the high slopes of the Santa Lucia Mountains above the Big Sur coastline. These giant human-shaped phantoms stand silhouetted against the sky, staring out to sea or across the rugged mountains before vanishing into the growing night. The Dark Watchers were first seen by the Chumash Indians, who painted them on rock art galleries.

The great California novelist John Steinbeck described them in the short story "Flight": "Pepe looked up to the top of the next dry withered ridge. He saw a dark form against the sky, a man's figure standing on top of a rock, and he glanced away quickly not to appear curious. When a moment later he looked up again, the figure was gone."

Even still hikers and campers see the Watchers gazing into the great nothingness, often wearing a black hat and cloak. They are not malevolent and usually vanish after being noticed or called to by humans. Keep your senses alert and perhaps you too will become aware that you are being watched.

but rather a new way of looking at things." Another thought to consider as you drive through Big Sur country.

The library also hosts theater, poetry readings, concerts, workshops, and lectures year-round. Check the schedule at the website henrymiller.org or call (831) 667-2574. The center is open every day except Tuesday 11 a.m. to 6 p.m.

**Finding the library:** The library is on the east side of the highway; park in a roadside lot (GPS: 36.220751 N / -121.754145 W; mile marker 43.6).

## Julia Pfeiffer Burns State Park

**Julia Pfeiffer Burns State Park,** a 3,762-acre parkland, is one of the most beautiful sections of the central coast with a rocky shoreline, a waterfall that plunges into surf, towering redwood trees, and the soaring Santa Lucia Range. It offers excellent wildlife-watching with gray whales passing close to shore during their biannual migrations, as well as sea otters, harbor seals, and sea lions basking in rocky coves. The endangered California condor, back from the brink of extinction, also soars the skies above the coast.

The park is named for Julia Pfeiffer Burns (1868–1928), who grew up here in the 19th century and leased grazing land from Lathrop and Helen Brown in

today's park. They were so taken with Julia that they eventually donated their Saddle Rock Ranch as a state park in 1962 to be named after her.

The 4-square-mile park is a wonderland of ecologic diversity. The redwoods, including both old- and second-growth trees, flourish within 300 feet of the ocean and are among the southernmost redwoods on the California coast. Three creeks dash down steep canyons to the ocean, including McWay Creek which eventually falls 80 feet off a sheer cliff onto a golden beach in a cove. Four seabird colonies are here, including the only one for double-crested cormorants on the central coast. The park's rich underwater environments, including kelp forests, are preserved in the **Monterey Bay National Marine Sanctuary** and the **California Sea Otter State Game Refuge.**

You can explore the park on many trails. The most popular one is the 0.5-mile **Overlook Trail** to **McWay Falls.** The trailhead is found on the west side of the highway (GPS: 36.220751 N / -121.754145 W); park in designated areas along the highway or in parking lots to the east. Follow the wide easy trail to a spectacular overlook of McWay Falls and McWay Beach. The beach and falls themselves are off-limits to visitors. Other good trails include **Canyon Falls Trail, Ewoldsen Trail, Tan Bark Trail, and Partington Cove Trail.** The park has two tent-only walk-in campsites (reservation only), picnic facilities, and winter nature programs, including whale-watching.

**Finding the park:** The park is on CA 1/Cabrillo Highway 37 miles south of Carmel and 12 miles south of Pfeiffer Big Sur State Park (don't confuse the two parks!) at mile marker 35.9. It's open from a half-hour before sunrise to a half-hour after sunset. Dogs are not allowed on trails and must be leashed at parking areas. (831) 667-2315.

## Esalen Institute

The **Esalen Institute,** spilling down steep slopes above the ocean south of Julia Pfeiffer Burns State Park, is a magical place that is essential California. People come to this remote residential community and retreat center to find themselves, to lose themselves, to become themselves. The institute, founded in 1962 by Michael Murphy and Dick Price on 120 acres, offers hundreds of workshops as well as conferences every year, with a focus on human potentiality, psychology, personal growth, yoga, massage, and spirituality. There is also a hot spring bath that hugs a cliff above the ocean. Visitors come for a day or night or stay for a month or more at this adult summer camp. Reservations are required.

*McWay Falls, one of Big Sur's most dramatic wonders, plunges 80 feet onto sand and surf on McWay Beach.*

**Finding the institute:** Esalen is about 45 miles south of Carmel and 9 miles north of Lucia. Turn west off CA 1 (GPS: 36.127935 N / -121.642081 W) to the institute. For more info, visit esalen.org or call (831) 667-3000.

## Landels-Hill Big Creek Reserve

The 4,328-acre **Landels-Hill Big Creek Reserve,** part of the University of California Natural Reserve System, protects a variety of unique ecosystems on narrow ridges, separated by deep canyons, which drop steeply down to the rocky shoreline. The extreme topography creates diverse flora and fauna, making it an ideal area for scientific research, including archaeology; insect studies on bees, walking sticks, and butterflies; crustal geology; intertidal communities; and fish studies of both the ocean and the southern steelhead trout. The reserve also offers 13 miles of trails and three campgrounds.

**Finding the reserve:** To visit the reserve, turn east from CA 1 at Big Creek (GPS: 36.069819 N /-121.598981 W) to the gatehouse and entrance. A couple good overlooks are both north and south of the turnoff. Contact the reserve for more information at bigcreek.ucnrs.org or (831) 667-2543.

## China Basin Beach

This pocket beach, tucked into a wide cove below the Cabrillo Highway, is flanked by cliffs and jutting rock formations scoured by crashing surf. The beach with its broad stretch of sand is usually private and quiet, except for the crying of seagulls.

**Finding the beach:** Park in a gravel pullout on the west side of CA 1 (GPS: 36.053136 N / -121.587666 W), walk south on the asphalt shoulder, then follow an old road down steep open slopes to the beach.

## New Camaldoli Hermitage

Do you crave solitude, quiet, and fabulous views of the Big Sur Coast? If you answered yes, then you might consider staying overnight at the **New Camaldoli Hermitage.** The hermitage, perched at 1,200 feet in the Santa Lucia Mountains above the coast, is home for a group of Camaldolese Benedictine monks, an obscure and ancient Catholic order whose members are dedicated to seeking God through a life of solitude, silence, work, and study. Visitors are welcome to stay at the heritage for a contemplative retreat up to 2 weeks long in either private rooms or trailers with dramatic coastal views. It's extremely quiet, remote, and has no Internet access or phone service. Vegetarian meals are served but must be eaten in your quarters. The monks and other visitors are rarely seen so you are alone most of the time.

*Big Creek Bridge, a double-arched concrete span built in 1937, was retrofitted for earthquakes in 1999.*

The hermitage has a small bookstore and gift shop, where they sell their excellent brandy-dipped fruit cakes and date nut cakes, fudge, Holy Granola, books, religious items, and cards. There's also a simple chapel where you are welcome to attend services, but there is no obligation. Prices are extremely reasonable for Big Sur but be prepared for rustic accommodations and no air-conditioning. Reservations are recommended, but there is last-minute availability.

**Finding the hermitage:** The hermitage is just south of Lucia and north of Limekiln State Park. Find it by turning northeast off CA 1 (GPS: 36.019752 N / -121.540069 W) and driving 2 miles up a steep road. For more information and reservations go to hermitagebigsur.com or call (831) 667-2456.

## Limekiln State Park

**Limekiln State Park** is a gorgeous but small 716-acre parkland that protects the dramatic meeting of mountain and coast about 52 miles south of Carmel. The park packs a lot in a small area, including pretty **Limekiln Falls,** redwood trees, a rocky shoreline and small beach, fern-lined trails, and a 24-site campground (11 sites with an ocean view). On Limekiln Creek are the park's four namesake kilns that were used in the late 1800s to process lime, which was carried by wagon to

Rockland Landing where it was shipped to the Bay Area for concrete. The limestone quarry was exhausted in only 3 years, and most of the redwoods were cut down for firewood.

Explore the park by hiking a couple good easy trails—half-mile **Limekiln Trail** through redwoods to the kilns and **Falls Trail,** which climbs to the base of a 100-foot-high waterfall. You can also picnic and camp; reservations are necessary for camping from reserveamerica.com or by calling the park. Dogs must be leashed and are not allowed on trails. Swimming is not recommended at the stony beach because of dangerous currents, high surf, and rogue waves.

**Finding the park:** Drive south 2 miles on CA 1 from Lucia and make a turn east (GPS: 36.008607 N / -121.51815 W; mile marker 20.95) to the park entrance just past a high bridge. Past the entrance station, make a sharp left turn to a large parking area below the bridge by the beach. The campground and trails are straight from the entrance; the trailhead at end of the short road. (805) 434-1996.

## Kirk Creek Campground

**Kirk Creek Campground,** perched on a high bluff overlooking the restless Pacific Ocean, is simply one of the most stunning settings for a campground anywhere. The campground, administered by Los Padres National Forest, is sandwiched between the Cabrillo Highway and the ocean. Get a site above the cliffs and you'll never forget the sunset from your table. The 33-site campground offers both large spots for RVs and trailers as well as quiet walk-in tent-only locations. The campground, shaped like a lazy 8, has half its sites on a first-come first-served basis and the others by reservation through recreation.gov or calling (877) 444-6777. Come early to grab a site if you don't have a reservation. A short trail heads north from the campground and drops down to a narrow beach.

A prison labor camp for 150 well-behaved San Quentin inmates once sat at Kirk Creek. The inmates' sentences were reduced 3 days for every 2 worked, and escape attempts into the dry, unpopulated surrounding country were rare.

**Finding the campground:** The campground is on the west side of the highway a couple miles south of Limekiln State Park and 80 miles north of San Luis Obispo. Turn west off the highway (GPS: 35.990067 N / -121.494962 W; mile marker 19.0) into the area. (805) 434-1996.

## Nacimiento-Fergusson Road

The 24.5-mile-long **Nacimiento-Fergusson Road,** the only road over the Santa Lucia Range, twists east over the crest from CA 1 to US 101. This breathtaking scenic drive is a roller-coaster road that quickly climbs to its 2,780-foot high point before beginning a long downhill. This beautiful drive accesses a remote part of central California and yields spectacular views of the Pacific Ocean as it climbs away from Cabrillo Highway. For one of the best views, stop at the Mano Seco Group bench at a large pullout a few miles up the road. The narrow paved road is popular with motorcyclists, wildflower aficionados, and steering-wheel adventurers. Near the summit the drive intersects Cone Peak Road. Head north on this back road, which ends just below the summit of 5,755-foot Cone Peak. Two campgrounds—**Nacimiento and Ponderosa**—are on the drive.

**Finding the road:** The drive begins just down the road from Kirk Creek Campground. Turn east on the marked road (GPS: 35.988678 N / -121.493991 W; mile marker 18.9). The last part of the road on the east side passes through Hunter-Liggett military reservation; you may be stopped and asked for your driver's license, auto registration, and rental car contract to pass through. Large vehicles, RVs, and cars pulling trailers are not recommended. Inquire at the Los Padres National Forest office for road conditions and closures (831) 385-5434.

## Mill Creek Picnic Ground

**Mill Creek Picnic Ground,** 0.4 miles south of the turn onto Nacimiento-Fergusson Road, makes a good ocean-view stop. Turn west just north of a bridge spanning wooded Mill Creek (GPS: 35.984012 N / -121.491524 W) and drive down a short paved spur road to a parking area. Several picnic tables offer great views of a stony beach and the rugged coastline. The area, administered by Los Padres National Forest, also has restrooms.

## Sand Dollar Beach & Plaskett Creek Campground

**Sand Dollar Beach,** one of the largest Big Sur beaches, stretches across a crescent-shaped cove northwest of Plaskett Creek Campground. A steep bluff covered with low brush backs up the beach while rock piles, white with guano, poke above the surf and cliffs line the shore north and south of the beach. The popular beach, reached by a steep trail and wooden steps, is a mixture of sand, coarse gravel, and rounded cobbles. Bits of smooth jade can be found on the beach. Look below the tide line to find glinting jade pieces. The beach can be busy, especially on weekends, but is usually quiet and deserted on weekdays. It's popular for fishing, hiking, and surfing, which is best in autumn at mid-high tide.

Across the highway from the beach is **Plaskett Creek Campground** (mile marker 13.7), a convenient and comfortable stopover. All the sites are grassy and shaded by Monterey pine and cypress trees. The crash of surf can usually be heard from the campground. The campground offers 41 sites, with drinking water and toilets. Make reservations at reserveamerica.com. For info, call (805) 434-1996.

**Finding the beach:** The beach is 31 miles northwest of San Simeon off CA 1. Park in a large lot on the west side of the highway (GPS: 35.921137 N / -121.466774 W; mile marker 13.8). A parking fee is charged. From the northwest corner of the parking lot, follow a trail out to an overlook and down the steep bluff to the beach. The beach is dog-friendly but your pup needs to be leashed.

## Jade Cove Beach Recreation Area

**Jade Cove,** a Los Padres National Forest recreation site, is a rugged coastal area that yields fine pieces of water-polished jade to rock hounds and scuba divers. The area includes two rocky coves—North Jade Cove and South Jade Cove—that are just south of Plaskett Creek Campground. There are two parking areas on the west shoulder of the Cabrillo Highway that access each of the coves; these are about 0.1 mile apart. The south parking area is opposite a roadside sign for the site. It seems best to park at the larger northern area, which is opposite Plaskett Point, a jagged promontory above North Jade Cove.

After parking, hike west along obvious trails to the cliffed rim above the coves. Look around and locate obvious used paths that descend down the steep rocks to the stony beach below. Use caution since the rocks can be slick; also watch for poison ivy.

When you're on the beach, search for jade, which is found on most area beaches. Unless you know what you're looking for, it's difficult to locate good pieces. The serpentine rock that composes the cliffs is sometimes mistaken for jade. To differentiate jade from serpentine, use a pocketknife to scratch the surface. Serpentine will scratch; jade will not. The best time to look is at low tide when more rock is exposed; after big storms in winter; and in morning before others pick it over. Look for rocks that are wet since jade is easier to spot. By the time you get to the parking area, the rocks will be dry and appear dull. This is usually a salt veneer. Lick it off to temporarily see the jade color beneath. Most jade here is green, shines in the sun, and feels greasy. Two types of jade are found—rare nephrite jade and common green Monterey jade. In 1971, three divers excavated an 8-foot-long, 9,000-pound boulder of nephrite jade valued at $180,000. Good luck!

**Finding the beach:** Jade Cove is 9.7 miles south of Lucia and 29.8 miles north of the Hearst Castle turnoff. Park on the west shoulder of CA 1 (GPS South Lot: 35.913653 N / -121.468341 W; North Lot: 35.917055 N / -121.46906 W).

*Highway 1 twists across steep mountain slopes above the rocky and rugged Big Sur Coast south of Mill Creek.*

# Willow Creek Picnic Ground & Beach

This roadside pullout offers a great vista point above rocky **Willow Creek Beach** as well as picnic tables and restrooms. This scenic spot is popular with surfers, surf fishers, photographers, and beachcombers. Willow Creek drains from the Santa Lucia Range into the ocean here.

    **Finding the beach:** Find the vista point and beach, about 28 miles north of the Hearst Castle turn, by turning west off CA 1 (GPS: 35.892506 N / -121.460764 W; mile marker 11.6) and parking in the first lot or driving down to a lower lot by the beach.

# Willow Creek Trail

Willow Creek Road, which accesses the interior of the Santa Lucia Range, begins just under a mile south of the lookout point. Turn east on the marked road (GPS: 35.885629 N / -121.458667 W), which is also marked for Treebones Resort. Go left at the immediate junction. A great hike is up **Willow Creek Trail.**

    **Finding the trail:** Drive 2.4 miles up the rough road to the trailhead, an old road that goes left. The 3.6-mile out-and-back hike, following the old road and a trail, drops down to Willow Creek, then climbs up through the largest Douglas fir forest on the central coast to a redwood grove and an old homestead.

# Ragged Point Vista

**Ragged Point Vista** offers one of Big Sur's most spectacular and most popular viewpoints. Ragged Point, a usual stop for tour buses, actually is a small resort community (Ragged Mountain Inn and Resort) perched atop 400-foot cliffs above the raging ocean with a hotel, gas station, restaurant, and wedding pagoda for those who want to tie the knot in front of what is often called the "Million Dollar View."

    If you stop, walk out to the viewpoints above sheer cliffs for the great view. You can also follow a steep **Ragged Point Cliffside Trail** for a half-mile down switchbacks to a pocket beach covered with black sand and a great view of 300-foot-high **Black Swift Falls,** the tallest waterfall on the Big Sur Coast.

    **Finding the point:** Ragged Point is on the west side of CA 1 north of San Simeon and Point Piedras Blancas (GPS: 35.781433 N / -121.329725 W). For more information, contact the resort at (805) 927-4502.

# Point Piedras Blancas

**Point Piedras Blancas,** named for three white, guano-covered rock islands at the end of a blunt promontory, is protected by the BLM as a 19-acre Outstanding Natural Area. Perched at the tip of the promontory is a 70-foot-high lighthouse built in 1875. It was originally 115 feet high but the top section was removed after a 1948 earthquake. It's still in use, with the beacon flashing every 10 seconds. Guided tours of the lighthouse are regularly offered. A perimeter trail offers great views of cliffs, surf, and ocean.

The area is also used for marine wildlife studies, including the thick kelp forest that covers the bay south of the lighthouse. The kelp is anchored to the ocean floor and grows to heights of 100 feet, serving as home to numerous sea creatures. A walk along the beach here reveals tangles of kelp with remains of life clinging to the damp seaweed, including baby octopi, skeleton shrimp, sea spiders, sponges, and kelp crabs. The area also offers good spots to sit above the ocean and watch sea otters frolic in the kelp beds.

**Finding the point:** The point is just west of CA 1 about 5.5 miles northwest of San Simeon. Turn west from CA 1 (GPS: 35.670162 N / -121.278377 W) and drive to parking at the point by the lighthouse. Access to the area is by tour only; Monday to Saturday in summer and Tuesday, Thursday, and Saturday the rest of the year. A fee is charged. BLM: (805) 927-7361. Tours: piedrasblancastours@gmail.com.

# Piedras Blancas Elephant Seal Rookery

The largest elephant seal rookery on the California coast is a mile south of Point Piedras Blancas. Pull off the west side of CA 1 into a large parking lot (GPS: 35.662958 N / -121.256849 W) for an amazing glimpse into wild America at **Piedras Blancas Elephant Seal Rookery.** Sprawled on the sandy beach below lie thousands of elephant seals, huge sea mammals that come here for a few months each winter and spring to molt, mate, give birth, and rest. After being hunted almost to extinction, the seals lived only in remote places, but in 1990 they began coming to these unspoiled beaches. The first birth here was in 1992, and then the seal population exploded, with over 600 born in 1995 and thousands now. It's estimated that over 15,000 elephant seals land here annually.

The seals are seen year-round, but the best months are December through March during the mating and birth seasons. Usually docents from Friends of the Elephant Seal are present and offer lots of information. You get great views of the seals from overlooks by the parking area. A good trail heads north along the coast, passing through private property by permission, to more beaches and coves

*The Point Piedras Light Station, completed in 1875, perches on the windswept tip of a promontory to warn mariners of dangerous rocks.*

teeming with seals. Human access to this coastal section is very limited. Don't go down to the beaches to view them; elephant seals are wild unpredictable animals and adult males can weigh up to 5,000 pounds. Observe from a safe distance and don't disturb these marine giants.

**Finding the rookery:** The elephant seal rookery is 1 mile south of Point Piedras Blancas and about 5 miles north of the Hearst Castle turn. Open daily. There are no admission or parking fees nor restrooms or trash cans. For more information, visit elephantseal.org.

## William R. Hearst Memorial State Beach & Coastal Discovery Center

The **William R. Hearst Memorial State Beach,** opposite the turn to Hearst Castle and just north of San Simeon, is a popular and pleasant beach at the head of a cove in San Simeon Bay. It's popular for swimming, lazing, beachcombing, and

*As many as 17,000 elephant seals form colonies to birth, breed, molt, and rest from long migrations at the Piedras Blancas rookery.*

fishing. Most anglers head onto a 495-foot-long pier that begins at the parking lot. There are 24 picnic sites, restrooms, barbecue grills, and water. A concession rents kayaks and boogie boards.

Also here is the **Coastal Discovery Center,** an education facility operated by California State Parks and Monterey Bay National Marine Sanctuary. The free center offers exhibits and programs about the area's unique marine ecosystems, human history, and geography. Days and hours are limited so call (805) 927-6575 for more info.

**Finding the beach:** Find the state beach and Coastal Discovery Center on the west side of CA 1 opposite the Hearst Castle Road. Turn west to the large parking lot (GPS: 35.643835 N / -121.186645 W). (805) 927-2020.

## Hearst San Simeon State Historical Monument

The **Hearst San Simeon State Historical Monument,** perched on a high hill above San Simeon, is one of California's busiest tourist attractions. The extravagant **Hearst Castle,** built by publishing magnate William Randolph Hearst and architect Julia Morgan beginning in 1919, has 115 rooms including 56 bedrooms, 31 bathrooms, two libraries, a movie theater, and a billiards parlor, and is adorned with art treasures from around the world. The grounds include 127 acres of gardens, an airfield, swimming pools, tennis courts, and what was then the world's largest private zoo. The first-floor vestibule is decorated with 2,000-year-old mosaic tiles from Pompeii. The mansion cost more than $10 million, or as much as the total expenses for CA 1 when it was built. The total square footage of all the buildings exceeds 90,000, while Casa Grande, the main castle, is 60,645 square feet.

The castle, named *La Cuesta Encantada* or The Enchanted Hill, straddles a 1,600-foot-high hill in the southern Santa Lucia Range about 5 miles east of the coast. The estate, donated to California by the Hearst Corporation in memory of its maker in 1957, can be toured daily. It takes almost 2 days to see the entire place.

Several daytime tours, which last 45 minutes, as well as a seasonal night tour, are offered daily except on Thanksgiving, Christmas, and New Year's Day. Tours, which are somewhat pricey, are usually sold out, especially in summer. Plan ahead by making reservations online or by phone. Pets and strollers are not allowed. It's usually best not to bring children on the tours since they get bored and restless. When you visit, plan on at least a half-mile walk to the castle and a climb up 400 steps. It's as much as 30 degrees hotter at the castle than at the parking lot and coast below in summer. All tours start at the visitor center just off CA 1. Visitors take a bus from here for the 5 miles to the site.

*Casa Grande, with 60,645 sqaure feet of floor space, was publishing magnate William Randolph Hearst's personal mansion.*

**Finding the park:** Hearst Castle is about halfway between Los Angeles and San Francisco or about 230 miles from each city; allow 5 hours to drive there. It is 39 miles north of San Luis Obispo and 93 miles south of Monterey. Turn east off CA 1 (GPS: 35.644027 N / -121.185371W; mile marker 57.8) opposite WR Hearst Memorial State Beach and drive a short distance to the park visitor center (open 8 a.m. to 5 p.m.). Park in one of the large lots; then tour the free visitor center with exhibits about Hearst and his castle and a gift shop. It's advisable to view a film about the site before your tour. For more info visit hearstcastle.org or call (800) 444-4445.

## Hearst San Simeon State Park

The 2,309-acre **Hearst San Simeon State Park,** straddling CA 1 with a long beach on the west and wooded hills on the east, is a popular area for hiking, camping, and beach activities. The park also includes the **Santa Rosa Creek Natural Preserve** with riparian woodlands and coastal wetlands; **San Simeon Natural Preserve** with wetlands, riparian zone, and a monarch butterfly wintering site; and the **Pa-nu Cultural Preserve,** an archaeological area that protects an ancient habitation site that dates to almost 6,000 years ago. The park offers several fine trails that explore the area and two campgrounds—**San Simeon and Washburn**—with water, restrooms, showers, and tables. There are also a Junior Ranger program and seasonal campfire talks. The park includes a long stretch of cliff-lined beach that is perfect for walking, sunbathing, wildlife-watching, and beachcombing.

**Finding the park:** The park is on CA 1/Cabrillo Highway 5 miles south of the Hearst Castle turnoff or 35 miles north of San Luis Obispo. To access the inland park section and campgrounds, turn east off CA 1 on San Simeon-Monterey Creek Road (GPS: 35.59893 N / -121.127459 W), then turn right into the park. The main beach section is accessed from a parking lot on the west side of the highway (GPS: 35.59893 N / -121.127459 W) just south of the park turn. (805) 927-2020.

## Moonstone Beach

**Moonstone Beach** is a long stretch of sand backed by low cliffs that parallels CA 1 and Moonstone Beach Drive in Cambria south of the Hearst Castle. The beach, part of **Hearst San Simeon State Park,** is bordered on the east above the cliffs by Moonstone Beach Drive. Lots of parking areas on the drive offer easy access to the beach. There are also hotels and restaurants on the east side of the road, making it perfect for a beach stay with visits to Hearst Castle and the elephant seal rookery. The peaceful beach offers great hiking along a boardwalk and along the sandy tidal zone; exploring tide pools; watching wildlife including birds, sea otters, and seals; surfing when the waves are high; and swimming if it's hot. There are also lots of bouldering spots on the low cliffs in coves and on a few blocks, offering fun for climbers. The beach is named for water-polished milky agates that look like opals.

**Finding the beach:** There are two ways to access Moonstone Beach from CA 1. From the north, turn west on Moonstone Beach Drive (GPS: 35.585471 N / -121.121172 W) and drive south. Several good viewpoints and parking areas are encountered. One of the best is right on State Park Road to a large parking lot with great views of surging surf on bedrock. From the south, turn west on Windsor Boulevard (GPS: 35.585471 N / -121.121172 W) then turn immediately right on Moonstone Beach Drive. Park in a large parking area on the left when the road reaches the beach for easy access; restrooms are at this lot. This is the Santa Rosa Day Use Area. Other lots are farther north.

# Cambria

**Cambria** is a pleasant village with a population of 6,032 (2010) on CA 1 about halfway between Los Angeles and San Francisco. Moonstone Beach and the Pacific Ocean form Cambria's western border. It was originally settled in 1869 as a mining boomtown when miners flocked in to dig cinnabar which would be processed into quicksilver or mercury. For 20 years Cambria alternately boomed and busted with the mining until it finally settled into middle age as a quiet dairy community.

Now the village economy is based on tourism, with lots of hotels, B&Bs, restaurants, the long stretch of **Moonstone Beach,** and nearby attractions, including the famous **Hearst Castle** 6 miles to the north. There are lots of outdoor recreation options in the area—hiking, beachcombing, climbing, bicycling, wildlife-watching, camping, surfing, and fishing. Cambria makes a good base camp for exploring the southern Central Coast region.

Besides welcoming tourists, Cambria also welcomes your dog to tread the **Moonstone Beach Boardwalk,** hike area trails, and stroll through the picturesque downtown. Many restaurants offer seating for owners and their pups. There are also a dog park and kennels where you can board your dog while visiting Hearst Castle, which doesn't allow any pets.

For more information, contact the **Cambria Chamber of Commerce** (805-927-3624; cambriachamber.org).

## Monterey Pine

Groves of wind-sculpted Monterey pines are mixed into open grasslands on the bold, rolling hills surrounding Cambria. The Monterey pine is endemic to California and grows in a very restricted range around Monterey, **Año Nuevo Point,** two islands off Baja California, and around **Cambria.** It prefers sandy soils from marine sediments and water-laden summer fogs for moisture rather than rainfall. The Monterey pine, along with its close relatives the knobcone pine and bishop pine, once grew across much of coastal California in a milder climate. All three pines grow today in relict stands left over from those earlier times. The Monterey pine, however, is widely used worldwide for reforestation and ornamental purposes.

# Fiscalini Ranch Preserve

The 430-acre **Fiscalini Ranch Preserve** on the southwest side of Cambria protects a mile-long swath of coastline as well as a unique stand of Monterey pine, freshwater wetlands along Santa Rosa Creek, and a long ocean-side bluff that reaches heights of 400 feet with dramatic views of the rocky shore. The compact preserve is easily visited, offers fun hiking trails, and yields good wildlife-watching for whales, dolphins, seals, and sea otters that frolic in kelp beds.

The preserve, sometimes called East-West Ranch, was bought by local residents and the Coastal Conservancy to protect it from development and then turned over to Cambria for habitat protection and recreational use. Two main trails—**Bluff Trail** and **Marine Terrace Trail**—access the area. Both are easy 1- to 2-mile hikes that are wheelchair-accessible (most of Bluff Trail is a boardwalk), with benches for resting and viewing. The two trails can be combined for a good loop hike. The Bluff Trail requires dogs be leashed, while the upper trail does not.

**Finding the preserve:** Find the preserve's north trailhead by exiting west from CA 1 onto Windsor Boulevard. Follow the road west then south for a couple miles through a neighborhood to a parking area at the road's end on the property boundary (GPS: 35.556103 N / -121.102327 W).

# Pasos Robles Wine Region

The Central Coast around Cambria offers numerous wineries from large operations to small family-run vineyards that are tucked into the rolling hills east of the village and the Cabrillo Highway. This California wine region, called **Pasos Robles** for a small city 25 miles inland from the coast, is a premier wine area with over 40 varieties of grapes grown at more than 180 wineries on over 26,000 acres. Some of the best wines made are award-winning cabernet sauvignon, merlot, syrah, and zinfandel, making up about 75 percent of the wine production. The region has a long growing season with hot days and cool nights; the Santa Lucia Range blocks most marine fogs from filtering into the area.

**Finding the area:** For a good tour of the Pasos Robles wine region from the coast, drive south from Cambria and turn east on CA 46 (GPS: 35.527245 N / -121.044665 W). This scenic highway dips and rolls through hills and valleys dotted with oaks, passing 15 wineries that beckon you to stop and taste their wines. Contact the Cambria Chamber of Commerce at cambriachamber.org or call (805) 927-3624 for information about area wineries.

## Estero Bluffs State Park

The undeveloped 355-acre **Estero Bluffs State Park** lies west of CA 1 just north of the town of Cayucos. The primitive parkland is mostly a coastal terrace covered with grassland that ends at a steep bluff that plunges abruptly to surf, sand, and rock. The park, bisected by a couple perennial streams, is easily accessed from large parking areas on the west side of the highway. About 4 miles of trails explore the edge of the bluffs and the interior grassland. Lots of wildlife can be seen in the rich ecosystems, including seals, otters, sea lions, pelicans, and the endangered snowy plover. Be extremely careful on the cliff tops since they are actively eroding into the ocean.

**Finding the park:** The park is a mile north of Cayucos on CA 1. The best parking is a large lot opposite San Geronimo Road (GPS: 35.449879 N /-120.932565 W). A wide trail heads directly west here to the top of the bluff, then turns south and follows the cliff edge to more dramatic viewpoints.

## Cayucos

**Cayucos,** spreading along the northeast corner of scallop-shaped Estero Bay, is a historical beach town with a population of 2,592 (2010). The town has an old California ambience with main streets lined with 19th-century buildings instead of tacky souvenir and T-shirt shops. In 2009 Cayucos was listed by *Frommer's Budget Travel Magazine* as one of the "Coolest Small Towns in America." There are lots of hotels, bed-and-breakfast inns, and restaurants along Ocean Avenue. Cayucos is also one of the best places on the south central coast for antiques with several shops; it hosts antique fairs every year. It's a popular place to set up base camp to explore the surrounding area, include wineries and Hearst Castle to the north.

The area was originally inhabited by the Chumash Indians, who lived here for thousands of years. One of their largest settlements was south of Cayucos along Morro Creek. The name Cayucos is from the Chumash word for the boats they used to fish in Estero Bay.

Recreation at Cayucos centers around its long beachfront, including **Cayucos State Beach** and the long wooden **Cayucos Pier,** built in 1875. Visitors come to swim, explore tide pools, walk the beach, surf, try sea kayaking, and fish from the pier. The pier is also the northernmost spot on the coast where the grunion run in summer, coming ashore to spawn after the full moon during high tide.

**Finding the town:** Cayucos is on CA 1 4 miles north of Morro Bay and 31 miles south of the Hearst Castle turn. If you're driving north, the highway is 4 lanes until the northwest side of Cayucos where it narrows down to 2 lanes.

*Pacific rollers crash onto surfers at Cayucos State Beach, a popular sandy beach in Cayucos.*

## Cayucos State Beach

**Cayucos State Beach,** on the west side of the town, is a long crescent-shaped sand beach lined with houses and businesses. The 16-acre state beach is Cayucos' recreation center, offering swimming, surfing, sunbathing, boogie boarding, and fishing off a 19th-century wooden pier. The Cayucos Pier, which is wheelchair-accessible, is lit at night for fishing. A beach wheelchair is available. Lifeguards are on duty during the summer. Dogs are allowed but must be leashed.

    **Finding the beach:** Access the beach from CA 1 by taking the Cayucos Drive exit. Follow the road for about a half-mile until it dead-ends at the pier. Go right to a large parking lot (GPS: 35.449514 N / -120.906834 W) or left to a long strip of diagonal parking on Ocean Front Avenue. This beach does not accept the Annual Day Use Pass. (805) 781-5930.

## Morro Bay

**Morro Bay,** dominated by humped **Morro Rock,** is a picturesque city that evolved from a fishing village to a tourist destination. This small city, with a population of 10,234 (2010), is sandwiched between a long strand and the ocean on the west and

*The town of Morro Bay, despite its many natural attractions, is still a fishing village at its harbor heart.*

low grassy hills on the east. The Cabrillo Highway bisects the city from south to north. Morro Bay has lots to offer the traveler, including lots of accommodations; a wide variety of restaurants, some serving excellent local seafood; miles of sandy beach for walking, swimming, surfing, and fishing; a busy shopping district; the state park's 18-hole **Morro Bay Golf Course;** and a museum of natural history. **Morro Bay Estuary** offers rich habitat, particularly for birds with over 250 species seen here.

The city has some great local parks, including **Morro Rock Beach** off Coleman Drive at the base of Morro Rock's northeast face; 3.2-acre **Bayshore Bluffs Park** with a cormorant nesting area, bike path, and viewpoints of Morro Bay; and **North Point Natural Area.**

The **Morro Bay State Park Museum of Natural History** is a great stop with lots of informative exhibits about Morro Bay and its wildlife and ecosystems. It particularly appeals to children with hands-on and interactive exhibits. (20 State Park Rd., Morro Bay, CA 93442; 805-772-2694; slostateparks.com).

Don't get hooked, however, into going to the Morro Bay Aquarium. It's a sad place that is supposed to be a rehabilitation center for seals and sea lions. Other visitors feel the same, calling it "The Saddest Aquarium in the World," a "Seal Guantanamo," and an "Aquatic Auschwitz."

Other attractions here are **Morro Bay State Park, Morro Strand State Beach,** the town of **Los Osos** on the southeast shore of Morro Bay, and, of course, the city's own skyscraper—Morro Rock. Farther south spreads **Montaña de Oro State Park,** a huge parkland of rugged hills and remote coastline.

Morro Bay has a remarkably mild climate throughout the year, with November being the warmest month and March the coolest. November's average high is 70°F while March's average high is 61. Monthly low temperatures generally range from 43°F to 55°F. Annual precipitation averages 17.6 inches, with December through March being the rainy season. Rainfall is almost nonexistent in summer.

**Finding the town:** Morro Bay is on CA 1 about 12 miles northwest from San Luis Obispo and US 101, the main north-south artery close to the coast. The city is about 4 hours north of Los Angeles and 6 hours south of San Francisco. For more information, contact **Morro Bay Chamber of Commerce & Visitor Center** (805-225-1633; morrobay.org).

## North Point Natural Area

**North Point Natural Area,** on the far north side of the town of Morro Bay, is a 1.3-acre parkland on **North Point Beach.** From an easily accessed parking lot, you can descend a stairway from the bluff-top to the beach. There are excellent tide pools here at low tide. You can hike north along the beach to Cayucos or south along the wide beach to Morro Point State Park. In spring, colorful wildflowers blanket the bluff. It's also a great spot to watch an ocean sunset.

**Finding the area:** From CA 1 turn west on Beachcomber Drive, then immediately north on Toro Lane. Drive a short distance until the road ends at a parking area above the beach (GPS: 35.406358 N / -120.870351W). The park is administered by the City of Morro Bay. (805) 772-6200.

## Morro Strand State Beach

**Morro Strand State Beach,** not to be confused with Morro Bay State Park farther south, is a 3-mile-long stretch of sand and surf on the west side of the town of Morro Bay. The park has two entrances at each end. Most folks visit the north end with easy beach access and a 75-site campground. Don't expect plush accommodations here; there are few trees, little privacy, and the sites are better suited for RVs or trailers than tents. Most sites can be reserved at reserveamerica.com. Popular activities are beach walking, swimming, surfing, windsurfing, and wave watching.

*A lone gull perches below the north flank of Morro Rock,*
*a huge rock dome at Morro Bay.*

**Finding the beach:** From CA 1 turn west from the highway onto Beach-comber Drive (right turn is Yerba Buena Street). Drive a block and continue straight into the park to a pay kiosk (GPS: 35.402252 N / -120.867945 W). The campground is straight ahead. To access the southern entrance, go west from CA 1 on Atascadero Road. Follow it west, then continue south on Embarcadero to a large parking area by the beach (GPS: 35.376778 N / -120.862688W).

## Morro Bay State Park

**Morro Bay State Park** sprawls across 2,700 acres on the east side of Morro Bay and the town of Morro Bay. This fabulous state park has it all—excellent trails, pleasant camping, rock climbing, mountain biking, the 18-hole **Morro Bay Golf Course,** and a small boat marina on Morro Bay.

A variety of species-rich ecosystems are found in the park, including grasslands, freshwater riparian habitats, salt marshes, coastal shrub habitats, and rolling hills. The Morro Bay area and Morro Rock are both natural and wildlife preserves, inhabited by numerous birds, including endangered peregrine falcons, great blue herons, egrets, and over 250 other avian species. The bay, sitting on the **Pacific Flyway,** is an important rest stop for migrating birds in spring and autumn. This area, including the Morro Estuary in the park's center, is one of the nation's best bird-watching spots. The park protects several unique natural areas: Heron Rookery Natural Preserve, Morro Rock Natural Preserve, and Morro Estuary Natural Preserve.

**The Heron Rookery Natural Preserve,** on the eastern edge of Morro Bay west of the golf course, is a small eucalyptus and cypress woodland that is alive with great blue herons, egrets, and double-crested cormorants that nest in the trees from February to June.

The **Morro Rock Natural Preserve** protects the unique dome of Morro Rock, a 23-million-year-old coastal landmark that was sacred to local Native Americans. The rock, protected as part of the state park, is closed to all visitors to protect nesting birds, including peregrine falcons.

The **Morro Estuary Natural Preserve** is a triangular-shaped, 800-acre wet-land where Chorro Creek drains into Morro Bay. The freshwater creek mixes with salt water to form a lush ecosystem where many birds thrive. Estuary life is easily seen from State Park Road on the west side and South Bay Boulevard on the east side. Look for pullouts where you can safely stop for wildlife-watching. Don't forget your binoculars.

At White Point on the eastern shore of Morro Bay and west of the golf course is the park's fine **Natural History Museum** with interactive exhibits and displays about the area's natural history, human history, geology, and marine ecology. It's a perfect stop for kids. The museum also offers nature walks, puppet shows, and lectures.

# Morro Rock

Morro Rock is a 581-foot-high (177-meter) volcanic plug or neck that dominates the coast of Estero Bay and gives its name to an estuary below the formation as well as a coastal town. Morro Rock, nicknamed the "Gibraltar of the Pacific," is the interior remains of an ancient volcano that lifted its cone here over 23 million years ago. Morro Rock is one of the Nine Sisters, a row of volcanic plugs that dot the Los Osos Valley between Morro Bay and San Luis Obispo. The dome-like rock, jutting above the ocean and sandy coastline, has long served as a coastal landmark for sailors.

Portuguese explorer Juan Rodriquez Cabrillo and his crew first documented it during a voyage along the California coast in 1542. Cabrillo named it El Morro since it resembles a Moor with a head scarf. Local Native Americans, including the Chumash and Salinan tribes, considered Morro Rock sacred. The Chumash lived in a large village near the mouth of Morro Creek near the rock for almost 7,000 years and south of the rock are large middens or piles of broken shells left by the early Chumash. Even today they are sometimes allowed to climb to the rock summit for a solstice ceremony, while the formation remains closed to all other visitors.

Morro Rock, protected in Morro Rock Natural Reserve and as a California Historical Landmark, was once an island, but a causeway was built on its northeast side to connect it to land and serve as protection to the harbor in Morro Bay. The rock was sporadically quarried until 1969. Now Morro Rock is a wildlife preserve, particularly for the endangered peregrine falcon which nests on the formation, and is closed to climbing and hiking.

*Clouds swirl around Morro Rock, a 581-foot-high volcanic plug that rise above Morro Bay.*

The park also offers lots of hiking trails on both sides of the estuary. One of the best hikes climbs 1.5 miles up a good trail to the summit of 640-foot **Black Hill.** The top offers stunning views of the entire Morro Bay region. Look for monarch butterflies in winter on eucalyptus trees on the hill. Good trails on the east side of the bay include **Quarry Trail, Live Oak Trail,** and **Portola Trail.** Ask at the museum for a trail map or download one off the park website.

A popular rock climbing area is on the south side of **Cerro Cabrillo,** the park's high point. **Rock Land, Ghost Rock,** and **El Dorado** are good cliffs that offer a fine selection of both lead and top-rope routes, mostly of easy and moderate grades.

The park campground has 135 shade campsites for tents, trailers, and RVs on the northwest side of the estuary near the museum and marina. The campground has water, showers, barbecue pits, tables, and restrooms. All facilities including a grocery store, restaurants, and shops are close by in Morro Bay. **Bayside Cafe** by the marina is close to the campground for a quick meal. For info and reservations call (800) 444-7275 or visit parks.ca.gov.

**Finding the park:** Access Morro Bay State Park by driving 10 miles northwest from San Luis Obispo on CA 1 or east from the town of Morro Bay for a half-mile. Exit from CA 1 on South Bay Boulevard. Drive 0.75 mile to the park entrance. All the attractions and activities are easily accessed from there. (805) 772-2560; slostateparks.com.

## Elfin Forest Natural Preserve

The **Elfin Forest** is a 90-acre preserve on the southeast edge of Morro Bay and bordering the town of Los Osos. The small area packs a lot of ecological diversity, with coastal marsh, riparian woodland, coastal dune scrub, oak and manzanita and its namesake pygmy oak woodland. All grow on stabilized sand dunes in poor soil. The coast live oak has adapted superbly to this relatively harsh environment and its persistent winds by growing very slowly. The oaks, miniature versions of their cousins growing in better climes, are stunted, twisted, up to 20 feet tall, and as old as 200 years. You can explore the forest by walking a 0.8-mile boardwalk that encircles the preserve. The wheelchair-accessible trail threads through the pygmy forest; offers marvelous views across Morro Bay to Morro Rock; and has viewing platforms and interpretative signs. Bring binoculars to see over 110 bird species and 25 mammal species. Watch for poison oak. Wear a hat and bring water in summer because there is little shade. Dogs must be leashed.

**Finding the preserve:** Reach the preserve from either Morro Bay or San Luis Obispo by driving on CA 1 to exit 277. Drive south on South Bay Boulevard for 2.5 miles to Santa Ysabel Avenue on the north side of Los Osos. Turn right and drive 2 blocks to 16th Street. Turn right on 16th and drive a block where it dead-ends at a gravel parking area (GPS: 35.33177 N / -120.82552 W). The board-walk trail begins here. slostateparks.com.

## Sweet Springs Nature Preserve

**Sweet Springs Nature Preserve** is a 24-acre wetland area on the south side of Morro Bay in the town of Los Osos. The preserve, a sanctuary for migrating and nesting birds on the **Pacific Flyway,** has two freshwater ponds, a salt marsh habitat, and groves of eucalyptus and Monterey pine. Monarch butterflies winter over here in the eucalyptus trees from November to March. A mile of easy trails, including a boardwalk, explores the area. At the end of the boardwalk on the bay edge is a large wildlife viewing platform, so bring binoculars to see shorebirds, egrets, pelicans, ducks, and other birds.

**Finding the preserve:** Reach the preserve from either Morro Bay or San Luis Obispo by driving on CA 1 to exit 277. Drive south toward Los Osos on South Bay Boulevard for about 3 miles to Pismo Avenue in Los Osos. Turn right and drive a block to 18th Street. Turn left on 18th and drive a block where it bends right as Ramona Avenue. Follow Ramona west to the preserve on the right between 4th Street and Broderson. Park in designated spots on the paved shoulder by the trailhead. (GPS: 35.320448 N / -120.841663 W). The free area is managed by the Morro Coast Audubon Society (805-772-1991; morrocoastaudubon.org).

## Los Osos Oaks State Natural Reserve

The **Los Osos Oaks,** a California State Park unit, is a magical forest of stunted and gnarled ancient oaks on the southeast side of the town of **Los Osos** just south of Morro Bay. The 90-acre reserve protects an undisturbed woodland of old-growth coast live oak trees, most only 6 to 8 feet tall and some as old as 800 years. The trees grow on a field of relict sand dunes with poor soil. Larger oaks grow in better and wetter soils here, some as tall as 25 feet with massive trunks and twisted branches.

The Chumash and Salinan Indians lived in the area, leaving large midden piles or trash dumps scattered around. After the area was colonized by Spanish settlers, much of the Morro Bay area was deforested for agriculture. This special oak woodland was somehow spared the ax and hoe. In 1972 this reserve was bought and turned over to the state park department for preservation.

Three trails—**Chumash Loop, Los Osos Creek Trail,** and **Oak View Trail**— explore about 1.5 miles of the reserve. Keep your eyes open for a variety of birds, mammals, and reptiles that live in the forest, including hummingbirds, flycatch-ers, owls, opossum, and deer. Lots of poison oak is here; avoid it by staying on the trails. Pets are not allowed. The park is open in daylight hours only, and there are no facilities.

**Finding the reserve:** Find the reserve from CA 1 by taking exit 277 just east of Morro Bay or 10 miles west of San Luis Obispo. Go south, following signs toward Los Osos, and follow South Bay Boulevard into the town of Los Osos. Continue to Los Osos Valley Road. Turn left or east and follow the road for less than a mile to a large marked parking lot on the right (south) side of the wide street and park (GPS: 35.30629 N / -120.813495 W). (805) 772-7434.

## Montaña de Oro State Park

**Montaña de Oro State Park** is one of the largest state park units in California with about 8,400 acres. This somewhat remote and little known parkland spreads along the hilly coast south of Morro Bay, offering 7 miles of rocky shoreline, pocket beaches, wave-sculpted headlands and arches, high rolling hills, and carpets of brilliant yellow flowers, including yellow mustard and poppies, in springtime that give the park its name—"mountain of gold."

The park offers over 50 miles of trails for hiking and mountain biking that explore the coastline, pass through scented groves of eucalyptus trees, and climb to lofty summits like 1,076-foot **Hazard Peak,** named for early settler Alexander Hazard, and 1,347-foot Valencia Peak, the park high point. Expect lots of solitude and silence on the trails. Recommended hikes include the 2-mile **Valencia Peak Trail** and **Bluff Trail,** a pleasant 2-mile ocean-side hike. Watch for rattlesnakes and poison oak along the trails. You can pick up a trail map at the visitor center.

The park's developed area is at **Spooner's Cove,** a pocket beach flanked by cliffs. Park in a large lot off Pecho Valley Road (GPS: 35.274875 N / -120.887268 W) for the beach. Swimming is discouraged along the park coast because of strong riptides and cold water. The cove and other rock benches along the coastline are great for looking at tide pools and beachcombing. Watch for rogue waves and the incoming tide if you're on remote sections of the shore. Several surfing spots are also along the coast. One is about a half-mile north of Spooner's Cove.

A small visitor center at the old **Spooner Ranch,** open year-round on weekends and daily in summer, sits on the bluff above the cove. Stop by for park info and maps. East of the visitor center and cove is 56-site **Islay Creek Campground** that's open year-round. Reservations are recommended for summer through reserveamerica.com, otherwise call the park or just show up.

**Finding the park:** Access the park from CA 1 by taking exit 277 for Los Osos just east of Morro Bay or 10 miles west of San Luis Obispo. Drive south on South Bay Boulevard to the town of Los Osos. On the south side of town, go right on Los Osos Valley Road, which eventually bends southwest on Pecho Valley Road. Follow the road for 7 miles to the shoreline, the park visitor center, and Spooner's Cove. There is no park entrance fee, and parking is free. (805) 528-0513.

*A quiet afternoon on the rocky shore of San Luis Obispo Bay south of Avila Beach.*

# 3
# SOUTH CENTRAL COAST DRIVE

# San Luis Obispo to Santa Barbara

**General description:** A 113-mile-long highway that twists down the south central California coastline from San Luis Obispo to Santa Barbara.

**Location:** Western California. Between San Luis Obispo and Santa Barbara.

**Drive route number and name:** CA 1 (Cabrillo Highway) and US 101.

**Travel season:** Year-round. Weather is mild most of the year. Watch for heavy rain at times in winter.

**Camping:** Many campsites are in state parks, beaches, and private campgrounds along the drive. Reservations, particularly in summer, are strongly recommended.

**Services:** All services in San Luis Obispo, Pismo Beach, and Santa Barbara. Services are in other towns along the drive.

## The Route

This 113-mile-long (181-kilometer) scenic drive, following CA 1 (Cabrillo Highway) and US 101, begins at the small city of San Luis Obispo, 11 miles east of the Pacific Ocean, and ends in the old mission city of Santa Barbara. The drive follows CA 1, a winding 2-lane highway, bypassing the fast divided highway US 101 between the two cities, passing by a spectacular area of coastal sand dunes, remote and hidden beaches, and a stretch of south-facing coast with great beaches, camping, and scenic ocean views.

While the drive can be done in a few hours, allow a full day or longer to stop, linger, and discover its many hidden treasures and pleasures. The highway follows quiet stretches of coastline, passes through fertile farm fields and pastures, and traverses hilly country on the edge of the Santa Ynez Mountains, one of the few east-west mountain ranges in the US.

The drive ends at Santa Barbara where California's wild Pacific coast also ends and its developed shoreline of wide sandy beaches flanked by the Los Angeles metropolis, one of the world's largest urban areas, begins. This section of coastline, which stretches to San Diego and the Mexican border, has no great mountain ranges along its edge but instead offers many great beaches along its broad crescent with only occasional headlands and rocky points to tease the restless surf. Check out other travel guides from Globe Pequot Press for coast and beach information on the greater Los Angeles area and San Diego.

# San Luis Obispo to Santa Barbara

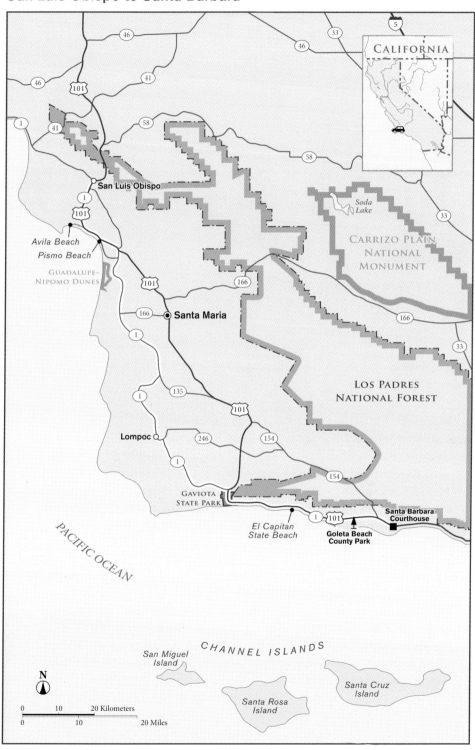

*Anchored boats bob in San Luis Obispo Bay beside a pier that juts south from Avila Beach.*

### Weather

The Mediterranean climate along the south central coast offers mild year-round temperatures with warm, sunny summers and pleasant winters. It can be foggy along the coast on summer mornings. Most rain falls from November through April, but it is usually erratic with occasional heavy downpours or light scattered showers. Summer high temperatures, moderated by offshore breezes, are generally in the mid-70s but can climb into the 90s and even low 100s on occasion.

## Avila Beach

The drive begins in **San Luis Obispo,** a city of 45,119 in 2010, that nestles in a hill-lined valley 11 miles inland from the Pacific Ocean on CA 1 (Cabrillo Highway) and US 101. This pleasant city, once called "America's Happiest City" by Oprah Winfrey, is not included here since it isn't located on the coast. Its best points of interest are the **Mission San Luis Obispo de Tolosa,** the **San Luis Obispo Museum of Art,** and hiking 2.2 miles up **Bishop Peak,** one of the Nine Sisters chain of local peaks. The drive heads south from SLO on CA 1/US 101 to the Pacific shoreline and Avila Beach.

*Gentle waves lap against a rocky headland at Avila Beach and Point San Luis Obispo.*

The town of **Avila Beach,** with a population of 1,627 (2010), is a seaside village at the northern head of San Luis Obispo Bay, formed by Fossil Point to the east and San Luis Point to the west. The shallow bay is usually warmer than other coastal areas since it's blocked from persistent westerly winds.

The main attraction is Avila Beach, a wide stretch of sand that's popular with sunbathers, swimmers, and beginning surfers on the edge of the town. The family-friendly beach is less crowded than ones down the coast like Pismo Beach, and there are swing sets in the sand and a nearby park for the kiddies, picnic tables next to the beach, generally clean public restrooms, and lots of free parking. The beach also has lifeguards when it's busy. Avila Pier runs out to sea from the south side of the beach.

The rest of Avila Beach stretches west across the north end of the bay to Point San Luis, a rocky headland that juts south and provides protection from the winds. Three other long piers, including one at the point itself, are on the long beach. The smallest pier at **Port San Luis Harbor District** has restaurants, fishing charters, and **SLO Coast Kayaks** where you can rent a boat or take a sea kayaking tour.

Along **Front Street** facing the beach and side streets are numerous restaurants, including several wine-tasting rooms, and gift shops. Other attractions are the **Avila Beach Golf Resort** and **Avila Hot Springs** with a swimming pool and a smaller soaking pool.

The **Bob Jones Trail** is a popular path for walkers, joggers, and bicyclists that follows the old railroad right-of-way for 2.5 miles between a trailhead next to CA 1/ US 101 and Avila Beach. The paved trail begins at a large parking area (GPS: 35.18568 N / -120.702863 W) on Ontario Road north of Avila Beach Road.

**Finding the town:** From CA 1/US 101, take exit 195 and go west of Avila Beach Road, which bends around a hill and goes south to the town of Avila Beach. Continue on the road past Avila Beach Golf Resort to the state beach on the left. Park off 1st Street on San Juan Street or Front Street (GPS: 35.179846 N / -120.735902 W) to access the beach and Avila Pier. avilabeachpier.com.

## Port San Luis Lighthouse

The **Port San Luis Lighthouse,** listed on the National Register of Historic Places, sits above ragged bluffs at the tip of Point San Luis west of Avila Beach. The lighthouse was built in 1890 after several shipwrecks, including that of the *Queen of the Pacific* which sank in 1888 while trying to navigate into Hanford Harbor on the east side of the point.

The lighthouse, decommissioned in 1974, is now open for limited tours seasonally. Trolley tours run by the nonprofit Point San Luis Lighthouse Keepers operate three times every Saturday. Call (805) 540-5771 for reservations. Pacific Gas and Electric (PG&E), which oversees the nuclear Diablo Canyon Power Plant 6 miles up the coast, offers guided hikes on the scenic coastal **Pecho Trail** (3.5 miles round-trip) out to the lighthouse. Preregister by calling (805) 541-TREK. For more info, visit sanluislighthouse.org or call (806) 540-571.

## Pismo Beach

**Pismo Beach,** with a population of 7,655 (2010), sprawls across an outwash plain backed by hills along the ocean shore south of San Luis Obispo. The town, nicknamed the "Clam Capital of the World," was established in 1891, taking its name from a Chumash Indian word for "tar," which was gathered along the coast to seal canoes. The famed Pismo clams were once so numerous on the beach here that they were harvested with plows. Pismo Beach takes its clams seriously with a giant clam on the edge of town and a clam festival every October with a clam parade and clam chowder cook-off. Pismo Beach usually refers not only to the village to the north but also to the neighboring communities of Grover Beach, Arroyo Grande, and Oceano on the south.

There are lots of outdoor activities here, including five golf courses; horseback riding on **Oceano Beach,** fishing off the 1,250-foot-long **Pismo Pier** for red

*Ths Pismo Dunes south of Pismo Beach is at the northern end of the second largest sand dune field in California.*

snapper and cod, surfing at Pismo Beach (lots of surf shops to rent boards or get lessons), sea kayaking along the rocky coast (again rent a kayak), and strolling on the long stretch of white sand beach. Pismo Beach is also like the good old days since you can still buy a permit from the ranger and drive your car onto the sandy shore to set up camp. It's the only beach in California with sand that is firm enough to drive a 2-wheel-drive vehicle on. You can also drive ATVs; rent one on Pier Avenue.

Attractions in town include **Price Historical Park,** the 1893 ranch and house of town founder John Price. **Pismo Beach Monarch Butterfly Grove,** one of California's largest monarch butterfly wintering sites, is at the southeast corner of **North Beach Campground** on South Dolliver Street (CA 1); free parking at the campground. The grove features thousands of butterflies from October through February. For more info visit monarchbutterfly.org.

The town has lots of restaurants, shops, and accommodations, including campgrounds. For great clam chowder, try **The Splash Cafe's** bread-bowl full of steaming chowder with seafood topping.

**Finding the towns:** The towns of Pismo Beach, Grover Beach, Arroyo Grande, and Oceano are along US 101 and CA 1. Pismo Beach is 13 miles south of San Luis Obispo and 20 miles north of Santa Maria.

# Pismo State Beach

**Pismo State Beach** is a 6-mile-long strip of glistening white sand that forms the western border of the town of Pismo Beach. The north end of the beach, which can be crowded, offers lots to do including walking, sunbathing, swimming (water can be cold), wading, surfing, and driving and camping on the beach. Lifeguards are on duty in summer. The remoter and more primitive south end of the beach features hiking in a gorgeous field of sand dunes and clam digging. It's more private and quiet than the north end.

The park offers a couple campgrounds with easy access to town and to the beach. **North Beach Campground** at Pismo State Beach on South Dolliver Street (CA 1) has 103 sites, easy beach access, restrooms, and showers. Farther south is 80-site **Oceano Campground,** also in Pismo State Beach, off Pier Avenue. Half the sites are RV only. **Lagoon Trail** encircles a large freshwater lagoon in the campground.

**Finding the beach:** Pismo State Beach stretches along the coast west of the towns. To access the beach, exit from US 101 onto CA 1 on either the north or south end of the towns. The northern beach is reached from South Dolliver Street (CA 1). The southern beach is also from CA 1 which is Pacific Boulevard in Grover Beach and Oceano. Plenty of parking is found at the different access points. (805) 489-1869.

# Guadalupe-Nipomo Dunes

The **Guadalupe-Nipomo Dunes** are a spectacular field of sand dunes that stretches for 18 miles along the coast from Pismo State Beach in the north to Point Sal State Beach in northern Santa Barbara County. This long strip of coastal sand, covering 15,000 acres, is the largest dune field south of San Francisco, the second largest in California, and one of the largest coastal dune systems in the world. The relatively undisturbed dunes, ranging from 1 to 3 miles wide and over 500 feet high, were built by prevailing northwest winds over the last 18,000 years. The dunes, a National Natural Landmark, are administered as several different units by various agencies. Parts of the dunes are protected as natural areas while others are open for recreation including off-road vehicles and camping. For information and maps, contact **The Dunes Center** (1065 Guadalupe St., Guadalupe, CA 93434; 805-343-2455).

**Pismo Dunes Natural Preserve** is south of Pismo State Beach and the town of Oceano. This large dune field, sometimes called Oceano Dunes, offers a remote beach experience with few other people and no facilities. The area is closed to all vehicles. **Finding the area:** Access it by parking at Pier Avenue in Pismo State

Beach and hiking south or driving south on the beach to marker #1. Park and hike east into the dune field.

**Oceano Dunes State Recreation Area** is a popular 3,600-acre site with compacted sand that is open to off-road vehicles and primitive camping; 1,500 acres are open for OHV driving. If you come here, be prepared for the full redneck experience. Go to other parts of the dune field if you want peace and quiet. It's loud and the off-roaders drive fast and recklessly. Everyone seems to be having a lot of fun though. If you want to share in that fun, get an ATV for a 2-hour rental at one of the shops at Pier Avenue in Oceano. Be warned that if you drive your vehicle, you might get stuck in sand. **Finding the area:** Drive west on Pier Avenue from Pacific Avenue/CA 1 in Oceano. Pay an entrance fee at a park kiosk and drive south a mile to the OHV area. Speed limit is 15 mph.

**Oso Flaco Lake Natural Area** is an 800-acre protected area just south of the OHV area and Oceano Dunes. A trail follows a bridge over the large freshwater Oso Flaco Lake to a boardwalk that heads west for about a mile to the beach, traveling through vegetation-stabilized dunes next to a riparian ecosystem. The handicap-accessible trail is great for bird watching with lots of species sighted at the lake. At the end of the trail is a high overlook with views from Point San Luis to Mussel Rock. No dogs allowed. **Finding the area:** Reach the area from CA 1 by driving 3 miles north of Guadalupe or about 4 miles south of Callender to Oso Flaco Lake Road. Turn west and drive 3 miles to the natural area parking (GPS: 35.029087 N / -120.617362W). Pay a parking fee and hike.

**Guadalupe-Nipomo Dunes National Wildlife Refuge** is a 2,553-acre protected area in the midsection of the dune field. The refuge, with a 1.8-mile section of coast, lies north of the Santa Maria River and includes the wildest dune section and lots of undisturbed wildlife habitat. The area provides protection for over 150 species of plants and animals, including several endangered and threatened species like the California least tern and western snowy plover. Other animals are pelicans and nesting peregrine falcons as well as deer and mountain lion. Recreational opportunities are limited to hiking and nature study. **Finding the area:** The refuge is easily accessed from CA 1 and Guadalupe to the east. There are two entrances. The north entrance is at the Oso Flaco Lake parking area described above. Hike south across the dunes or beach to the refuge. To access from the south, drive west from Guadalupe on paved West Main Street to a parking area where the road is closed (GPS: 34.95956 N / -120.641593 W). Hike north to the refuge. (805) 343-9151.

**Rancho Guadalupe Dunes Preserve,** anchoring the southern end of the dune field, is a mostly unspoiled natural area that offers hiking, bird watching, picnicking, and fishing. The preserve has 1.5 miles of coastline as well as a 550-foot-high dune, the highest on the west coast, and the estuary of the Santa Maria River. From the parking area, it's easy to access both the beach and the dunes, allowing for a solitary experience with the lonely sea and the sky. Out there in the dunes lies a buried Egyptian city with pyramids and the Sphinx, the massive film set for Cecil B. DeMille's 1923 silent-screen epic *The Ten Commandments.* Afterward the sets were toppled and buried with sand. It's illegal to dig for artifacts or to take them. **Finding the area:** From Guadalupe and CA 1, drive west on West Main Street on a narrow paved road to a parking area where the road is closed (GPS: 34.95956 N / -120.641593 W), same parking as the refuge. (805) 343-2354.

   **Point Sal State Beach,** at the southern end of the dune field in Santa Barbara County, is an 80-acre area with 1.5 miles of beach. The state beach is a remote park that is one of the southern coast's best. The day-use beach, reached by a long hike, is a lonely and rewarding wild place of surf crashing on exposed rock at Point Sal's headland, tide pools teeming with sea life, wave-swept rocks that attract seals and sea lions, and fine sand on a beach tucked into a rocky cove. Springtime brings carpets of wildflowers. Until 1998 when storms washed the road out, hikers could drive to an overlook above the beach. Now you have to park farther away by a farm and hike the old road on the **Point Sal Trail** about 6 miles to the beach, losing 1,200 feet of elevation from ridgetop to beach. The no camping rule in the area is strictly enforced not only by park rangers but also military police from nearby Vandenberg Air Force Base. Open from sunrise to sunset.

   **Finding the area:** From Guadalupe, drive south on CA 1 to Brown Road and turn west. Follow Brown Road until it ends at a gate by a farm (GPS: 34.912426 N / -120.619374 W). Do not block the gate at the parking area. (805) 733-3713.

## Ocean Beach County Park

**Ocean Beach** is an off-the-beaten-track beach that is mostly a Lompoc (pronounced lom-POKE) locals beach. The 5-mile-long sandy beach, facing the open ocean, gets big waves as well as wind so swimming isn't recommended. Surfing is reserved only for experts since big waves regularly occur. Vandenberg Air Force Base sandwiches the 36-acre park and the beach on both the north and the south sides, isolating it from the base's beaches south of here. The public can access 1.5 miles north of here and 3.5 miles south.

   The Santa Ynez River, draining into the ocean here, is backed up in a 400-acre freshwater lagoon that teems with birds. The endangered snowy plover also nests here, so beach access may be restricted from March through September. At the parking area above the lagoon are restrooms and picnic tables protected from the wind by berms. No dogs allowed.

   **Finding the beach:** Drive to Lompoc from US 101 on CA 1. From the middle of Lompoc, head west on West Ocean Avenue/CA 246. After about 8 miles, go right on Ocean Park Road and drive another mile or so to a large parking area at the beach (GPS: 34.690169 N / -120.60047 W). (805) 934-6123.

## Jalama Beach County Park

**Jalama Beach,** a Santa Barbara County Park, is a popular but off-the-beaten-track beach at the end of a long back road. It's a great spot to explore with miles of beach backed by high bluffs. Most visitors stick to the main beach, indulging in sunbathing, walking, fishing, and surfing. The water is often too cold for swimming, and there is a nagging wind here so make sure your tent is staked well. The park has a 98-site, first-come first-served campground with showers, cabins, picnic area, playground, and the **Jalama Beach Store and Grill,** serving its famous Jalama Burger. If you're visiting when a satellite is being launched from nearby Vandenberg Air Force Base, you will be treated to the roar of the rocket overhead. There is no cell phone service here, so bring a phone card to call out on the two pay phones. The excellent **De Anza Trail** begins here and follows the coast for 5 miles to **Point Concepcion** to the south, making a 10-mile out-and-back hike.

**Finding the beach:** From Santa Barbara or San Luis Obispo, follow US 101 to exit 132 for CA 1/Lompoc/Vandenberg. Head west of CA 1 for 14 miles to Jalama Road. Turn south and follow the scenic winding road for 14.5 miles to the beach. (805) 736-3504.

## Point Concepcion

**Point Concepcion,** marking the geographic boundary between the southern California coast and the central coast, is a rocky promontory where the Santa Barbara Channel meets the Pacific Ocean. Here two climates and several ocean currents converge. The native Chumash revered the point, calling it the "western gate," a place where dead souls passed into the next life, called *Similaqsa*.

Since October 18, 1542 when explorer Juan Rodríguez Cabrillo was turned back by heavy seas, the point has been one of the most dangerous spots for boats on the coast. Ships coming from the north would round the point into the channel and were often dashed on rocks by heaving seas, especially in fog.

The point, nicknamed Cape Horn of the Pacific by early mariners, is the site of the still-active Point Concepcion Lighthouse. The first lighthouse was built in 1856 and later moved to its present location on a lower platform above cliffs in 1881. The 52-foot-high lighthouse, listed on the National Register of Historic Places, is not open to the public. You can, however, hike to it on the 5-mile-long **De Anza Trail** from Jalama Beach to the north, for a 10-mile round-trip hike.

# Gaviota State Park

**Gaviota State Park,** 30 miles west of Santa Barbara, is a 2,787-acre parkland that extends north from the rugged coast to high hills coated with oaks and chaparral. US 101 bisects the park. Most visitors come to sprawl on the sandy beach, surf, swim, and picnic. A long Southern Pacific railroad trestle spans the mouth of Gaviota Creek above the day-use parking area near the beach. A pier on the west side of the beach is used by anglers, surfers, and divers. The name *gaviota* or seagull was given by sailors on the 1769 expedition led by Gaspar de Portolà who killed a gull while camping here. The name is also applied to this section of coast, which contains almost half of southern California's rural coastline.

The park offers lots of other activities including camping at a 41-site campground (can be noisy and sites are close together), mountain biking, and hiking on 34 miles of trails. Recommended hikes are the 1.5-mile **Overlook Fire Road** to a scenic view of the **Channel Islands;** a 3-mile trail to the summit of 2,458-foot **Gaviota Peak** in adjoining Los Padres National Forest; and a short steep trail to **Gaviota Hot Springs,** two sulfur spring baths. Keep alert when hiking for Pacific rattlesnakes and mountain lions. The park was closed for a month in 1992 after a lion almost killed a 9-year-old boy.

The thing that gets most visitors attention and usually lessens their enthusiasm for the park is the fierce and persistent winds that often occur. The wind begins in the afternoon, funneling down the canyon and blowing over tents.

**Finding the area:** Drive west from Santa Barbara on US 101 for about 30 miles to a marked left turn into the park. Follow Gaviota Beach Road down to the park entrance, beach, and large parking area (GPS: 34.471713 N / -120.227849 W). (805) 968-1033.

# Refugio State Beach

**Refugio State Beach,** the middle of three state beaches west of Santa Barbara, is a popular spot for locals with a 1.5-mile stretch of sand in a shallow shelter cove as well as some tide pool areas and rocky bluffs. The beach has an exotic feel to it with lots of palm trees waving in the wind. The best thing about Refugio is the great beachside 67-site campground, which offers outstanding ocean views and the sound of surf to lull you to sleep. The downside is the highway din from US 101 and the occasional train rolling past. There is also day-use parking, camp store, and lifeguards in towers during summer. Beach wheelchairs are available. Make camp reservations in advance by calling (800) 444-7275 or visiting reserveamerica.com.

**Finding the beach:** Drive west from Santa Barbara on US 101 for about 20 miles or 2.5 miles west of El Capitan State Beach. Take exit 120 for Refugio Road to the beach area and parking lot (GPS: 34.463197 N / -120.070438 W). (805) 968-1033.

# El Capitan State Beach

**El Capitan State Beach,** a 133-acre park on a blunt triangular-shaped promontory, is a very popular south-facing beach and campground alongside the coastal highway. The long sand beach, backed by a bluff, is narrow, so high tide almost covers it. There are also rocky sections with tide pools. Visitors enjoy walking on the beach, swimming if the water's not too cold, surfing on a few high wave days, and frolicking with dolphins in summer. Sycamores and oaks line El Capitan Creek as it runs through the park; good tide pools are at the mouth of the creek. The 133-site campground is good, with well-spaced sites and general quiet. It's hard, however, to get a reservation so plan well ahead of time to book at reserveamerica.com. No dogs are allowed on the beach.

**Finding the beach:** Drive west from Santa Barbara for about 17 miles on US 101 to exit 117 and go left on El Capitan State Beach Road to the parking area (GPS: 34.459548 N / -120.025289 W). (805) 968-1033.

# Santa Barbara

## *Location*

Santa Barbara and its suburbs spread across slopes between the Santa Barbara Channel to the south and the Santa Ynez Mountains to the north. This sunny section of coast trends from east to west, the longest transverse section of the West Coast. Santa Barbara lies 92 miles northwest of Los Angeles and 105 miles south of San Luis Obispo. US 101/CA 1 passes through the city, paralleling the coast and allowing easy access to the city's attractions and beaches.

## *About Santa Barbara*

The pleasant city of Santa Barbara, population 88,410 (2010), and its section of Pacific coast are a premier coastal destination with an almost perfect climate; a wide range of visitor attractions, museums, and cultural venues; historic landmarks; five colleges and universities; great sandy beaches; lots of restaurants and accommodations; and an unrivaled outdoor life. This California gold coast is nicknamed the American Riviera for its bucolic Mediterranean climate and similarities to the French Riviera.

Santa Barbara is, however, quintessential California with a laid-back atmosphere. Reflecting its Spanish colonial history, Santa Barbara's streets are lined with whitewashed stucco buildings and homes topped with red-tile roofs and rows of palm trees.

Paleo-Indians inhabited the area as long as 13,000 years ago, leaving behind fluted spear points as evidence of their passage. When explorer Juan Rodriquez Cabrillo sailed up the Santa Barbara Channel in 1542, thousands of Chumash

*The Santa Ynez Mountains scrape the horizon beyond a Santa Barbara beach lined with palm trees.*

lived here. The area was named in 1602 by Spanish explorer Sebastian Vizcaino after his ship and crew narrowly averted disaster in a channel storm on December 3, the eve of the feast day of Santa Barbara.

The town was established by Spanish colonists in 1782 as a presidio surrounded by crude adobe houses. Among the first settlers was Franciscan Padre Junípero Serra, who had established a mission at Monterey 12 years earlier. He died in 1784, 2 years before Mission Santa Barbara was completed. The mission was intended to convert the native Chumash and teach them European ways. Many Chumash, however, died from diseases like smallpox or were enslaved by the Spanish. Much of the town was destroyed in 1812 by an earthquake accompanied by a huge tsunami.

In the 1830s the Franciscan Mission lands were divided into land grants which were given by the Mexican government to notable citizens to create huge rancheros. The author Richard Henry Dana Jr., on a 2-year voyage to California, stopped by Santa Barbara on January 14, 1835, after 150 sea days from Boston. He described Santa Barbara in his book *Two Years Before the Mast*: "The town . . . is composed of one-story houses built of brown clay–some of them plastered–with red tiles on the roofs. I should judge that there were about an hundred of them; and in the midst of them stands the Presidio, or fort, built of the same materials, and apparently but little stronger. The town is certainly finely situated, with a bay in front, and an amphitheatre of hills behind."

Santa Barbara became American soil after it was taken by soldiers led by John C. Fremont on December 27, 1846 in the Mexican-American War. It quickly became a growing and prosperous town, but with the Gold Rush crowd it was also dangerous and lawless. After English became the official language in 1870, Stearns Wharf was built and Santa Barbara was promoted as a resort destination. In the early 20th century the Summerland Oil Field was discovered and the coastal area became the world's first offshore oil field. Even today black gold is pumped from offshore derricks seen from town beaches. A big earthquake in the Santa Barbara Channel in 1925 destroyed much of the city. It was decided that rebuilding would be in the current Spanish Colonial style of white buildings with tiled roofs.

For more information contact the **Santa Barbara Conference & Visitors Bureau and Film Commission** (500 E. Montecito St., Santa Barbara, CA 93103; 805-966-9222; santabarbaraca.com).

## Santa Barbara Climate & Weather

Santa Barbara, like the rest of the central and southern California coast, has a pleasant Mediterranean climate with warm summers and cool winters. The Santa Ynez Range to the north, rising to 7,000 feet, protects the city from cold north winds. The climate is generally mild and temperate, allowing flowers to bloom year-round and tropical trees like palms, which usually grow in greenhouses, to grow along the streets. The average daily high varies by only 12°F between January's 64.7°F and August's 76°F. Summer temperatures are usually moderated by persistent offshore breezes while the Santa Ynez Mountains create a rain shadow effect, bringing erratic rainfall. The city receives an average of 18.5 inches of precipitation, with February the rainiest month and July the driest. Occasionally a dusting of snow falls on the mountains, but the last time Santa Barbara received any snow was a few flakes in 1939.

## Santa Barbara Shopping & Restaurants

Santa Barbara is a prime shopping target for travelers. The best place to go is downtown along **State Street,** the city's main street and the heart of downtown, from the beach and **Stearns Wharf** to **Victoria Street.** Lots of stores and shops line the street as well as adjacent malls and shopping complexes. If shopping is your thing, you'll enjoy strolling up the cobbled sidewalks and checking out the stores. **Paseo Nuevo** (E. De La Guerra Street, Santa Barbara, CA 93101; 805-963-8084; paseonuevoshopping.com), with over 50 stores, is an old-world pedestrian mall with both department stores and local merchants. **La Cumbre Plaza** (121 S. Hope Ave., Santa Barbara, CA 93105; 805-687-6458; shoplacumbre.com) is another open mall with both restaurants and retail stores and a farmers' market.

*California Highway 1 twists through Santa Barbara along the Pacific coastline.*

### Santa Barbara Attractions

Santa Barbara, one of California's most beautiful cities, offers lots to do and see. It's a great place to walk around and explore the many attractions along palm-lined streets set with whitewashed buildings topped with red-tile roofs. Most of Santa Barbara's attractions are within walking distance of downtown as well as most hotels. Instead of driving places, park your car and take an urban hike. If you need refreshment, there are lots of restaurants, cafes, and coffee shops where you can stop and rest tired feet.

## Santa Barbara Courthouse

The **Santa Barbara Courthouse,** a classic public building in Spanish Revival style, is a beloved Santa Barbara landmark that was built after the 1925 earthquake and completed in 1929. The U-shaped complex, composed of four buildings, is an architectural masterpiece with tiled floors, arching corridors, high beamed ceilings, and a series of murals on the second floor depicting local California history from its discovery by explorer Cabrillo to the building of the local mission. Take

*The historic Santa Barbara Courthouse was rebuilt after a massive earthquake destroyed much of the town in 1925.*

time to stroll around the manicured grounds of this functioning courthouse and look at both native and exotic plants or have a picnic on the lawn. The highlight is to climb to the top of the clock tower for a wide view across all of Santa Barbara from one of the city's highest points, including the offshore Channel Islands. Free guided tours are offered every day. 1100 Anacapa Street; (805) 962-6464; santabarbaracourthouse.org.

## Santa Barbara Historical Society Museum

The museum, housed in an adobe building with a red-tile roof, offers a collection of local historical artifacts and memorabilia and fine art from the city's colorful past and diverse cultures, including Chumash, Spanish, Mexican, and American. A carved gold-leaf Chinese tong shrine that belonged to the Chee Kung Tong, a Chinese political group here in 1900, is a prized exhibit. On the museum grounds are two historic adobe houses from 1817 and 1836. (805) 966-1601; santabarbaramuseum.com.

## Santa Barbara Museum of Natural History

This museum, located behind the Mission Santa Barbara, is a worthwhile stop, especially for kids. The museum offers a good introduction to local flora and fauna with great exhibits of birds, a collection of Chumash Indian artifacts, and a planetarium. Out front is a 72-foot blue whale skeleton. (805) 682-4711; sbnature .org.

## Santa Barbara Museum of Natural Art

The museum of art in downtown Santa Barbara is a fine regional museum with a permanent collection of 27,000 objects, covering American art, impressionism, California artists, Pacific Rim photography, and Buddhist art from China, Japan, India, and Tibet. The Asian collection on the third floor is particularly nice. Both permanent and traveling exhibits are displayed on a rotating basis. The museum is open Thurs through Sun; closed on Mon and major holidays. (805) 963-4364; sbmuseart.org.

## Old Mission Santa Barbara

This picturesque mission, sitting on a hill overlooking downtown Santa Barbara, offers not only great views of the **Channel Islands** but is one of the best preserved and most elegant of all the California missions. The mission, built from native sandstone, is dominated by twin towers topped with domes and crosses. The current mission and outbuildings were finished in 1820, although the mission was founded in 1786 and four sets of buildings previously inhabited the site. This is also the only California mission that has been continuously operated by the Franciscan padres for over 225 years. Besides viewing the chapel, also check out the flower gardens with a fountain and the cemetery, with over 4,000 Chumash converts buried under the spreading shade of a large fig tree. (805) 682-4713; santabarbaramission.org.

## Moreton Bay Fig Tree

The massive **Moreton Bay fig tree** *(Ficus macrophylla),* west of US 101 at the corner of Chapala and Montecito Streets, is the largest of its species in the US. The fig tree, native to Moreton Bay in Australia, spreads a shady 176-foot-wide crown

*The Old Mission Santa Barbara, established in 1786, is called the*
*"Queen of the Missions" for its position and elegant lines.*

over an equally broad root system that snakes across the ground. The tree, a designated historic landmark, was originally planted on State Street by a local schoolgirl in 1876 and then replanted a few years later at its present site. The 80-foot-high tree has a circumference of almost 500 inches or 42 feet. Take a half-hour to stop and visit this ancient giant—it's worth the time.

**Finding the tree:** Located on a triangular-shaped block near the corner of Chapala Street and West Montecito Street just off CA 1/US 101 at the Santa Barbara Amtrak Station. (GPS: 34.41363 N / -119.693998 W).

## Santa Barbara Urban Wine Trail

If you don't want to travel an hour by car to visit any of the Santa Barbara County wineries, you can stay in downtown Santa Barbara and do your own wine-tasting tour. The **Santa Barbara Urban Wine Trail** features almost 20 tasting rooms for local vintners within a few blocks of the downtown, the beach, and US 101. It's easy to taste your way across Santa Barbara, stopping and sampling the wares (typically $10 for five or six wines) from the **Santa Barbara Winery,** the city's oldest and largest with 45,000 cases annually, to boutique producers like **Whitcraft Winery** that make less than a thousand cases. Besides tasting, you can see wine-making at some of the facilities. Before going, visit the trail's website urbanwine-trailsb.com and download an essential map. It's best to park and walk to a few of the rooms rather than drive and find parking. Better yet, rent a beach cruiser bike and pedal your way along the trail. Remember to eat, drink water for hydration, and look both ways before crossing the street!

## Santa Barbara Waterfront

The **Waterfront,** one of Santa Barbara's top visitor attractions, lies on the sheltered west side of a crescent-shaped beach near downtown. **Stearns Wharf** forms the east border of the harbor. It's a bustling place filled with all kinds of boats, their spiked white masts rising like a barren forest. It's fun to stroll alongside the harbor beneath palm trees, watch pelicans and gulls, or visit the nearby **Santa Barbara Maritime Museum.** For a more adventurous day, you can charter a fishing boat, go whale-watching, or take a guided sea kayak trip around the harbor through an outfitter like **Santa Barbara Adventure Company.**

**Finding the area:** The Waterfront is accessed from Shoreline Drive by turning south on Harbor Way. Park in one of many lots in the area and walk to the harbor.

*The widely distributed brown pelican, often seen on Santa Barbara beaches, nest on nearby Santa Barbara Island, one the few breeding colonies in California.*

## Santa Barbara Maritime Museum

The harborside **Santa Barbara Maritime Museum** is a great stop for both kids and adults. The museum's 8,000 square feet of space boasts lots of interesting exhibits. Trace Santa Barbara's seafaring past with a Tomol wood canoe made by native Chumash; smuggling and Chinese fish camps on the Channel Islands; Spanish explorers; famous shipwrecks; naval history; abalone diving; and sea otters, seals, and whales. Then you can watch films in the hull-shaped Munger Theater or scan the waterfront through a submarine periscope. An interesting surfing history exhibit and another one that details human impact on the oceans round out your educational experience.

**Finding the museum:** Turn south off Shoreline Drive and park along Harbor Way or in front of the museum (GPS: 34.40367 N / -119.694111 W). (805) 962-8404; sbmm.org.

## Stearns Wharf

**Stearns Wharf,** California's oldest working wharf or pier, juts into the Santa Barbara Waterfront. The wooden wharf, named for its builder John Stearns, was the longest pier between Los Angeles and San Francisco when it was completed in 1872. The wharf was used to load and unload passengers and freight from ships, instead of having to row them ashore through surf and swells, for the next half century. The construction of the Harbor Restaurant in 1941 marked the beginning of the wharf as an attraction.

Today it's Santa Barbara's most visited landmark. Start at the famous leaping dolphin sculpture and fountain at the head of the wharf off Cabrillo Boulevard and stroll south past restaurants and gift shops. At pier's end you can fish with tackle and bait from a nearby shop. The views of Santa Barbara and the Santa Ynez Mountains are outrageous, especially if you trek out in the early evening when the city lights are twinkling and waves slosh against the wood pilings.

**Finding the wharf:** Stearns Wharf is opposite the intersection of Cabrillo Road and State Street at the Dolphin Fountain. Park nearby and walk or on the wharf itself (GPS: 34.410074 N / -119.686196 W). stearnswharf.org.

## Santa Barbara Zoo

The **Santa Barbara Zoo,** on 30 acres with over 500 animals and 160 species, is considered one of America's best small zoos, especially with its ritzy seaside views. Exhibits include Cats of Africa, African Veldt with giraffes, the endangered Channel Island fox, Penguin House, two Asian elephants, two gorillas, aviaries filled with

*Stearns Wharf, California's oldest working wharf, offers spectacular views of the city lights at night.*

birds, and four majestic California condors. The zoo is intimate, family-friendly, and has a kids' play area. It is small, so it doesn't take long to check out the animals.

**Finding the zoo:** The zoo, sitting adjacent to CA1/US 101, is easily accessed from East Cabrillo Boulevard on the east side of Santa Barbara. Turn north on Niños Drive and drive a couple blocks to the zoo entrance on the right. Park in a large lot (GPS: 34.420253 N / -119.66741 W). (805) 962-5339; sbzoo.org.

## Santa Barbara Botanic Gardens

The 78-acre **Santa Barbara Botanic Gardens**, lying in Mission Canyon north of Santa Barbara, is a good stop to view native plants in a wild setting. You can explore the gardens on 5.5-miles of trails, passing cultivated displays, riparian woodlands along a trickling creek, and a unique grove of redwoods, which grow naturally farther north. The area also has the historic 1807 Mission Dam and an aqueduct, which delivered water down to the mission, and a Japanese teahouse and tea garden. There is free parking, a nominal entrance fee, and a gift shop. It's best to come in spring when all the flowers are blooming, especially the California poppies.

**Finding the gardens:** Access the botanic gardens by driving north from Santa Barbara on Mission Canyon Road. Park in a long lot on the west side of the road (GPS: 34.45689 N / -119.709247 W). 1212 Mission Canyon Rd.; (805) 682-4726; sbbg.org.

## Coal Oil Point Natural Reserve

The 150-acre **Coal Oil Point Natural Reserve,** administered by the University of California's Natural Reserve System, protects a coastal strand ecosystem with various dune, shoreline, and estuarine habitats. The area includes sand dunes covered with scrub and brush, forming a nesting site for the endangered snowy plover, as well as tidal Devereux Lagoon which seasonally floods. The reserve provides refuge for wildlife, including thousands of migratory birds. The area is used for research at nearby University of California, Santa Barbara and for nature study by students, birders, and hikers. A trail encircles the preserve, providing wildlife viewing. The sand beach below the sand dunes is open to public use. Some areas may be closed to protect wildlife habitat.

**Finding the reserve:** From US 101, take exit 108 and drive south on Storke Road. At its L-junction with El Colegio Road, continue straight on Slough Road. Follow it along the eastern edge of the lagoon to a turnaround and parking area at Coal Oil Point (GPS: 34.407624 N / -119.878124 W). Several pull-offs allow bird watching. (805) 893-5092.

## Isla Vista County Park

The 1.4-acre **Isla Vista County Park,** perched atop a high bluff, overlooks **Isla Vista Beach** in the suburb of Isla Vista, which is mostly populated by college students. The small rectangular park, hemmed in by apartment buildings, offers great ocean views as well as benches, picnic tables, and a sand volleyball court. A stairway leads down to the sandy west end of Isla Vista Beach.

**Finding the park:** From US 101, take exit 107 and drive south on Los Carneros Road to El Colegio Road. Turn left and drive to Camino Corto. Turn left and drive to the park. Parking is on the street (GPS: 34.409754 N / -119.866135 W).

## Goleta Beach County Park

**Goleta Beach,** part of a 29-acre Santa Barbara County Park, stretches for over a half-mile south of the suburb of Goleta and the Santa Barbara Airport. The day-use park and beach, hosting over 1.5 million visitors annually, is justifiably popular with its golden sands (regularly replenished since the beach is eroding), sand volleyball court, picnic tables, barbecue grills, playground, and horseshoe pits.

It's also popular with bicyclists who ride paved trails and anglers who congregate on a 1,450-foot-long pier called **More's Landing** to catch halibut, bass, rockfish, corbina, and even occasional small sharks; it's considered one of California's best fishing piers and offers great views of the coastline. Activities, besides sunbathing, include birding, whale-watching, surfing, and swimming. The beach is also dog-friendly, although Fido needs to be leashed.

**Finding the beach:** From US 101, take exit 104 and drive southwest on Clarence Ward Memorial Boulevard to the Sand Spit exit at a sign for Goleta Beach County Park. Turn left and drive into the park. There are almost 600 parking spaces in several parking lots next to the beach (GPS: 34.417416 N /-119.829796 W). The free park is open 8 a.m. to sunset. Santa Barbara County Parks (805-568-2461).

## Arroyo Burro Beach County Park

This beach, also called Hendry's Beach, is a long spread of sand hemmed between a towering bluff and the Pacific surf, which, despite being only a 10-minute drive from downtown Santa Barbara, has a somewhat private feel. The beach is popular with families, kids wading in the waves, sunbathers, and surf anglers. Dog-lovers especially enjoy it since the beach south of the creek on the west side of the park allows unleashed dogs to romp in the surf; the beach north of the creek is for leashed dogs. The park has free parking (come early on busy days), a grassy picnic area, restrooms, outdoor showers, a restaurant, and snack bar. The park is open 8 a/m/ to sunset. Watch the tides because the beach considerably narrows at high tide.

**Finding the park:** The park and beach is 5 miles west of downtown Santa Barbara on Cliff Drive. From US 101/CA 1, take exit 100 and drive south on Las Positas Drive to Cliff Drive. Turn right and drive 0.5 mile to the park entrance on the left and a large parking area (GPS: 34.40411 N / -119.743198 W).

## Shoreline Park

**Shoreline Park,** a Santa Barbara community park, is a long bluff-top strip of land that offers beach access and great scenic views. With its green grass and shade trees, it's perfect for picnicking, walking, and people-watching. There is a playground, 2 free parking lots, whale-watching in winter, views of the Channel Islands, and a stairway down a steep bluff in the middle of the park to narrow **Mesa Beach.** The beach is best in summer at low tide with its hard-packed sand; winter storms often rage on the beach, limiting visitation.

**Finding the park:** The park is west of the marina on Shoreline Drive. Park at large free lots on the west side of the park (GPS: 34.396017 N / -119.710727 W) or on the east side of the park (GPS: 34.397876 N / -119.703877 W).

# Leadbetter Beach

**Leadbetter Beach** is a long crescent-shaped sand beach that stretches from the east end of Shoreline Park to the marina. The popular and wide beach, free and family-friendly, is convenient to downtown Santa Barbara and easy to access since it's alongside Shoreline Drive. The beach is usually crowded with locals and tourists, so plan on going to a different one on the weekend. Activities include sunbathing, strolling, surfing, and people-watching. There are restrooms, parking, and picnic tables with grills.

**Finding the beach:** The beach is on Shoreline Drive just west of the marina and downtown. Make a left turn to 2 large parking areas (GPS: 34.402829 N / -119.697735 W).

# East Beach

**East Beach** is a long sand beach that runs east from Stearns Wharf and Mission Creek to the Andree Clark Bird Refuge; East Cabrillo Boulevard and some green grassy parks border it on the north. East Beach is great for walking, sunbathing, swimming on warm days, and surfing.

The **East Beach Volleyball Courts** are the place to be for beach volleyball, with about a dozen nets set up and some of the best beach volleyball players, including Olympic gold medalists, battling it out on the golden sand. The clean beach, lined with palm trees, is great for strolling, but watch for tar balls that stick to your bare feet.

**Skater's Point,** one of the best skateboard parks anywhere, is at the west end of East Beach. It offers lots of bowl riding and street skating and boarding. You can't skateboard without a helmet and pads.

There is plentiful scattered parking along the beach, but it can fill up fast so find neighborhood parking or ride a bike. Also watch the traffic along Cabrillo Boulevard, especially if you have small children.

**Finding the beach:** Access East Beach from US 101/CA1 by taking exit 96 and driving south on Garden Street a few blocks to East Cabrillo Boulevard. Turn left to access the beach and several parking areas. The first parking lot (GPS: 34.402829 N / -119.697735 W) is opposite the junction of Garden and Cabrillo. Farther east are more parking areas by the beach and volleyball courts. The volleyball courts are east of the junction of Niños Street and Cabrillo Boulevard.

# 4
# MARIN-SONOMA-MENDOCINO COAST SCENIC DRIVE

# The Golden Gate to US 101

**General description:** This 209-mile-long drive borders the Pacific coast north of San Francisco. The highway passes historic sites, redwood forests, abrupt headlands, sandy beaches, windswept coves, and numerous recreation areas.

**Special attractions:** Muir Woods National Monument, Point Reyes National Seashore, Golden Gate National Recreation Area, San Andreas Rift Zone, Sonoma Coast State Beaches, Fort Ross State Historic Park, Kruse Rhododendron State Reserve, Point Arena Lighthouse, Van Damme State Park, Mendocino Headlands State Park, Mendocino, Fort Bragg, hiking, redwoods, beaches.

**Location:** West-central California. The drive runs north on CA 1 from US 101 in Marin City just north of San Francisco to US 101 north of Willits.

**Drive Route number and name:** CA 1 (Shoreline Highway).

**Travel season:** Year-round. Summer mornings are often foggy. Winters are wet, windy, and cool. Watch for slick pavement.

**Camping:** Numerous campgrounds are along the route.

**Services:** All services at Stinson Beach, Bolinas, Point Reyes Station, Marin City, Bodega Bay, Jenner, Gualala, Manchester, Mendocino, and Fort Bragg.

## The Route

The 209-mile-long Marin-Sonoma-Mendocino Coast Scenic Drive follows paved CA 1 up California's spectacular Pacific coast from the Marin Peninsula north of the Golden Gate Bridge to US 101 south of Eureka. The highway traverses steep, wave-carved headlands; passes quiet sandy coves; crosses grassy terraces punctuated by grazing cattle; finds towering redwood trees in moist canyons; runs alongside long sweeping beaches; and plunges through dense woodlands of oak and pine.

The ragged Pacific coastline, called the Sonoma-Mendocino Coast for its two upper counties, is a wild and beautiful meeting of restless ocean and land and includes some of the California coast's most spectacular vistas and natural areas. Much of the coastline here is protected in numerous state beaches and parks, as well as Muir Woods National Monument, Golden Gate National Recreation Area, and Point Reyes National Seashore.

The drive begins in Marin City just north of San Francisco and the Golden Gate Bridge. Exit off US 101 and head west on CA 1, the Shoreline Highway. After a couple of miles, the highway leaves the town behind and passes along a rounded ridge lined with eucalyptus and oak trees. The road quickly narrows and begins winding across the hillsides—a character it assumes for the next 200 miles.

Vehicles over 35 feet in length are prohibited. The traveler will not encounter another traffic light until Fort Bragg, more than 160 miles up the coast. Just over

# Golden Gate to Leggett

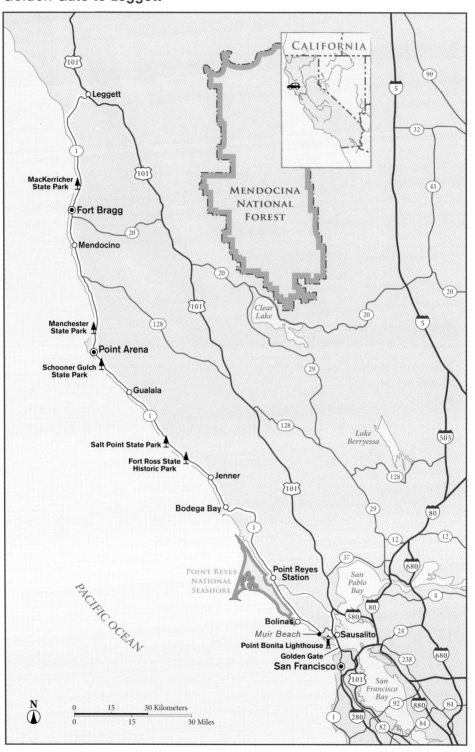

CALIFORNIA

MENDOCINA
NATIONAL
FOREST

Leggett

MacKerricher
State Park

Fort Bragg

Mendocino

Manchester
State Park

Point Arena

Schooner Gulch
State Park

Gualala

Salt Point State Park

Fort Ross State
Historic Park

Jenner

Bodega Bay

Clear
Lake

Lake
Berryessa

POINT REYES
NATIONAL
SEASHORE

Point Reyes
Station

San
Pablo
Bay

Bolinas

Muir Beach

Point Bonita Lighthouse

Golden Gate
San Francisco

Sausalito

San
Francisco
Bay

PACIFIC OCEAN

N

0    15    30 Kilometers
0    15    30 Miles

*Alamere Falls drops 50 feet off a cliff onto a pristine sand beach at Point Reyes National Seashore.*

3 miles from the drive's start, the route intersects the Panoramic Highway, which climbs north into 6,300-acre Mount Tamalpais State Park and the Muir Woods Road.

## Weather

The Marin-Sonoma-Mendocino Coast lies in California's fog belt. Thick fog, particularly in summer, hangs over the shoreline and backs up against the coastal mountains. The fog is the result of moist air blowing over cold offshore currents. Fog forms when the air condenses into tiny water droplets.

Inland, even just a few miles, the fog dissipates as the sun warms the air. Point Reyes northwest of San Francisco is considered one of California's foggiest and windiest spots. Some coastal areas, notably the Point Arena headland, are "banana belts" that are warm and virtually fog free because of protective mountains to the east and ocean currents.

Expect cool temperatures year-round, with summer highs ranging from 60°F to 70°F. Afternoons along the shoreline are usually breezy so pack a sweater and wind jacket. September and October generally bring glorious, balmy days. In September, the daily high temp averages 65°F with temperatures occasionally climbing into the 80s. Clear skies dominate, with fog occurring on only one out of every 8 days.

Winters are cool and rainy, with most of the coast's annual precipitation falling during wet storms that sweep off the Pacific Ocean. December and January both average 7 inches of rainfall along the Mendocino coast. Temperatures are moderate, falling between 40°F and 60°F. Expect heavy rain, slick roads, and stiff winds during stormy weather. A raincoat over a sweater provides plenty of protection for winter hikers, beachcombers, and whale-watchers. Wet weather continues into spring, but greenery adorns the grasslands and forests.

## Marin Headlands Area

The **Marin Headlands** is a blunt peninsula of grass- and oak-covered hills and valleys that juts southeast like a blunt finger to the north side of the Golden Gate strait, the entrance to San Francisco Bay. Much of the area lies within Golden Gate National Recreation Area, protecting beaches, redwood forests, abandoned military fortifications, lighthouses, hiking trails, and picturesque towns.

The southern end of the headlands offers expansive panoramic views of the Golden Gate Bridge, San Francisco Bay, and the skyline of San Francisco. Several fine beaches are found along the southern shoreline, including Kirby Cove, Rodeo Beach, and Muir Beach, as well as some great overlooks. Hawk Hill is one of the best places on the Pacific coast to witness the autumn migration of raptors. Nearby is beloved Mount Tamalpais State Park with over 200 miles of hiking trails and spectacular views.

## Golden Gate National Recreation Area

The 80,002-acre **Golden Gate National Recreation Area** (GGNRA), stretching for 60 miles along the California coast and San Francisco Bay, is one of the largest and busiest urban parklands in the world. The park, encompassing many distinct attractions and areas in San Francisco, Marin County, and San Mateo County, sees almost 15 million visitors a year. The GGNRA, administered by the National Park Service, includes many of the San Francisco area's best coastal attractions, including **Muir Woods National Monument, Alcatraz Island,** the historic **Presidio of San Francisco,** the **Golden Gate Bridge** area, beaches, overlooks, hiking trails, and old military forts. The park's areas are detailed below.

Golden Gate National Recreation Area's various sites are easily accessed from CA 1. Detailed information, maps, books, and interpretative activities can be found at the area's visitor centers, including at park headquarters at **San Francisco Maritime National Historic Park, Presidio Visitor Center, Marin Headlands Visitor Center,** and **Muir Woods Visitor Center.** Contact the park at (415) 561-4700 or visit the park website at nps.gov/goga.

# Golden Gate Bridge

The **Golden Gate Bridge** is an iconic California landmark, one of the Wonders of the Modern World, the most photographed bridge in the world, and one of the California coast's must-see attractions. The span with its graceful lines, international orange color (constantly maintained by 38 painters), and beautiful natural setting, is arguably the most beautiful bridge in the world.

The art deco bridge, built in 4 years between 1933 and 1937, stretches 8,981 feet or 1.7 miles across the Golden Gate, the strait that separates the Pacific Ocean from San Francisco Bay. The strait was originally named "Chrysopylae" or "golden gate" by Captain John C. Fremont in 1846. The twin suspension towers rise 746 feet above the water and support the 6-lane, 90-foot-wide roadway with two giant cables, each composed of 27,572 separate wire strands woven together, that are anchored on each end of the bridge.

Besides its beauty and aesthetics, the Golden Gate Bridge harbors a darker side—suicide. The bridge has more suicides than any other place in the world, with one every 2 weeks. It's estimated that as many as 1,500 people have jumped from the bridge deck, falling 245 feet to the water at 75 mph where they either die on impact or drown in the frigid water. Many jumpers come to San Francisco specifically to make the 4-second leap from the bridge to the water. Many bodies are never recovered from the 372-foot-deep water in the channel below the bridge.

The Golden Gate Bridge is open to auto and bicycle traffic 24 hours a day but only during daylight hours for pedestrians. An auto toll is charged for the southbound lanes only.

There are two bridge vista points. On the south or San Francisco side is **South Vista Point** with a metered parking lot with restrooms, a gift shop, and cafe. If the lot is filled, look for nearby lots. **North Vista Point** next to the northbound lanes at the end of the Marin Headlands has a large free parking area that's a popular tour bus stop and restrooms.

You have to walk across the bridge to truly appreciate its size, height, and beauty. The distance between the two vista points is 1.7 miles, making it a 3.4-mile round-trip walk. If that's too far, consider walking out to the middle only. Only the east side of the bridge is open for pedestrians. Dogs must be leashed; no skateboards or inline skates allowed. goldengatebridge.org.

*Hendrik Point offers a stunning view of the iconic Golden Gate Bridge, a 1.7-mile-long span that connects San Francisco with the Marin Headlands.*

# North Vista Point

**North Vista Point** is the viewpoint directly north of the Golden Gate Bridge on the headland overlooking San Francisco Bay. The viewpoint offers a great view of the iconic bridge looking directly south at its tall towers. It is, however, usually crowded with tourists and tour buses, so be prepared to share the view. The best light for photography here is in the morning since later in the day the bridge is backlit by the sun. It's better to go to Hendrik Point (see below) on Couzelman Road for afternoon and evening photos and views of the bridge.

 **Finding the overlook:** Drive north from San Francisco across the Golden Gate Bridge on US 101/CA 1. Take the first turn to the right (just before exit 442) and drive into a large free parking area (GPS: 37.832478 N / -122.479574 W). The viewpoint is at the south end of the lot. Restrooms are in the middle of the parking area. Remember that there is a $6 toll if you return south to San Francisco over the bridge.

# Kirby Cove

**Kirby Cove,** lying a scant 8 miles from San Francisco, sits on the north side of the strait and just west of the Golden Gate Bridge. The secluded cove and beach includes a coveted four-site National Park Campground with stunning views and a sense of isolation despite the city and the iconic Golden Gate Bridge looming nearby. Battery Kirby between the campground and the beach is a historic military site operated from 1898 to 1934 to help protect the entrance to San Francisco Bay. The artillery battery and beach were named for First Lieutenant Edmund Kirby, who was killed at the Battle of Chancellorsville in 1863 during the Civil War.

 The campground is available by reservation only and for limited periods of time so others can also enjoy this crown jewel camping area. Make reservations well in advance of your planned stay at recreation.gov. A park ranger will give you a code to open the gate lock, allowing you to drive to the campground. No water is available. Sites are limited to 10 people and three vehicles.

 **Access Kirby Cove** by taking exit 442 off US 101 north of the Golden Gate Bridge. Go left on Alexander Road, then right on Couzelman Road; follow a mile or so to the trailhead (GPS: 37.829493 N / -122.483537 W) on the southeast side of the road. From a trailhead on the west side of the parking area, hike or bike down the closed mile-long Kirby Cove Road through a cypress, pine, and eucalyptus woodland to the beach.

## Hendrik Point

If you drive out to Kirby Cove, take the short walk from the parking area out to **Hendrik Point** and its stunning view of the Golden Gate Bridge and San Francisco. You stand level with the giant towers and the great orange cables at the overlook, framing the city skyline beyond. Come at sunrise or sunset for the best photo ops. This viewpoint is a great alternative to busy North Vista Point on the east side of US 101 north of the bridge. Lots of tour buses stop at North Vista Point, disgorging camera-pointing tourists, but Hendrik Point is reserved for locals who know its special view. Battery Spencer, an old artillery fortification, is also at the overlook. Remember to bring a coat since it is often windy and cool at the overlook.

**Access Hendrik Point** by taking exit 442 off US 101 north of the Golden Gate Bridge. Go left on Alexander Road, then right on Couzelman Road; follow a mile or so to the parking area (GPS: 37.829493 N / -122.483537 W) on the southeast side of the road

## Bay Area Ridge Trailhead

The **Bay Area Ridge Trail** is a proposed 550+-mile-long multiuse loop trail that encircles the entire San Francisco Bay, crossing ridges, hills, and valleys. Over 340 miles of the trail are now completed. A northern trailhead for the Bay Area Ridge Trail begins on the north side of the Golden Gate Bridge just west of US 101 and opposite North Vista Point. A good 4.6-mile hike begins here and ends at Tennessee Valley Trailhead to the northeast. The hike combines several trails, beginning on SCA Trail to Rodeo Valley Trail to the Bobcat Trail. Expect marvelous views as you cross open grasslands and chaparral and an elevation gain of 600 feet along singletrack trail and closed service roads.

**Access the trailhead** by taking exit 442 off US 101 north of the Golden Gate Bridge. Go left on Alexander Road, then make the first right on Couzelman Road, then an immediate left to the trailhead (GPS: 37.832497 N / -122.482093 W). Find out more about the Bay Area Ridge Trail and download maps at ridgetrail.org.

## Hawk Hill

**Hawk Hill,** a 920-foot-high mountain on the southern end of the Marin Headlands, offers a lofty vantage point to observe the autumn migration of thousands of raptors, including hawks, falcons, eagles, vultures, and ospreys, on the Pacific Flyway. From August to December, the migrating birds follow the coastline, taking advantage of coastal thermals to soar high. The most common species seen are red-tailed hawks and turkey vultures. The best viewing times are on fog-free days between 10 a.m. and 2 p.m. from September through November. Bring warm clothes, binoculars, and a field guide. Leashed dogs are allowed. There are also great views of the Golden Gate Bridge and San Francisco from the hill.

**Access Hawk Hill** in Golden Gate National Recreation Area from Couzelman Road southeast of US 101/ CA 1 just north of the Golden Gate Bridge. Take Exit 442 onto Alexander Road on the west side of US 101 and turn right on Conzelman Road, the first road on the right, and follow it to marked Hawk Hill. Park at a designated lot on the east side of the road (GPS: 37.827273 N / -122.499071 W) and walk up to a viewing area and visitor center.

## Point Bonita Lighthouse

The **Point Bonita Lighthouse** lives up to its name: It's simply beautiful. The lighthouse perches on the end of Land's End, a narrow rocky peninsula that juts south from the Marin Headlands and marks the entrance to San Francisco Bay. The lighthouse was originally built farther inland in 1855, but the light was too high to be easily seen so it was moved onto the rocky point in 1877, where it still perches 124 feet above sea level. The site was also very remote and lonely, so seven keepers quit during the first 9 months of operation.

The active lighthouse, maintained by the US Coast Guard, is open to visitors. For info on public tour times, check the GGNRA website, visit the **Marin Headlands Visitor Center,** or call (415) 331-1540. Full moon and sunset tours are occasionally offered. The lighthouse is reached by a 0.5-mile trail, with a tunnel and suspension bridge over the final broken rock section. Near the parking area at old Fort Barry are a couple batteries that offered artillery protection for the entrance to San Francisco Bay as well as small **Bicentennial Campground,** the **YMCA Point Bonita Outdoor and Conference Center,** and **Marin Headlands Hostel** (415-331-2777) with its scenic and affordable accommodations.

**Finding the lighthouse:** From San Francisco, drive over the Golden Gate Bridge and take exit 442 onto Alexander Road just past North Vista Point. Go right on Alexander to Bunker Road; turn left on Bunker and follow it for 3 miles to Fields Road. Turn left on Fields and drive 0.8 mile to Fort Barry and the lighthouse parking (GPS: 37.821906 N / -122.529372 W). Marin Headlands Visitor Center (GGNRA) (415) 331-1540.

## Rodeo Beach

**Rodeo Beach,** lying just north of Point Bonita and a couple miles northwest of Golden Gate Bridge, is a long gravel bar that separates crescent-shaped Rodeo Cove from Rodeo Lagoon, an inland estuary that is habitat for the endangered California brown pelican. The pretty beach is also unique since it is composed of smooth wave-polished pebbles of red and green chert rather than fine sand. Rodeo is not the best beach for lolling in the sun or walking barefoot, but it is great for walking, sunsets, views of cliffs that flank the beach, rocky sea stacks, and surfing. Summer offers the best surfing conditions, with the best winds out of the northwest. Watch for sharks. The beach can also be cool, windy, and is often draped in fog so bring a coat.

Lots of hiking trails are in the area including the **Coastal Trail,** which heads north toward Muir Beach. A good moderate hike with great views is to follow the Coastal Trail for about 1.5 miles to Hill 88 (the big hill to the north), then return via **Wolfback Ridge and Miwok Trails** to the parking area. On the north shore of the lagoon are the remains of old **Fort Cronkhite** and the **Marine Mammal Center.**

**Finding the beach:** From San Francisco, drive across the Golden Gate Bridge. Take exit 442 onto Alexander Road just past North Vista Point. Go right on Alexander to Bunker Road; turn left on Bunker and follow it for about 4 miles to a parking area on the north side of the lagoon (GPS: 37.83170 N / -122.536198 W). A handicapped-accessible bridge crosses the lagoon outlet to the beach. Marin Headlands Visitor Center (GGNRA), (415) 331-1540.

## Tennessee Valley & Beach

The **Tennessee Valley** is a broad valley that slopes gently westward to a pocket beach at Tennessee Cove on the western side of the Marin Headlands. The area, part of Golden Gate National Recreation Area, offers lots of wonderful hiking trails in the valley and across surrounding hills. The best hike wanders 1.7 miles down Tennessee Valley to end at remote **Tennessee Beach.**

This lonely spot conjures up wild California at its best, with waves crashing on the sand beach and towering cliffs that crowd against it on both sides. An iconic natural arch in a rock fin on the north end of the beach suddenly collapsed on December 29, 2012 before an astonished group of almost 20 hikers, including a couple geologists who documented the fall—a reminder of changes that constantly occur along the shoreline. Besides beach walking, hiking, and sunbathing, Tennessee Beach also offers limited bouldering on small boulders above the sand.

The valley was originally called Elk Valley for its Tule elk herds but after the SS *Tennessee* accidently turned ashore in thick fog in 1853 and was beached in the cove, the area was renamed for the lost ship. Some 550 passengers along with 14 gold-filled chests were saved from the wreck. The ship's engine can still be seen at low tide.

**Finding the beach:** From US 101 north of Golden Gate Bridge, take exit 445 to Stinson Beach on CA 1. Follow CA 1/Shoreline Highway to the marked

Tennessee Valley turn and drive west on Tennessee Valley Road to a parking area (GPS: 37.860552 N / -122.535938 W) and the trailhead at Miwok Livery Stables. The trail to the beach continues down the closed road, while the Miwok and Marincello Trails begin east of the parking area. **Marin Headlands Visitor Center** (GGNRA; 415-331-1540).

## Muir Beach

**Muir Beach** is both a small unincorporated town (2010 population was 310) and a popular sand beach on the Marin County coast about 16 miles northwest of San Francisco. The Shoreline Highway (CA 1) leaves Mill Valley and US 101, twisting over a high ridge and descending west down Redwood Creek past the **Green Gulch Farm Zen Center,** a Buddhist retreat with comfy accommodations, to the village of Muir Beach. You know you're there when you reach a long row of mailboxes at the town turnoff.

There's not much to the town except 150 or so houses and the **Pelican Inn,** the only commercial business here. The Pelican Inn, an authentic English pub and hotel at the corner of Shoreline Highway and Pacific Way, opened in 1979 after the owner wrangled with citizens for 8 years before he could build. The pub was named for Sir Francis Drake's 70-foot galleon which sailed by in 1879; it was later renamed *The Golden Hinde.* The inn offers a dining room, bar with a dart board, and upstairs rooms for overnight guests.

Muir Beach, named of course for famed naturalist John Muir, lies in a curved, south-facing cove south of the town. The beach, 1,000 feet long and 200 feet long, is covered with coarse sand and scattered boulders. The beach can be crowded on good weekends, so plan accordingly and come during the week. It also seems warmer and less windy than nearby beaches since it's in a deep cove and protected by a rocky headland.

Parking is free but the lot fills quickly on weekends. Part of the beach is clothing optional, so bring blinders if that offends. No glass bottles are allowed; leashed dogs allowed only on trails; toilets are at the parking; and swimming is discouraged because of cold water and strong currents. Besides enjoying the beach, take a hike south along the scenic **Coastal Trail,** which follows the ragged shoreline down to Point Bonita. Another good hike is up **Dias Ridge Trail** to breathtaking views of the coastline. The trailhead is opposite the Pelican Inn.

**Finding the beach:** From US 101 and Mill Valley, drive west on CA 1 for about 6 miles to Muir Beach. Turn left at milepost 5.7 on Pacific Way by the Pelican Inn. Follow the street down to the parking area (GPS: 37.861073 N / -122.575504 W). A pedestrian bridge allows access to the beach and trails. Don't hike down the stream to the beach.

# Muir Beach Overlook

**Muir Beach Overlook,** perched on a high cliff edge on the north side of the town of Muir Beach, offers a spectacular ocean view from its lofty vantage point. Restrooms and picnic tables are at the small parking area. A boardwalk trail descends a narrow ridge down to a small fenced viewpoint. On a clear day you can spot the **Farallon Islands,** one of the largest seabird nesting areas in American waters, jutting like haystacks above the ocean horizon to the southwest. Closer at hand to the south is the rugged coast ending at Point Bonita Lighthouse and the entrance to the fabled Golden Gate. It's also a good spot to view migrating whales in the winter.

    **Finding the overlook:** From the Pelican Inn on the south side of Muir Beach, follow CA 1 north to a signed left turn and drive a short distance to the parking lot (GPS: 37.863108 N / -122.585559 W).

# Muir Woods National Monument

**Muir Woods National Monument,** a scant 12 miles north of San Francisco, protects a virgin stand of old-growth coast redwoods in a hidden valley on the southern flank of **Mount Tamalpais.** This small 554-acre national parkland was spared from logging when Congressman William Kent bought it in 1905; he later donated the land to the federal government. After President Theodore Roosevelt established the national monument in 1908, Kent urged the new park be named for famed California naturalist and writer John Muir. Muir later told Kent, "This is the best treelover's monument that could possibly be found in all the forests of the world."

    The tall trees nestle in **Redwood Canyon,** lifting their towering crowns high above the damp forest floor. This relatively small redwood grove, the most visited redwoods in California, thrive in the cool moist environment, absorbing crucial summer moisture from fog. The tallest tree here measures 258 feet high; it's a giant but still considerably shorter than the 380-foot redwood farther north. Ferns, including sword fern, lady fern, California polypody, and bracken fern, moss, and redwood sorrel blankets the forest undergrowth, while red alders line trickling Redwood Creek.

    The best way to explore the monument is to stop at the visitor center, then get out and hike the park's 6 miles of trails. Recommended hikes are the easy **Main Trail Loop** (wheelchair-accessible), which follows the creek up to the **Cathedral Grove,** and the moderate 3-mile **Fern Creek Trail,** which heads into the heart of the redwoods. The main canyon floor trails are paved with bridges over the creek.

    Muir Woods is extremely popular since it's one of San Francisco's iconic landmarks. The crowds (a million people annually), jammed parking lots, and trails filled with weekend throngs distract from the reverence you feel here. Come on a weekday or before 9 in the morning for quiet time. The parking lots quickly fill on weekends and holidays. Consider stopping at a Park and Ride lot and catching a free shuttle to the park. A visitor center, snack bar, and gift shop are at the parking area.

**Finding the park:** From US 101, take exit 445 in Mill Valley and head west on CA 1 toward Stinson Beach. At Muir Beach, go right on signed Muir Woods Road to the parking and visitor center (GPS: 37.891211 N / -122.568846 W). (415) 388-2595.

## Slide Ranch

**Slide Ranch** is a 134-acre educational nonprofit farm that teaches folks about the environment, sustainable food, and health. The organization, open to the public, offers workshops, seminars, summer camp for kids, and family programs, including sheep shearing, ocean exploration, and toddler days. The farm, perched on a headland above the shoreline, offers not only educational opportunities like milking a goat or making cheese but also great views and a 5-minute hike down to the shore for beachcombing and a picnic. It's best to make reservations ahead of time to visit.

**Finding the ranch:** Drive north from Muir Beach on CA 1 for a couple miles to a left turn (GPS: 37.875114 N / -122.595285 W) to the farm. Park in a spacious lot (GPS: 37.874292 N / -122.596859 W) and walk down to the ranch. (415) 381-6155.

## Steep Ravine Beach & Hot Springs

**Steep Ravine Hot Springs** is one of those locals-only places that was discovered by the unkempt masses, much to the chagrin of the locals. The springs are among rocks next to picturesque Steep Ravine Beach, a wild rocky beach tucked in a cove a couple miles south of popular Stinson Beach. Access is by a mile-long steep closed road that twists down to 10 rustic cabins and a park campground (available by reservation at reserveamerica.com) and then a rocky trail to the beach or down a very steep singletrack trail from CA 1.

The hot springs bubble up through sand, warming your butt in shallow sulphur-scented pools fashioned from sand and rocks. The secluded springs can only be visited at extreme low or negative tides (minus 1.0-foot mean tide or lower). Soaks last at the most only 2 hours before the rising tide drowns the pools. The area is dangerous with slippery rocks and poison oak on the trail; it can be too crowded; and rangers do give tickets for nudity.

**Finding the hot springs:** For the easy approach, park in a small area on the east side of CA 1 (GPS: 37.863108 N / -122.585559 W) opposite a gate. Hike down

*Pale dawn light and a relentless surf break on massive boulders that hide Steep Ravine Hot Springs.*

the closed road for about a mile to cabins, then follow a rough trail north to the beach. Hike to the north end of the beach and thread through boulders for about 500 feet to the springs. Alternatively, park in a large pullout on the west side of the highway (GPS: 37.863108 N /-122.585559 W) and descend a mile down a steep path to the hot springs.

## Red Rock Beach aka Mickey's Beach

**Red Rock Beach,** also called Mickey's Beach, is a quarter-mile-long stretch of narrow sand and giant boulders that is backed by a towering bluff. The beach is one of the best and most popular nude beaches in the San Francisco area as well as a wonderful ocean-side rock climbing and bouldering area. Most of the folks here are well-mannered and have fun relaxing on the sand or playing naked Frisbee, but be prepared for some gawkers.

Lots of climbing is found on the many beach boulders as well as on small cliffs on the hillside above. Look for boulders at both the north and south ends of the beach. Chalk stains mark the best boulder problems, unless they have been washed off by rain. There are often other climbers here who can give you bouldering beta. For more information, get the guide book *Rock Climbing the San Francisco Bay Area* (FalconGuides).

**Finding the beach:** Drive north on CA 1 from Muir Beach to the turn to Steep Ravine Beach. Continue north another third of a mile and park on the left (west) side of the highway in a large lot (GPS: 37.888745 N / -122.629507 W). This parking is 1.5 miles south of Stinson Beach. If the main parking is full, another lot is on the east side of CA 1. Follow a steep trail downhill to the beach. Allow at least 15 minutes to walk down and wear good shoes.

## Stinson Beach

The Shoreline Highway twists north from Muir Beach, but straightens out at Stinson Beach, an old resort town. **Stinson Beach** itself stretches alongside the highway, attracting swimmers, sunbathers, and surfers, while climbers work out vertical problems on boulders at the beach's south end. The 3-mile beach, one of the best near San Francisco, is justifiably popular with emerald-colored waves washing across its broad expanse of sand. On a sunny summer day, mingling among the crowds, you can almost imagine you're basking on a southern California beach. It's an illusion though since it is often foggy and cool here. Summer water temperatures warm to a chilly 58°F.

Besides its glorious sand and views, another reason that Stinson Beach, part of Golden Gate National Recreation Area, is popular is because it has free parking. Plan on arriving early in summer since the parking lots fill by midday. The beach is open every day, with the gates opening at 9 a.m. but close at different times depending on the season. There are picnic tables, restrooms, grills, and showers; a snack bar is open in summer. Dogs are not allowed on the national park beach but are, if they're leashed, on the county part of the beach farther north.

Swimming is recommended only in summer when the beach is staffed with lifeguards. The water is cold, and there are strong undertows. Watch children in the water and don't turn your back to the ocean since sneaker waves can knock you down. Also watch for sharks, which have attacked people here. The last attack was in 2002 when a great white shark attacked a surfer; the young man survived but required over 100 stitches to close the bite wounds.

**Seadrift Beach** is at the north end of Stinson Beach. This long stretch of sand and surf is backed by ritzy beach houses. Park at the top of the beach where Seadrift Drive ends (GPS: 37.907305 N / -122.678804 W). Remember that this is not a private beach but the access road may be gated.

The town of **Stinson Beach** (population 632 in 2010) is the closest thing you'll get to a beach town here. It began as Willow Camp in the early 1890s when Nathan and Rose Stinson rented out tents to tourists. The town offers limited services, with accommodations and dining, including the popular **Stinson Beach**

**Grill.** A lasting tradition is the 7.5-mile Dipsea Race, the second oldest footrace in the US. The race, which began in 1905, is run on the second Sunday of every June from Mill Valley to Stinson Beach, crossing over Mount Tam.

**Finding the beach:** From US 101 north of San Francisco, take exit 445 onto CA 1/Shoreline Highway at Mill Valley. Follow the twisting highway for about 20 miles to Stinson Beach. This road section makes some folks queasy; drive slowly and carry extra bags. In Stinson Beach, look for a marked left turn that leads to the parking lots (GPS: 37.897259 N / -122.639989 W).

## Mount Tamalpais State Park

**Mount Tamalpais,** towering over the Bay Area, is the centerpiece of 6,300-acre **Mount Tamalpais State Park,** a protected enclave with over 60 miles of hiking trails, camping, picnicking, and amazing scenic views. The 2,572-foot mountain, its profile resembling a sleeping lady, is a Marin County landmark that's usually just called Mount Tam. The view from atop Tamalpais encompasses the entire Bay region; on a clear day you can see the San Francisco Bay and its cities, the Fallon Islands 25 miles offshore, and even the snowcapped Sierra Nevada almost 150 miles away.

The park is easily accessed on Panoramic Highway, which runs between CA 1 just west of Mill Valley to Stinson Beach. The twisty scenic road threads through the sprawling park, offering access to hiking trails, camping and picnic sites, viewpoints, and Ridgecrest Boulevard, which climbs to a visitor center and overlook on the summit of Mount Tam's East Peak. The mountain is clad in second-growth redwood forest, oak woodlands, and tawny grasslands. Spring brings gorgeous wildflower displays.

The best way to explore Mount Tamalpais is on foot or mountain bike. It is, after all, the place where mountains bikes were developed. The trails range in difficulty from easy to hard, but all are easy to follow as they cross through all kinds of ecosystems. Recommended hikes include **Matt Davis Trail, Dipsea Trail, Steep Ravine Trail,** and **Coastal Trail.** The 0.5-mile handicapped-accessible **Verna Dunshee Trail** at East Peak offers amazing views of San Francisco and the Bay Area. Ask at **Pantoll Ranger Station** for a trail map and suggestions for loop hikes.

The state park opens daily at 7 a.m. and closes between 6 p.m. and 9 p.m., depending on the season. The park has several year-round campgrounds, including 16-site **Pantoll Campground; Steep Ravine Campground** with seven sites and nine cabins; **Alice Eastwood Group Camp;** and **Frank Valley Group Horse Camp.** For reservations go to reserveamerica.com or call (800) 444-7275.

**Finding the park:** The best way to access the heart of the park is from CA 1 in Stinson Beach. As you come into town from the south, look for a right turn onto Panoramic Highway. Follow the scenic road up to Pantoll Ranger Station. Mount Tamalpais State Park, (415) 388-2070.

# Audubon Canyon Ranch

A great blue heron, great egret, and snowy egret rookery lies in a shallow canyon at the 1,000-acre **Bolinas Lagoon Nature Preserve** at **Audubon Canyon Ranch** just east of the lagoon. From March to July, visitors can hike into the canyon and view the birds' nests high atop the **Schwartz Grove** redwoods in Picher Canyon. The best views are from hillside blinds opposite the trees where you can peer through mounted telescopes or your own binoculars at the birds. The preserve offers numerous plant communities including redwood and Douglas fir forest, open grasslands, chaparral, and riparian zones along creeks and marshes. The area has 8 miles of trails, a picnic area, bookstore, and display hall. It's open from mid-Mar through mid-July on weekends and holidays and by appointment Tues through Fri. No dogs allowed.

**Finding the preserve:** Drive to Stinson Beach on CA 1. Continue northwest on CA 1 for about 3 miles to the preserve on the right (GPS: 37.929907 N / -122.682631 W). (415) 868-9244; egret.org.

# Bolinas Lagoon Nature Preserve

**Bolinas Lagoon,** a shallow 1,100-acre tidal estuary, is protected from ocean waves by a sand spit at the head of south-facing, 5-mile-wide Bolinas Bay. At low tide, the 3.5-mile-long lagoon is a tidal mudflat inhabited by numerous birds, waterfowl, and sea lions. The San Andreas Fault runs up the middle of Bolinas Lagoon. The lagoon, designated a Marin County Open Space District wildlife preserve, is bordered on the east by the Shoreline Highway, on the west by the Olema-Bolinas Road and the town of Bolinas; and Stinson Beach on the sand spit on the south. Over 3 million cubic yards of water alternately fill and then empty the lagoon with each tide. Bring binoculars and park along CA 1 on the lagoon's shoreline to watch wildlife and birds or rent a kayak to paddle around.

# Bolinas

**Bolinas,** spreading across the end of a blunt peninsula, is a quintessential California beach town that folks either adore or abhor. Visiting Bolinas, with a 2010 population of 1,620, is like stepping back in time to 1969 with its hippies, hermits, funky houses, organic bakery, and little grocery store. It's a contradictory place at

*Historic Smiley's Schooner Tavern, a landmark Bolimas watering hole, has served thirsty customers since Captain Isaac Morgan built it in 1851.*

the end of the road where residents like their privacy but also embrace the surfers who come for its gentle waves and visitors who stop for its cool art scene. Rusted VW buses parked beside brand-new BMWs typify the Bolinas vibe.

But unless you're in the know, you'll probably speed by the turn to Bolinas on the Shoreline Highway since the road sign pointing the way has been missing since 1990. In the 1960s, locals started removing the signage to their town. After 36 highways signs disappeared, the highway department decided in 1990 that they weren't going to waste any more money on signs.

Despite the hubbub, Bolinas isn't much to write home about. There's an eclectic mix of businesses and houses dappled across the hilltop above Bolinas Lagoon and a couple pleasant sand beaches—**Bolinas** and **Agate Beaches**—below a bluff. The town lies on the west side of 5-mile-wide Bolinas Bay, with Stinson Beach anchoring the east side.

The **Bolinas Museum,** established in 1982, is a surprisingly fine art museum that specializes in Marin County artists, exhibiting work in five galleries. Also check out the **Bolinas-Marin Botanical Gardens** with over 2,000 species spread across 15 acres. The garden specializes in succulents, including aloes. Another popular stop is 2-story, whitewashed **Smiley's Schooner Saloon,** reputedly the oldest working tavern in California, which dates from 1851. For a great ocean view, head to **Bolinas Overlook** at the end of Overlook Drive on the west side of town.

**Finding the town:** From Stinson Beach, drive north on CA 1/Shoreline Highway for 4.5 miles to the north end of the lagoon. Turn left (west) at the first road, then go left (south) at a T-junction on Olema-Bolinas Road. The highway turnoff is unmarked. Follow Olema-Bolinas Road south alongside the west edge of the lagoon for a couple miles to Bolinas. At the 3-way junction, go straight on Wharf Road for the main business sector and Bolinas Beach or right on Brighton Avenue, the main drag through town. Parking is a big problem on busy weekends.

## Bolinas Beach

**Bolinas Beach** is a popular sand beach on the south side of Bolinas. The beach is divided into two sectors. The east section is accessed from Wharf Street, while the west section is at a boat ramp at the end of Brighton Avenue. A seawall built against the tall bluff separates the two. Don't attempt to walk between them unless the tide is low. High tide covers both beaches. The water is cold and the weather can be foggy. Beach is dog-friendly.

*The San Andreas Fault runs up Bolinas Lagoon, a tidal estuary*
*that provides habitat for birds, waterfowl, and sea lions.*

The west section, also called **Brighton Beach,** is the best one to visit since access is easy and it's good for walking and sunbathing if the sun is out. It's great for surfing since it's sheltered and has low surf—perfect for beginners. Get lessons or surf gear at **Bolinas Surf Shop** (415-868-1935) or **2 Mile Surf Shop** (415-868-0264).

**Finding the beach:** At the 3-way junction in town, go right on Brighton Avenue and follow it to the boat ramp. The beach is to the left of the ramp. Parking on busy days is the crux. Find a parking spot on Brighton and walk a couple blocks to the beach; you'll be happy and the locals won't be cranky.

## Agate Beach

**Agate Beach,** facing the open ocean on the far west side of Bolinas, is the other beach in town. Actually it's not much of a beach, so don't plan on sun and sand. Agate Beach allows access to **Duxbury Reef,** a long offshore rock outcrop that offers great tide pooling adventures. The reef is filled with intertidal and marine life, including hermit crabs and starfish. Explore and look, but don't touch or take the sea critters. The narrow pebbly beach below the parking and overlook and the bluffs yield translucent oil agate along with petrified wood and whalebone, jasper, and abalone shell. Plan on visiting at low tide and know the tide tables so you can retreat before the tide comes in. Also be wary of the mudstone bluff above the beach. It's constantly eroding, with chunks of rock slipping down the cliff face.

**Finding the beach:** Just before reaching Bolinas, go right on Mesa Drive. Follow it to Overlook Drive and turn left (south). Drive to Elm Road and turn right (west) and drive to the Agate Beach parking lot (GPS: 37.896877 N / -122.708783 W). A trail to the beach begins at the north side of the parking. Keep back from the cliff edge west of the lot.

## Alamere Falls & Bass Lake Hike

The **Palomarin Trailhead,** northwest of Bolinas, allows access to the wild southern part of Point Reyes National Seashore on the scenic **Coast Trail.** The best out-and-back day hikes are to Bass Lake and then on to Alamere Falls. The 7.5-mile round-trip hike has minimal elevation gain and follows both closed fire roads and trails. Expect stunning views along the coast; pretty **Bass Lake** which invites a summer swim; and spectacular 50-foot-high **Alamere Falls** dropping off a cliff onto the beach below. Allow 4 hours to do the hike. Late winter and spring are the best times since the waterfall is rocking then. Watch for poison oak along the trail; it's advisable to wear long pants.

**The hike:** From the trailhead (GPS: 37.953889 N / -122.778123 W), hike north on the Coast Trail above cliffs along the shoreline before turning inland to shimmering Bass Lake. Continue on the trail, passing Pelican Lake on your left, to a junction at 3.5 miles (GPS: 37.953889 N / -122.778123W). Go left on the signed Alamere Falls Trail and descend the narrow path for a half-mile to the top of the falls (GPS: 37.953759 N / -122.783288 W). It's possible to scramble down the steep cliff below to the beach but use extreme caution since the rock is crumbling and rotten.

**Finding the trailhead:** From CA 1, drive south on Olema-Bolinas Road. About 0.3 mile before Bolinas, turn right (west) on Mesa Road. Follow Mesa Road about 5 miles to the Palomarin Trailhead (GPS: 37.934095 N / -122.747098 W). The last mile of the road is dirt and can be bumpy.

## Point Reyes National Seashore

Spectacular 71,028-acre **Point Reyes National Seashore,** administered by the National Park Service, preserves a magnificent slice of California's wild coastline on Point Reyes Peninsula. The region is geographically part of the coastal ranges with brushy, chaparral-coated hillsides, grasslands that waver under ocean breezes, and pine- and fir-choked ridges and vales. The park's wild 20-mile-long beach is pounded by Pacific breakers and scoured by winter gales. The national seashore was established in 1962 to protect the fragile and scenic area from a proposed residential development.

Triangular-shaped Point Reyes Peninsula is a scrap of southern California granite that's been hauled over 300 miles north by the San Andreas Fault. The fault zone forms the eastern border of the peninsula, separating it from the mainland along the diagonal fault from Bolinas Lagoon to Tomales Bay. Point Reyes is on the eastern edge of the Pacific Plate, which is slowly shifting to the northwest, while the land to the east is part of the North America Plate, which is being shoved west. The two plates push and lock against each other and then every so often the stressed plates shift and jump, causing huge earthquakes like the 1906 San Francisco Earthquake. The slippage along the fault zone here was almost 25 feet. Normally the fault slips 1.4 to 2 inches a year.

Point Reyes was named El Punta de Los Reyes ("the point of the kings") by Spanish explorer Don Sebastian Vizcaino on January 6, 1603. That day was Epiphany, the twelfth day of Christmas and the Feast of the Three Kings. A few years earlier in 1579, Sir Francis Drake anchored his ship *The Golden Hinde* to make needed repairs during his around-the-world voyage. Drake dubbed the land New Albion, and claimed it for England by placing "a plate of brasse, fast nailed to a great and firme post," and then 5 weeks later, sailed west into the sunset. While no definite proof exists, it's believed that he anchored in today's Drake's Bay.

Diverse ecosystems inhabited by varied plant communities and animals await the Point Reyes walker. The park, lying on the **Pacific Flyway,** boasts 361 bird

*A bicyclist pedals down Highway 1 in Point Reyes Station on a quiet Saturday summer morning.*

species, including eight hawk species, herons, egrets, ducks, and woodpeckers. Exotic deer, such as the fallow and axis deer, have flourished here since the 1940s. A Tule elk refuge is at **Tomales Point.** Sea lions colonize the rocky shore of Point Reyes itself; watch them from a nearby overlook. Point Reyes is also an excellent and popular whale-watching spot. More than 100 California gray whales a day are usually sighted during peak migration in January.

Point Reyes is a great place to explore. Before heading out though, stop at the **Bear Valley Visitor Center** off Bear Valley Road just west of CA 1 and Olema. You can stock up on maps, brochures, and books as well as get info and ranger advice. The park has two other visitor centers at Drakes Bay and Point Reyes Lighthouse. Four walk-in campgrounds scatter across the south park of the park. Almost 150 miles of trails lace Point Reyes, making it a superb hiking destination.

Several roads access the park's interior, leading to trailheads, points of interest, historic sites, and beaches. Sir Francis Drake Boulevard is the main road at Point Reyes. It accesses **Estero Trailhead, Point Reyes, North and South Beaches, Elephant Seal** and **Sea Lion Overlooks,** and **Point Reyes Lighthouse.** Visiting the historic lighthouse on a foggy day is atmospheric with waves crashing below. Point Reyes supposedly has the second thickest fog in the US. The lighthouse area is also the best place for whale-watching.

Pierce Point Road heads north from the boulevard, passing **Tomales Bay State Park, Kehoe and McClures Beaches,** and ends at the **Tomales Point Trailhead.** Tomales Point Trail wends north to the remote upper tip of Point Reyes. Limatour Road, leaving Bear Valley Road near Olema, heads out to **Limatour Beach** on the south coast. The beach is one of the best here for swimming since the water is calmer and the winds lighter than on the main coast. Along the road, you'll pass several trailheads as well as the **Point Reyes Hostel** (415-663-8811).

Two trails begin near **Bear Valley Visitor Center**—the 0.6-mile **Earthquake Trail** along the San Andreas Fault and the 0.7-mile **Woodpecker Nature Trail.** Nearby is **Kule Loklo,** a replica of a Coast Miwok village. The Miwoks were a hunting and gathering tribe that harvested this rich land for centuries before the Spanish and English arrived. Other popular trails include **Sky Trail** and the **Coast Trail.** The Sky Trail leads to the summit of 1,407-foot **Mount Wittenberg,** the park's high point. Cell phone service is limited at the Point Reyes area.

**Finding the park:** Point Reyes is about 30 miles northwest of San Francisco. To access the park from US 101 north of the Golden Gate Bridge, take exit 445 at Mill Valley and follow CA 1/Shoreline Highway to Olema and the park entrance. Alternatively, continue north on US 101 to Exit 450 and head west on Sir Francis Drake Boulevard for 21 miles to Olema. **Point Reyes National Seashore** (1 Bear Valley Rd., Point Reyes Station, CA 94956; 415-464-5100, ext. 2; nps.gov/pore).

## Olema

**Olema,** the gateway to Point Reyes National Seashore, is an almost inconspicuous crossroads at the junction of the Shoreline Highway and Sir Francis Drake Boulevard (GPS: 38.04197 N / -122.788824 W), which connects Point Reyes with US 101. The quiet unincorporated community, now just a handful of shops, a few bed-and-breakfast inns, and a couple restaurants, was a raucous lumber town back in the 1800s until the railroad bypassed it and ran through Point Reyes Station.

Olema, named with the Miwok Indian word for "coyote," has long been considered the epicenter of the big 1906 earthquake, although some geologists now think it was in Daly City. The San Andreas Fault jumped an astounding 16 feet here, causing immense damage to San Francisco. If you want to see the rupture, take the short wheelchair-accessible **Earthquake Trail** east of the Bear Valley Visitor Center just west of town.

For information, contact **West Marin County Chamber of Commerce** (415-663-9232).

## Samuel P. Taylor State Park

**Samuel P. Taylor State Park,** southeast of Olema on Sir Francis Drake Boulevard, is a quiet off-the-beaten-track parkland. The 6,700-acre park includes 600 acres of towering old-growth coast redwood trees, which shade 59-site Madrone Campground. Lots of trails explore the fern-festooned redwood groves and wooded hills and grasslands. The best ones include the 1.7-mile **Pioneer Tree Trail,** which explores the redwood forest, and **Bill's Trail** up to the treeless summit of 1,466-foot **Barnabe Peak,** which offers an incredible view. The popular paved **Cross Marin Trail** bike path, following the abandoned grade of the Northern Pacific Coast Railroad, traverses 3 miles through the park.

The park is named for Forty-Niner Samuel Taylor, a New Yorker who came west in 1849 and struck gold in 1852, panning 21 pounds of gold dust which he sold for $5,691,99. He then bought 100 acres of land here and in 1856 built the first paper mill on the West Coast along Lagunitas Creek, making newsprint and the world's first square-bottomed paper bags. After the railroad came through in 1874, he also built a bustling town named Taylorville, as well as a resort and Camp Taylor as a busy weekend rural refuge for San Franciscans. Taylor died in 1886 and is buried on the property above the creek.

**Finding the park:** From the junction of CA 1 and Sir Francis Drake Boulevard in Olema, drive east on Sir Francis Drake Boulevard for about 3 miles to the park entrance (GPS: 38.019638 N / -122.729572 W). Or drive 15 miles west from San Rafael and US 101 on Sir Francis Drake Boulevard. (415) 488-9897.

## Point Reyes Station

**Point Reyes Station,** a small unincorporated town on the Shoreline Highway, is, along with Olema to the south, the gateway to Point Reyes National Seashore. The town, beginning as a railroad stop in 1875, has a small downtown along Main Street with several restaurants including the **Station House Cafe,** the **Old Western Saloon,** a bakery, and an assortment of accommodations. At **Cowgirl Creamery** you can watch its award-winning cheeses being made. As the main commercial center for the area there are the requisite grocery store, hardware store, auto repair shop, and pharmacy as well as a surf shop. **Point Reyes Outdoors** (415-663-8192) offers kayak rentals as well as guided kayak trips in Tomales Bay and hiking tours across Point Reyes.

For information, contact **West Marin County Chamber of Commerce** (415-663-9232).

# Tomales Bay

From Point Reyes, CA 1 runs north along the east shore of **Tomales Bay,** a long narrow sea arm that separates Point Reyes Peninsula from mainland California. The 15-mile-long bay, averaging a mile wide, formed along the San Andreas Fault, which runs diagonally northwest along the coastline here. The fault is submerged beneath the bay but is visible south of Point Reyes Station at the epicenter of the great earthquake of 1906. The rounded hills of Bolinas Ridge, blanketed by open grassland and woods, stair-steps eastward from the highway.

Besides being a geologic point of interest, Tomales Bay is also a rich ecological zone with over 250 species of birds, salt marshes and tidal flats, and oyster farms. **Tomales Bay Ecological Reserve,** administered by the California Department of Fish & Wildlife, protects 483 acres at the south end of the bay. The bay also offers good sea kayaking, sailing, fishing, bird watching, and motorboating.

Oysters are the big business at Tomales, with six players, including **Tomales Bay Oyster Company** (tomalesbayoysters.com) and **Hog Island Oyster Company** (hogislandoysters.com). Both are open to the public. You can picnic at both, shucking and downing fresh oysters pulled from the bay a few hundred feet away. Oysters thrive in clean cold water, making Tomales Bay an ideal environment.

## San Andreas Fault

The Shoreline Highway joins the San Andreas Rift Zone at Stinson Beach and follows it north up to Olema Valley and Tomales Bay. The famed fault separates the North American crustal plate from the Pacific Plate and stretches some 650 miles from northern Mexico to Cape Mendocino, where it finally plunges into the Pacific Ocean. The two plates have been slowly creeping past each other for the last 30 million years at an annual rate of about 2 inches. Underlying rocks, contorted and broken by faulting, are easily eroded, forming the broad valley the drive traverses east of Point Reyes Peninsula. The coast range east of here is composed of sandstone and chert. The granite rocks on the low hills to the west were moved almost 350 miles from the south by the fault's gradual movement. During the great 1906 San Francisco earthquake, horizontal movement along the fault here was as much as 20 feet. The San Andreas Rift Zone contains numerous large and small faults besides the main one. As the two plates grind against each other, pressure builds to a breaking point and the faults jump and release the pressure, causing earthquakes.

The oysters here are close to perfect—plump with a salty brine taste offset by freshwater sweetness. The Tomales Bay Oyster Company has operated since 1909, making it the oldest continuously operating shellfish farm in California. They raise five different sizes of Pacific oysters for your tasting pleasure.

## Sonoma County Coastline

The Shoreline Highway (CA 1) bends inland near the north end of Tomales Bay, crosses rolling hills, and enters Sonoma County. This 1,768-square-mile county, the largest of the nine San Francisco Bay counties, offers 76 miles of pristine coastline that is mostly public land. The coast, however, is very rugged with steep headlands, rocky bluffs, and small wave-swept beaches (some of California's cleanest beaches), allowing for limited recreational opportunities. Instead the traveler relishes the undeveloped coast's gorgeous scenery, many viewpoints, and small towns.

After leaving Marin County and Point Reyes, the landscape subtly changes. Gone are the dense forest and high coastal peaks. Instead a bucolic countryside unfolds along the highway, with low grassy hills seamed by creeks and rivers. Eventually CA 1 turns abruptly west and descends northwest to the shore at Bodega Bay.

## Bodega Bay

The village of **Bodega Bay** is a charming seaside town that lies on the east shore of its harbor, a protected inlet enclosed by a hooked sand spit on the north end of Bodega Bay. The harbor is the busiest between San Francisco and Fort Bragg. The town, with a population of 1,077 in 2010, served as the backdrop for Alfred Hitchcock's classic 1963 thriller *The Birds,* with most of the filming in the towns of Bodega and Bodega Bay. In the film, flocks of birds violently and inexplicably attack local residents.

Bodega Bay itself is a great crescent-shaped bay south of the town and harbor. The 5-mile-wide bay straddles the border of Sonoma and Marin Counties. Bodega Head, named in 1775 for Don Juan Francisco de la Bodega y Cuadra, a lieutenant aboard the Spanish ship *Sonora,* is the tip of a sandy peninsula that marks the northern end of the bay and forms the western side of Bodega Harbor.

For more information, contact **Sonoma Coast Visitor Center** (707-875-3866). The next 10 miles from Bodega Bay to Jenner and the Russian River is lovely country. The highway rolls over grass-covered terraces backed by tawny hillsides. Coves and sandy beaches, broken by cliffs and bluffs, line the shoreline below the drive.

*The Catholic Church of the Assumption of Mary in Tomales was built with redwood lumber in 1860 for $4,000.*

# Sonoma Coast State Park

The 16-mile stretch of rugged Sonoma coast from Bodega Bay to Vista Point just north of Jenner and the Russian River is a breathtaking piece of state real estate dubbed **Sonoma Coast State Park.** The parkland is actually a succession of coves, pocket beaches, rocky cliffs, and craggy headlands that scatter along the Shoreline Highway. The highway rolls across grassy terraces backed by tawny hillsides above the coast, allowing easy access to beaches, overlooks, and some of California's best coastal scenery.

**Bodega Head,** a chunk of granite dragged north by the San Andreas Fault, is the southernmost part of the parkland. The southern end of the 4-mile-long promontory offers wonderful hiking across open grasslands above surf-washed cliffs. A good out-and-back trail heads north from the parking to **Horseshoe Cove Overlook.** The rocky headland and parking area is a great place to watch migrating whales in winter and spring; on weekends, volunteer naturalists help you spot the passing whales. A small pocket beach tucks in cliffs below the main parking area. On the inland side of the head is **Westside Regional Park,** with a campground, picnic area, and beach.

**Finding the area:** From Bodega Bay and CA 1, drive west and south around the enclosed bay on either Westshore Road or Bay Flat Road. Eventually they merge and become Westside Road. Follow it to a large parking area at the end of the road overlooking the ocean (GPS: 38.303788 N / -123.064309 W). **Sonoma Coast State Park,** 3095 CA 1, Bodega Bay, CA 94923; (707) 875-3483; parks.ca.gov.

**The Bodega Dunes** and 3-mile-long **South Salmon Creek Beach,** the longest beach on the Sonoma coast, form a great playground along the shoreline north of Bodega Bay. The dunes make up one of the largest intact dune fields along the entire California coast. **Bodega Dunes Campground,** lying west of CA 1 just north of Bodega Bay, offers 100 sites with restrooms, showers, and 4 handicap-accessible sites. Monarch butterflies overwinter in the campground. A 5-mile trail system explores the dunes and the wild beach.

**Finding the trailhead:** Turning on Beach Road near the campground and driving to parking by the beach (GPS: 38.34328 -123.066533 W). A great 2.2-mile hike heads south on a trail parallel to the beach to rocky Mussel Head, the northern end of Bodega Head, then returns along the beach.

**South and North Salmon Beaches** are south and north of the small town of Salmon Creek where the creek backs up behind sand, forming a lagoon. South Salmon is a long sand beach that stretches south to rocky Mussel Head, while North Salmon is a half-mile-long sand beach north of the creek. Both are popular,

*Gleason Beach is a narrow strand between flower-covered bluffs and rocky sea stacks at Sonoma Coast State Park.*

especially on weekends, with sunbathers, surfers when the waves are good, surf anglers, picnickers, and beach walkers. No fires and no dogs are allowed on the beaches because the area is a nesting ground for the endangered snowy plover. Swimming is not recommended due to frigid water (averages 50°F), strong rip currents, and great white sharks, which have attacked several people. In 2005 a 20-year-old woman was attacked while surfing. The 16-foot shark came behind her, biting her leg. She got away by hitting its tail and pushing off.

**Finding the beaches:** Drive a couple of miles north on CA 1 from Bodega Bay to the village of Salmon Creek. For South Salmon Beach, turn left (west) off CA 1 on Bean Avenue and drive a few blocks to a parking lot (GPS: 38.35031 N / -123.066369 W) by the beach. For North Salmon Beach, continue north across the creek past the park headquarters. Park on the left (west) side of the CA 1 in a large parking lot (GPS: 38.35031 N / -123.066369 W).

**Miwok, Coleman, Arched Rock,** and **Carmet Beaches** are below the Shoreline Highway in the 1.5-mile stretch past North Salmon Beach. They are all stony and difficult to reach, usually by a steep path down bluffs below roadside parking areas. They're generally reserved for those seeking a wild beach experience. Besides the signed beach parking, there are also designated overlooks.

**Finding the beaches:** All the beaches are accessed from CA 1. Miwok parking (GPS: 38.360339 N / -123.068284 W); 2.5 miles north of Bodega Bay. Coleman parking (GPS: 38.363492 N / -123.07006 W); 3 miles north of Bodega Bay. Arched Rock Beach parking (GPS: 38.366434 N / -123.071777 W); 3.3 miles north of Bodega Bay. Carmet Beach parking (GPS: 38.371901 N / -123.075956 W); 3.8 miles north of Bodega Bay.

## Schoolhouse Beach & Portuguese Beach

Schoolhouse and Portuguese Beaches are bigger pocket beaches than the ones to the south. **Schoolhouse Beach** is a gorgeous spot, with its wide sand hemmed in by cliffs and sea stacks on both sides. The parking lot offers a great view of the beach. Access is by a paved wheelchair-accessible trail; restrooms are near the beach. **Portuguese Beach** is a popular sand beach that's separated from Schoolhouse by a rocky headland. It's accessed by a couple parking areas and a paved wheelchair-accessible trail from the south lot. Both beaches offer great walking, wave-watching, surf fishing, rock fishing, and tide pooling among the rocks at low tide.

**Finding the beaches:** Both beaches are accessed from CA 1. Schoolhouse parking (GPS: 38.374904 N / -123.078077 W); 4 miles north of Bodega Bay. Portuguese south parking (GPS: 38.377924 N / -123.080209W); 4.3 miles north of Bodega Bay.

# Duncan's Landing & Wright's Beach

These two areas are both scenic and popular. **Duncan's Point** is a small rock-walled promontory that juts into the ocean, and **Duncan's Landing** is a small pocket beach tucked into the head of a cove next to the point. The Landing was used in the 19th century for loading and unloading cargo, including lumber from nearby Duncan's Mill. The point and beach are one of the most scenic places on the Sonoma coast. When you're driving up the highway, don't be lulled into thinking this site isn't special. Stop at one of three parking areas for great views of cliffs washed by surging surf. Besides its beauty, Duncan's Point is considered one of the most dangerous places on the California coast with its high, unpredictable surf. Many people have drowned here, washed away by sneaker waves and by storm surf that can reach the road above the point. A rock spur poking into the ocean on the west side of the point is aptly named Death Rock. A short road circles the point, offering parking and picnicking.

**Wright's Beach** is a long stretch of sand with 27-site **Wright's Beach Campground** in the middle. The campground is busy and the sites are cramped, but it is right next to the beach. Reserve early at reserveamerica.com and try to get a beachside site (1 to 8). The day-use parking area (fee is charged) is next to the campground.

**Finding the areas:** For Duncan's Landing, drive north from Bodega Bay on CA 1 for 5 miles and turn left (west) on Emry Road, which forms a short loop. There are 3 parking areas—one on CA 1, another above Duncan's Cove, and one on the west side of the point (GPS: 38.395063 N / -123.095868 W). For Wright's Beach, continue north a half mile and turn left to the campground and day use area. Park in a large lot south of the campground (GPS: 38.399544 N / -123.095085W).

# Shell Beach

**Shell Beach** is an isolated pocket beach composed of black sand. The beach area is well known by geologists who come to study the mélange of rocks, all mixed up by the grinding of the North American and Pacific Plates along the San Andreas Fault. The smorgasbord of rocks include greywacke sandstone with layers of shale and streaks of quartz; serpentine, California's state rock; peridotite; chert; greenstone; pillow lava; and amphibolite. You'll get more geology lessons at the parking lot, which is on an old marine terrace where waves once washed before it was uplifted. Look north across the level terrace toward two rock formations— **Mammoth Rock** and **Sunset Boulders.** These were sea stacks about 125,000 years, poking above the surf like the ones offshore now. **Sunset Rocks** also has mammoth rub where the great woolly mammoths scratched themselves on the rough rock surface. The beach is not the best for activities except surf fishing and hiking.

**Finding the beach:** Drive north on CA 1 from Bodega Bay for 7 miles. Make a left (west) turn on a marked road that descends to a large parking area (GPS: 38.418109 N /-123.104159 W). A trail and steps lead down to the beach.

## Goat Rock

**Goat Rock** is a dramatic meeting of land and ocean off a grassy peninsula between the Pacific Ocean and Russian River. The rock is a cliffed fortress lying just offshore and connected to land by a sand isthmus. Goat Rock Beach, a stretch of black sand, runs north from the rock to the Russian River mouth. Goat Rock is a Sonoma coast landmark along with Arched Rock just to the south. It's now illegal to climb Goat Rock, although goats were once herded onto its summit to graze. Sea lions and harbor seals often lounge along the rocky shore, while birds nest in the cliffs. Keep at least 150 feet away from the seals, especially during pup season. Dogs are prohibited at Goat Rock Beach to avoid disturbing the seals.

**Goat Rock Beach** is easily accessible, with restrooms and picnic tables by the parking area. It's a good beach for walking as well as tide pool exploration during low tide. Swimming is discouraged because of extremely powerful rip currents and treacherous waves; many people have drowned here. Plus the water is just darn cold.

One of the best coastal climbing areas is at **Sunset Boulders** off the road to Goat Rock. These boulders, some as high as 40 feet, offer about 50 different routes and boulder problems in a scenic setting on the grassy terrace above the beach. Some boulders have rock sections 10 feet above the ground that were polished by mammoths about 40,000 years ago. **Finding the boulders:** Drive a quarter-mile down the access road from CA 1 and park on the left (south) in a large pullout (GPS: 38.432407 N / -123.114248 W). Hike down a short trail to the obvious boulders in a meadow.

A great hike follows **Kotum Trail** from Goat Beach and Rock along the edge of the bluff above the ocean for 3.75 miles to Wright's Beach. For a shorter hike you can go 2.5 miles to Shell Beach.

**Finding the area:** Drive south from Jenner on CA 1; after crossing the river, the highway turns west and then south. At the southward bend, turn right on marked road to Goat Rock Beach. The beach parking is at the end of the road (GPS: 38.445758 N / -123.126038 W). Another parking area is below Goat Rock.

# Jenner Visitor Center & North Jenner Coast

The upper part of the state park includes a visitor center in Jenner and a rugged section of coast north of the Russian River. The visitor center is worth a stop to learn more about coastal and natural history, including the colorful logging days when harvested redwoods were floated down the river. **Jenner,** a small village (population 136 in 2010) clinging to the north bank of the Russian River, offers lodging, a few shops and restaurants (try **River's End, Jenner Inn,** and **Cafe Aquatica**), and a place to rent kayaks if you're inclined to paddle on the river. A couple state park campgrounds—11-site **Willow Creek** and 20-site **Pomo Canyon**—are east of Jenner off CA 116.

Jenner is also a major crossroads, with CA 1 joining CA 116 south of town by the river. CA 116 makes a good inland excursion. The highway winds along the 110-mile-long Russian River, its banks lined with willow, eucalyptus, cypress, and mixed conifer trees. At **Guerneville** the route leaves the river and plunges through dark woods to Santa Rosa and US 101.

Three miles north of Guerneville is 752-acre **Armstrong Redwoods State Natural Reserve** (707-869-2958), a majestic grove of towering coast redwood trees. The park includes 310-foot **Parson Jones Tree,** the 1,400-year-old **Colonel Armstrong Tree,** hiking trails, a wheelchair-accessible trail, a visitor center, and picnic facilities including a group area that is popular for weddings.

From Jenner, CA 1 heads north and, after crossing Russian Gulch, runs up Jenner Grade. This scenic highway section is one of the most dramatic on the northern coast with the road spiraling and edging across steep slopes almost 1,000 feet above cobbled beaches. **Russian Gulch Beach** is 2.5 miles north of Jenner. Turn left into a large parking area (GPS: 38.470002 N / -123.154839 W) and follow a trail to the stunning pocket beach below.

Past the beach parking, the highway switchbacks up steep hillsides and, 4 miles from Jenner, reaches a high grassy terrace and **Vista Point.** Turn left (west) off CA 1 at a marked junction just before Meyers Grade Road and drive to a parking area (GPS: 38.477864 N / -123.162843W). Follow a short wheelchair-accessible loop trail out to the viewpoint. This spectacular overlook offers a breathtaking view of the rugged and sheer coastline.

From Vista Point, continue north on CA 1. The highway drops onto an undulating terrace (watch for grazing cows!), crosses the San Andreas Rift Zone, and reaches Fort Ross State Historic Park.

# Fort Ross State Historic Park

Fort Ross, the site of imperial Russia's farthest American outpost, was initially settled by 95 Russians and 40 Aleuts of the Russian-American Company in 1812. The group built a 14-foot-high stockade from redwood timber that featured 40 cannons and corner lookouts. Warehouses, a jail, barracks, and the commandant's house were created inside the compound, while a village surrounded it. The place was named "Rossiya" or Little Russia, which was later corrupted to Fort Ross. The Russians set to work trapping sea otters and fur seals, quickly bringing the otters to the verge of extinction. The colonists then turned to farming, but the damp climate and rodents decimated their efforts. It was the site of the first windmill and the first ship built in California. In 1841 the Russians decided to cut their losses and sold the fort and all its property to John Sutter for $30,000. Sutter hauled everything, including 1,700 cattle, 940 horses and mules, and an arsenal of weapons to Sacramento.

Most of the fort is now reconstructed (only one original building remains) and is open as a living history exhibit in 3,400-acre **Fort Ross State Historic Park.** Buildings include a barracks, Russian Orthodox Church, blockhouse, and stockade. The park offers an excellent visitor center with numerous interpretative exhibits. Hiking trails meander around the park over grasslands, through cypress groves, and above the rocky shore. **Fort Ross Cove** has a small beach west of the buildings. Days and hours are limited; call ahead to make sure it's open. **Fort Ross Lodge** up the coast offers accommodations.

**Finding the park:** From Jenner, drive 12 miles north on CA 1 to a left (west) turn into the park. Drive past an entrance station to a large parking area (GPS: 38.516084 N / -123.246941 W). **Fort Ross State Historic Park** (19005 CA 1, Jenner, CA 95450; 707-847-3286; parks.ca.gov).

# Stillwater Cove Regional Park

The scenic coast drive runs northwest along grassy terraces from Fort Ross, passing Timber Cove with a good viewpoint on a headland and a nice small beach as well as Timber Cove Inn and Timber Cove Campground. About 16 miles north of Jenner, the highway swings past 363-acre **Stillwater Cove Regional Park** (707-847-3245), a pleasant overnight stop with 23 campsites, showers, and restrooms. The park is on the east side of the highway so there aren't any ocean view campsites. West of the highway is a small sandy beach at the head of the cove; no

*Sonoma Coast State Park is a 16-mile stretch of coves, pocket beaches, rocky headlands, and sea stacks that is simply some of California's best coastal scenery.*

*Fort Ross, imperial Russia's American outpost, operated from 1812 until 1841 when the colony was abandoned.*

parking here so use the parking lot in the park (GPS: 38.547683 N / -123.29558 W). The area is popular with abalone divers, who seasonally fill up the campground. Put away food at night, the raccoons are voracious seasonally.

## Salt Point State Park

**Salt Point State Park,** 4 miles farther up the coast from Stillwater Cove, is another great coastal stop that seems undiscovered by most travelers. The scenic 5,970-acre park encompasses abrupt headlands that plunge into foaming surf; shallow valleys dense with cypress, pine, and redwood; sandy beaches rimmed with sandstone cliffs; and rocky tide pools nestled in quiet coves. The park not only offers 7 miles of coastline, but includes the rolling hills east of the highway. Look at the cliffs along the coast for tafoni or sandstone that's been eroded into a honeycomb.

The park is great for hiking with 20 miles of trails threading across it. The 1.5-mile **Stump Beach Trail,** ending at a pocket beach, traverses bluffs above the ocean and yields great views for whale-watchers who see gray whales migrating between December and April. Mountain bikes are not allowed on singletrack trails.

Visitors also enjoy excellent beachcombing in rocky tide pools filled with starfish, sea urchins, and mussels; be sensitive to these fragile marine organisms and don't disturb their habitat. Others enjoy surf fishing and abalone diving (3 per person with a license). The Sonoma coast is famous for the red abalone, which takes 10 years to reach a 7-inch diameter. The park includes **Gerstle Cove Marine Reserve,** one of California's first underwater parks. All marine life is protected here and in other offshore park areas. Divers need to be experienced and careful since some occasionally drown after getting entangled in offshore kelp forests and panicking.

Salt Point also offers some unique climbing and bouldering on its rugged sea cliffs. Several bolted routes are found on **Sentinel Rock, Treasure Chest,** and **Shipwreck Wall at Fisk Mill Cove** in the north part of the park. Bouldering is found at many areas both on the coast, including Fisk Mill Cove, and in the woods.

The park offers lots of camping, including 30-site **Gerstle Cove Campground** and 99-site **Woodside Campground** (20 walk-in sites). Picnic at Fisk Mill Cove, Stump Beach, and Gerstle Cove Beach.

**Finding the park:** Drive north from Jenner on CA 1 for about 18 miles (90 miles from San Francisco). Turn left (west) into the park at the main park area at Gerstle Cove, including a visitor center and campground. Park for Gerstle Cove at a large parking lot (GPS: 38.56685 N / -123.332069 W). **Salt Point State Park** (25050 CA 1, Jenner, CA 95450; 707-847-3221; parks.ca.gov).

# Kruse Rhododendron State Reserve

**Kruse Rhododendron State Reserve** is in the hills east of the highway on the north side of Salt Point State Park. This 317-acre nature preserve yields one of the Sonoma coast's most beautiful natural wonders in April and May when its rhododendrons spread a canopy of pink blossoms throughout the second-growth redwood forest. Nowhere else in California do rhododendrons grow in such profusion or as tall as the 30-foot giants here. The reserve, reached via Kruse Ranch Road, can be explored by 5 miles of hiking trails. A small picnic area sits at the parking lot. Pets and mountain bikes are not allowed on trails and mushroom gathering is prohibited.

**Finding the park:** Drive north from Jenner on CA 1 for 20 miles and turn right (east) onto Kruse Ranch Road near milepost 43 (GPS: 38.595248 N / -123.345764 W) on the north side of Salt Point State Park. Drive east to a parking area (GPS: 38.593032 N / -123.339295 W). (707) 847-3221.

## Stewarts Point

The scenic Shoreline Highway (CA 1) continues north, running across a grassy shelf past Horseshoe Cove and Rocky Points to **Stewarts Point,** a small town above a bold promontory that juts into the ocean. Stop by **Stewarts Point Store** (707-785-2406), a rural country store since 1868, for snacks, great sandwiches, camping supplies, a restaurant, bakery with delectable chocolate cupcakes, gas pumps, and a front porch to watch the world go by.

**Stewarts Point Rancheria** is a 40-acre reservation for the 78 members of the Kashia Band of Pomo Indians, one of northern California's ancestral Native American tribes.

## Sea Ranch

The last 11 miles of the Sonoma Coast passes through **Sea Ranch,** a controversial luxury, vacation-home subdivision that was once part of a 17,500-acre Mexican land grant called Rancho de Herman. A battle between developers and conservationists culminated in the establishment of the California Coastal Commission after a ballot initiative was passed in 1972, allowing continued public access to 10 miles of state-owned beach that the developer wanted closed.

The compromise allowed for five trails to cross the property for coastal and beach access. The trails, all between a quarter- and a half-mile long, lead to pocket beaches along the scenic rocky shoreline. A parking fee is charged.

**Black Point Beach** is accessed from a parking area (GPS: 38.682068 N / -123.428752 W) off CA 1 near milepost 50.80 which is just north of Sea Ranch Lodge.

**Pebble Beach** is accessed from a parking area (GPS: 38.69998 N / -123.439792 W) west of CA 1 on Navigator's Reach near milepost 52.32.

**Stengel Beach** is accessed from a parking lot just north of a stable off CA 1 near milepost 54.0.

**Shell Beach** is accessed from a parking lot (GPS: 38.729173 N / -123.47256 W) off CA 1 just south of Whalebone Reach near milepost 55.20. Follow a half-mile trail to the beach.

**Walk-On Beach** is accessed from a parking lot and trailhead north of Leeward Spur Road near CA 1 milepost 56.5. The trail is wheelchair accessible, with a ramp to the beach. Alternatively the beach can be reach on the 3-mile **Blufftop Trail** which begins in Gualala Point Regional Park to the north and follows the coast to the beach.

# Gualala Point Regional Park

This 195-acre Sonoma County parkland protects a long narrow peninsula that points north to the mouth of the Gualala River where it empties into the ocean. The park has a visitor center, picnic area, a large sand beach, and hiking trails west of CA 1, and a spacious 20-site campground in a redwood forest along the river east of the highway. The visitor center offers interpretative displays about California history, Native Americans, and the 19th-century logging industry.

**Finding the park:** Drive 36 miles north from Jenner on CA 1 or a mile south from Gualala and turn west to the park. Continue to a large parking lot near the visitor center (GPS: 38.729173 N / -123.47256 W). A paved pathway, ADA compliant, heads northeast from here for beach access. (707) 785-2377.

# Mendocino Coast

Past Sea Ranch, the Shoreline Highway crosses the Gualala River and enters Mendocino County and Coast. For the next 90 miles, the serpentine drive winds across a brooding landscape, traversing steep ridges, crossing numerous creeks and rivers, and swinging around coves. The ocean, always in sight, dictates geography and climate. Strong winds constantly scour the sea-facing bluffs, rippling fields of grass and sculpting exposed trees. It's a land that seems in eternal motion—cloud shadows trailing across wooded hills; unceasing waves battering rocky headlands; and gray fog cloaking the earth's sharp edges, making forms uncertain and hazy.

Mendocino County, sprawling across 3,878 square miles, includes a big chunk of northern California's spectacular coastline. The county, with a 2010 population of 87,841, also has redwood forests, 9 Indian reservations, and a wine region with 12 different areas and 84 wineries. A major component of the county's economy is the cultivation of marijuana. For more information, go to Visit Mendocino County's website: visitmendocino.com.

# Gualala

**Gualala,** a derivation of the Pomo Indian word *wala'li* or *ah kha wa la lee,* meaning "meeting of the waters," is an unincorporated community of 2,093 (2010 census) that sits at the mouth of the Gualala River. Until the 1960s this small town, pronounced "WAH-la-la," was a bustling redwood lumber town; the last lumber mill here closed in 1970. The town offers a range of lodging choices, including the nostalgic old **Gualala Inn** on CA 1 (its saloon was a favorite of author Jack London), as well as restaurants like the unique **St. Orres Restaurant** in an onion-domed Russian-style building. Fishing is a popular activity on the Gualala River, with steelhead anglers coming November to March. Abalone diving is also popular along this section of coast.

**Redwood Coast Chamber of Commerce,** 39150 S. CA 1, Gualala, CA 95445; (707) 884-1080 or (800) 778-5252; redwoodcoastchamber.com.

## Schooner Gulch State Beach

**Schooner Gulch State Beach** is a wonderful undeveloped parkland a few miles north of Gualala on the rugged Mendocino coast. The area has two beach areas—Schooner Gulch Beach and Bowling Ball Beach, a stony beach littered with round rock balls.

**Schooner Gulch Beach** is a stretch of wide sandy beach backed by towering cliffs and bluffs. It's a great place to explore on foot, walking along the strand, examining tide pools, and finding polished pieces of driftwood. It's also great for watching the sunset and surf fishing. Some brave surfers in wet suits ride the waves. Most of the beach is submerged during high tide.

**Bowling Ball Beach,** just north of Schooner Gulch Beach, is a bizarre geological oddity that is worth visiting and photographing. Along the beach below towering bluffs squat long rows of rounded boulders that are remarkably uniform in size, shape, and spacing. These spheres are actually concretions composed of hard erosion-resistant rock that were deposited in the soft mudstone that forms cliffs above the beach. Relentless erosion has removed the surrounding soft rock, leaving the harder boulders to bask on the beach. It's only possible to see the bowling balls at low or negative tides, so consult the tide table before venturing down to the beach. You can only access the beach by walking north from Schooner Gulch Beach at low tide since the trail to the beach is closed due to severe erosion. For the best photographs, bring a tripod for long exposures and shoot the couple hours each side of low tide so that the rocks aren't dry but are instead partially covered with water.

**Finding the beaches:** Drive north on CA 1 for a few miles from Gualala or south from Point Arena for 3 miles to milepost 11.4. Park on the wide west shoulder of the highway (GPS: 38.869032 N / -123.653516 W). Start at a trailhead directly opposite Schooner Gulch Road. After a few feet, go left on a trail which leads southwest through redwoods and down to Schooner Gulch Beach. Do not go straight on the closed trail to Bowling Ball Beach since it is dangerous and eroding away. To reach Bowling Ball, walk north across rocks from Schooner Beach to the obvious beach.

## Moat Creek Beach

**Moat Creek Beach,** reached by a short trail from CA 1, is a rough stony beach hemmed in by towering twisted sandstone cliffs. It's fine for beachcombing, walking, and wave-watching. The beach area is great for birding, with ospreys hunting along the shore, brown pelicans bobbing on the waves, and cormorants, pigeon guillemots, tufted puffins, and rhinoceros auklets nesting in the cliffs. Bring binoculars. Migrating whales are often seen through the winter from the bluff top above. The 14-acre site is owned by the state of California and managed by Moat Creek Managing Agency, a nonprofit group dedicated to this coastal area. Parking is free; restrooms; no dogs allowed. A 3-mile loop trail follows the top of the bluff south to Ross Beach, passing a unique cliffed pocket cove.

**Finding the beach:** From Point Arena, drive south on CA 1 for a few miles. After crossing Moat Creek, go right (west) to a dirt parking lot (GPS: 38.88241 N / -123.673646 W). Follow a good trail west for 600 feet to the beach.

## Point Arena

**Point Arena,** lying 1.5 miles southeast of its namesake, is one of California's smallest incorporated towns with a 2010 population of 449. The town sits just east above **Arena Cove,** a natural harbor with the 322-foot-long **Point Arena Pier** jutting into the water. The pier's deck, 25 feet above the water, is considered one of California's best fishing piers, with anglers catching cabezon, striped sea perch, kelp and rock greenling, lingcod, walleye, and the occasional salmon in autumn. It's a working pier for commercial fishermen too. The first wharf here was in 1866 and within 10 years was one of the North Coast's busiest ports. Next to the pier is **Arena Cove Beach,** a small stony beach. Whales are often spotted offshore from the cove. Access the pier by driving west from CA 1 on Port Street.

Along CA 1, the town's Main Street, are lots of shops, restaurants, accommodations, and the historic 1929 **Arena Theater.** During the 19th century Point Arena was a busy place with saloons, brothels, and other entertainment for loggers and sailors. For more information contact the Redwood Coast Chamber of Commerce at (707) 884-1080 or (800) 778-5252 or visit the website redwoodcoast-chamber.com.

## Point Arena Lighthouse

Point Arena, a stubby peninsula sticking into the ocean, was first sighted by Captain George Vancouver and crew in 1792. The point is the closest spot on the mainland US to Hawaii, which lies 2,045 nautical miles or 2,353 statute miles to the west. The point was originally called Cabo de Fortunas by Spanish sailor

Bartolomé Ferrelo but was later renamed Punta Arena for a sandbar to the south. Just south of the point is **Sea Lion Cove State Marine Conservation Area,** an offshore 0.22-square-mile preserve that protects not only sea lions but also abalone and a fragile intertidal ecosystem.

Sitting on the tip of the grassy peninsula towers **Point Arena Lighthouse,** a 6-story, automated beacon which warns sailors of underwater dangers like rocky reefs. Until the first lighthouse was built in 1870, many ships found watery graves here, including 10 on a stormy November night in 1865. The original lighthouse was damaged in the 1906 earthquake and the present-day lighthouse, the first steel-reinforced lighthouse in the US, was built and opened in 1908.

Visitors can tour the old 115-foot-high lighthouse, the tallest on the West Coast, and march up its 147 steps to a spectacular coastal view. Besides touring the lighthouse, visitors can stroll around the point, visit a museum at the **Fog Signal Building,** or stay in the four guest cottages.

**Finding the lighthouse:** From Point Arena, drive north on CA 1 for a mile. Turn left (west) on Lighthouse Road and drive northwest for 2 miles to the lighthouse and parking area (GPS: 38.954169 N / -123.739649 W). **Point Arena Lighthouse Keepers,** PO Box 11, 45500 Lighthouse Rd., Point Arena, CA 95468; (877) 725-4448 or (707) 882-2809; pointarenalighthouse.com.

## Manchester State Park

**Manchester State Park** hugs the coast for almost 5 miles north from Point Arena to Alder Creek. The 760-acre park offers a long stretch of curving sand beach washed by rows of Pacific rollers. The rest of the park offers great coastal scenery, including marshes, bluffs, and a couple creeks. Bucolic fields and pastures dotted with grazing cattle and sheep border the park and CA 1. The San Andreas Fault heads out to sea in the park.

Most visitors come to Manchester to explore and enjoy its brown sand beach, picnicking and sunbathing in summer, finding waves for surfing, watching birdlife, and beachcombing. The beach, the longest north of Bodega Bay, is noted for polished driftwood and silver tree skeletons. The park also offers excellent steelhead fishing in Brush Creek and Alder Creek in winter. The park campground offers 41 sites off Kinney Road; it's often not too busy but make reservations at (800) 444-7275 or parks.ca.gov. The beach is a 15-minute hike from the campsites. A backcountry campground is reached by a 1.1-mile hike.

*The 115-foot-high Point Arena Lighthouse, tallest on the West Coast, has warned sailors of rocky perils since 1870.*

**Finding the beach:** There are 3 road access points to the park.

The first is Stoneboro Road north of Point Arena. Turn left (west) and drive for 1.6 miles to a parking area (GPS: 38.959953 N / -123.71453 W). Follow a good trail through a natural reserve of dunes and wetlands to the secluded beach.

Second is the main park entrance. Drive north from Point Arena on CA 1 through the village of Manchester. Continue a half-mile and turn left (west) on Kinney Road. Drive past the park campground to a parking area (GPS: 38.98304 N / -123.705406 W). The beach is directly west.

The third access is on Alder Creek Beach Road. It ends at a small parking area near the beach and Alder Creek. Check with the park for possible road closures. **Manchester State Park** (707-882-2463).

## Mallo Creek Pass Vista

**Mallo Creek Pass Vista** is a roadside overlook that yields spectacular views of the rugged coast north of Manchester. Mallo Pass derives from the early Spanish name Gran Mal Paso for a nearby creek that was difficult to cross with horses and wagons. If the track across was muddy, wagons were taken apart and hauled up with a block and tackle. The crossing was usually avoided until the 1930s when a stout bridge was built. The viewpoint (GPS: 39.033599 N -123.688207 W) is on the left (west) side of CA 1 about 4 miles north of Manchester.

## Elk

CA 1 runs north from Manchester along a wide grassy bench for 13 miles to **Elk,** a small scenic town (population 208 in 2010) that's perched on the edge of surf-swept cliffs and rocky mini-islands. The town, spreading along CA 1, has a lumber history that began in the 1880s with the construction of a wharf, sawmill, and railroad. Business boomed by 1890 when 80,000 board feet of lumber were produced daily. The lumber industry, however, collapsed in 1936 after the uninsured mill burned although two smaller mills were built and operated until the 1960s when the big redwoods and firs were gone. Now Elk is a charming village of Victorian homes along with an assortment of restaurants, B&Bs, inns, and a spa.

## Greenwood State Beach

**Greenwood State Beach,** a 47-acre state parkland patched onto the coast west of Elk, is a gorgeous mile-wide cove headed by a long sand and stone beach backed by tall bluffs. Numerous sea stacks, their rocky pinnacles white with bird guano,

*Cuffey's Cove was the picturesque site of a lumber town from 1870 to 1888, when the post office closed down.*

stud the broad cove. Note a sea arch in the blocky stack flanking the south end of the cove and the large stack in the middle of the cove. This is **Wharf Rock,** named for the old 19th-century Greenwood Wharf (also nicknamed Casket Wharf), which extended out to its near side, allowing lumber to be loaded onto schooners. The beach itself is the site of an old lumber mill. A few bits and pieces remain from that boisterous era.

Greenwood Beach, bisected by Greenwood Creek on its southern end, makes a great stop. Activities include walking the beach, staring out to sea, picnicking on a blanket, surf fishing, collecting driftwood, and whale-watching. After winter rains open the sand spit between the ocean and Greenwood Creek, steelheads head upstream for spawning. Bluff trails above the beach offer great views.

**Finding the beach:** Drive up CA 1 about 15 miles from Point Arena or 17 miles south of Mendocino. Park in an unmarked gravel lot on the left (west) side of CA 1 (GPS: 39.12930 N / -123.716794 W) opposite the Elk Store. Start on the west side of the parking lot and follow an old road south, gently descending down to the beach.

# Navarro Beach

From Elk, the highway runs north along an elevated marine terrace above the rugged coast, passing sea stacks, cliffs, coves, and hidden pocket beaches at places like Cuffey's Cove and Saddle Point. At the Navarro River, a 28-mile-long river that runs to the Coastal River, CA 1 meets CA 128 and Navarro River Redwoods State Park which threads east along CA 128 and the river for 11 miles. At the mouth of the Navarro River stretches **Navarro Beach,** a crescent-shaped beach and isthmus.

Navarro Beach, part of the state park, is perfect for overnight camping with its open 10-site campground along the east edge of the beach. All sites are primitive and available on a first-come first-served basis. The beach offers good walking and fishing, but it is often windy. It's also a good put-in point for kayaking and canoeing on the lower river.

A ramshackle building on the road to the beach is the historic **Captain Fletcher's Inn.** Fletcher was a Scottish sailor who settled here in 1851, sold his land for a lumber mill in 1860, then built the hotel in 1865. As many as 1,000 people lived here in the town of Navarro over the next 40 years, working in the lumber mill and loading wood on ships. The inn survived until the 1970s as a stagecoach stop, home for mill hands, and fishing resort. Now California State Parks and Navarro-by-the-Sea Center are raising funds to restore it.

**Finding the beach:** Drive north from Elk to the Navarro River or south from Albion for 2 miles. Just before the bridge over the river, turn left (west) on Navarro Beach Road. Follow the dirt road to a parking area and campground at the beach (GPS: 39.192073 N / -123.758342 W). **Navarro River Redwoods State Park** (707-937-5804).

# Navarro River Redwoods State Park

This ribbon-like 660-acre state park lines CA 128 and the Navarro River for 14 miles from Navarro Beach to the inland town of Navarro. The scenic highway, following the north bank of the broad river, is shaded by towering second-growth redwood trees. Beginning in 1850, the valley was heavily logged, leaving only stumps. These quickly regenerated with second growth fed by water in the moist valley floor into the towering trees now seen. To see virgin old-growth redwoods, continue southeast on CA 128 to nearby **Heady Woods State Park.**

Besides craning your neck to look up at redwood trees, the park offers swimming and wading in the river on hot summer days; kayaking and canoeing; steelhead fishing (barbless hooks and catch and release only), and camping at 26-site **Paul M. Dimick Campground** beneath tall redwoods. The campground is 6 miles east of the junction with CA 1.

**Finding the park:** Drive north from Elk for about a dozen miles to the junction of CA 1 and CA 128. Turn right (east) on CA 128 and follow it up the north bank of the Navarro River to the state park. **Navarro River Redwoods State Park,** CA 128, Albion, CA 95410; (707) 937-5804.

# Albion

The town of **Albion** (2010 population 168) sits on both banks of the Albion River where it drains into the Pacific Ocean 3 miles north of the junction of Shoreline Highway and CA 128. It got its start in the late 1840s after English sea captain William Richardson was given a large land grant by the Mexican government in 1845. He built a house and sawmill along the river estuary, which he named the Albion River after his homeland. Previously in 1579 Sir Francis Drake had sailed up the California coast and put in for ship repairs in a sheltered harbor, dubbing the land Nova Albion. Some historians say he possibly landed at Albion Bay but most agree it was on Point Reyes.

Albion is a pleasant village with a scenic harbor, the placid river, and a ragged coast that rivals anywhere on the north shore with cliffed headlands, a small beach, and sea stacks washed by tall waves. The Shoreline Highway runs through town, passing over the Albion River on the only wooden bridge that remains on the Pacific Coast Highway. The spectacular trestle bridge was erected during World War II in 1944 when concrete and steel was unavailable, so scrap lumber was used for its construction.

The **Albion River Inn** (707-937-1919 or 800-479-7944), on CA 1 above the protected cove, is one of the best places to stay on the North Coast with both guest rooms and cottages as well as a gourmet restaurant with stellar ocean views. The restaurant is part of the original hotel, built in 1916 from salvaged lumber from the wrecked steamer *Girlie Mahoney,* which sank in the cove with 400,000 feet of lumber. Nearby camping for tents and RVs is at **Albion River Campground** (707-937-0606) on the north bank of the river near the bridge. The beach on the west side of the highway bridge is called **Albion Flat.** This sand beach, forming the east border of Albion Cove, is accessed through the campground (entrance fee), with parking, a boat put-in on the river, concessions, and tables. It's not a swimming beach but rather used by anglers.

# Dark Gulch Beach

**Dark Gulch Beach** (GPS: 39.239732 N / -123.774054 W) is a lovely and secluded beach tucked at the head of a crescent-shaped cove just north of Albion. It's one of those places that only locals know about, especially since access to it became more

## Stay Alive! Stay Alert!

California State Parks, which manages Van Damme, Mendocino Headlands, Russian Gulch, and other North Coast beaches and parks offers these safety tips on its website at parks.ca.gov:

- Stay back from bluff edges. The edges of sea cliffs and bluffs are composed of loose rock, grass, and scree. They can easily break away beneath your feet. Keep a close watch on children close to cliffs.

- Large rogue waves can sweep you out to sea during **ALL** seasons and ocean conditions. Never turn your back on the water. Large waves can break on both rocky shores and sandy beaches without warning.

- Bluff- and ocean-related deaths are common.

- The water is very cold, swift, and unforgiving. The National Oceanographic Data Center (NODC) reports that the ocean temperature on the North Coast ranges between 50°F and 54°F. Rip currents are common and can sweep unsuspecting swimmers out to sea. Swimming is discouraged on almost all the NoCal beaches.

difficult after the Heritage House closed. The hotel had maintained a path with stairways and a bridge over a small creek. Now you need to find a place to park on the highway south of the cove and make your way to the path and beach. Best to ask in Albion for directions to avoid crossing private property.

## Van Damme State Park

**Van Damme State Park,** 3 miles south of the town of Mendocino, spreads its 1,831 acres for 5 miles along the Little River and a sheltered beach and cove protected by a rocky headland. The park, covered with second-growth redwood forest, is laced with 10 miles of hiking trails. The paved **Fern Canyon Trail** winds for 2.5 miles through lush undergrowth in the Little River Valley. The **Pygmy Forest** section, protected as a National Natural Landmark, boasts dwarfed Bolander and bishop pine, Mendocino pygmy cypress, and manzanita trees as old as 100 years that are 6 inches to 8 feet tall. Acidic soils and poor drainage stunt the trees. The fragile forest is viewed from a quarter-mile boardwalk to avoid damaging the trees. The trailhead is a couple miles east from CA 1 on Little River Airport Road, which starts south of the park entrance.

The **Van Damme Beach** at the river mouth is one of the few northern California beaches that is at the same elevation as the highway, making access easy from a large parking lot between road and sand. This small beach is popular because of its accessibility, scenic views, broad sand expanse, and protection from big waves and wind. It's also considered one of the best abalone-diving spots in northern California and a good beach to take little kids. The quiet cove is good for sea kayaking too.

Opposite the beach is the road into the rest of the park. Check out the visitor center, which offers exhibits about area history and natural history and provides summer interpretative activities like ranger-led hikes and a Junior Ranger program. The park has a popular 69-site campground, with showers and restrooms, spread along an open meadow and in a lush valley. Reservations are recommended in summer; call (800) 444-7275 or visit reserveamerica.com.

**Finding the park:** Drive 3 miles south from Mendocino on CA 1. The beach and parking is on the right (west) side of the highway (GPS: 39.273681 N / -123.790609 W). Many day hikers in the park leave their car at this free lot and make a donation at the visitor center across the highway. The main entrance to the park is directly across from the beach.

# Mendocino

**Mendocino,** perched atop dramatic bluffs above the ocean on a peninsula, is a quaint, rustic town with a New England ambience. Many of the town's Victorian homes were built by homesick pioneers who settled here during its 19th-century lumber boom. The town was founded in 1852 by shipwrecked German immigrant William Kasten and quickly became a logging center that shipped thousands of feet of redwood lumber to San Francisco. After the last sawmill closed in 1937, Mendocino's fortunes slowly ebbed until the 1960s when it became an artists' colony.

Today Mendocino, an unincorporated town with a 2010 population of 894, is a trendy, stylish place with boutiques, health-food restaurants, cozy B&Bs, and galleries. A walk around the town's designated National Historic District reveals the charm of its gingerbread architecture and the wild beauty of its coastline. Exterior shots for the popular television show *Murder She Wrote*, which aired from 1984 to 1996, were filmed here. The **Blair House,** a Victorian house built in 1888 and now a B&B, was featured as the home of sleuth Jessica Fletcher, played by Angela Landsbury, in the fictional Maine town of Cabot Cove.

Mendocino is a great place for walking around, exploring the quaint downtown with its eclectic collection of shops and restaurants. Some historic points of interest include the 1868 **Mendocino Presbyterian Church** on Main Street (44831 Main St., Mendocino, CA 95460; 707-937-5441; mendopres.org) and the **Temple of Kwan Tai** (45160 Alboin St., Mendocino, CA 95460; 707-937-1381;

kwantaitemple.org), built in 1854 by Cantonese immigrants and possibly the oldest Chinese worship center in California. Also on Main Street is the historic **Ford House** (707-937-5397), now a museum and visitor center for Mendocino Headlands State Park. You can also stroll out to the state park just west of town to watch the sunset if the fog lifts. The town offers the **Mendocino Music Festival** every July with a blend of musical genres (707- 937-2044; mendocinomusic.org) and the **Mendocino Film Festival** over Memorial Day weekend.

Mendocino, with its picturesque charm and beauty, is a popular place. It was even named one of the "Prettiest Towns in America" by Forbes.com in 2008. Congestion comes with that charm. Be prepared on busy summer weekends for crowded streets and a lack of parking spots. Remember to bring warm clothes since it is often cool and foggy in summer and rainy in winter.

For more information: Mendocino Coast Chamber of Commerce & Visitor Center, 217 S. Main St., Fort Bragg, CA 95437; (707) 961-6300 or (800) 726-2780; mendocinocoast.com.

## Mendocino Headlands State Park

**Mendocino Headlands State Park** is a spectacular 347-acre coastal parkland that is a monument to erosion with sea stacks, arched wave tunnels, and rocky head-lands carved by relentless waves. The park—offering hiking, gorgeous sunsets, whale-watching, abalone diving, sea kayaking, and excellent tide pools—forms a pristine 2-mile greenbelt along three sides of Mendocino and preserves the town's unique shoreline and open grassland from development. The park was established in 1974 to stop development and preserve the stunning scenery. Cliffs line the edge of the entire promontory from the mouth of the Big River on the south to Agate Cove on the north.

The headland has trails all around it, making it easy to access from town. If you're on Main Street, stop at the park's **Ford House Visitor Center** on the south side of the street to pick up maps and park information, then continue down Main until it ends at Hesser Street. Follow a well-worn path out to a rock-rimmed headland on the south. The trail continues up the wind-lashed coast to a parking area opposite Goat Island. If you're in a car, you can follow Hesser Drive, which borders the cliff edge, and park in four different lots to hike short trails to various viewpoints. The park is especially gorgeous in May when wildflowers bloom.

The park offers two beaches—Big River Beach on the south and Portuguese Beach on the west. **Big River Beach,** on the north side of the Big River's estuary and

*Mendocino, perched above rocky cliffs, is one of California's prettiest towns with its charming Victorian architecture.*

the northeast side of Mendocino Cove, is a spacious sand beach that's popular and protected from big waves. **Portuguese Beach** tucks into a small cove on the southern headlands below Main Street. It's reached by a staircase from a bluff-top path.

Inland from Mendocino is the **Big River Unit** of the state park. The area was originally intended to be a separate park but was attached to Mendocino Headlands because of state budget concerns. This 7,334-acre unit encompasses the mostly wild Big River watershed and its long undisturbed estuary. Access it by following Big River Road east from CA 1.

**Finding the beaches:** Big River Beach is easily reached by hiking down a trail that starts behind the Presbyterian Church on Main Street or from Big River Road on the south side of Mendocino. Park in a large lot on the right (GPS: 39.302879 N / -123.79133W). Portuguese Beach is directly south of the west end of Main Street. There is a small parking area on the shoulder at the end of the street. Follow a trail out to a headland. Look for a path and staircase that leads down to the beach (GPS: 39.303475 N / -123.803848 W). **Mendocino Headlands State Park** (PO Box 440, Mendocino, CA 95460; 707- 937-5804).

## Russian Gulch State Park

**Russian Gulch State Park,** 2 miles north of Mendocino and 7 miles south of Fort Bragg, features 7,630 feet of shoreline, a beach in a protected cove, a unique blowhole, second-growth redwood trees, numerous trails, and a 30-site campground (call 800-444-7275 or visit reserveamerica.com). One of the most unique features is the 60-foot-deep **Devil's Punchbowl,** a 100-foot wide blowhole. Waves are pushed through a 200-foot-long tunnel into the hole, creating a wild maelstrom when the surf is high. A small sandy beach below the highway bridge divides the ocean from Russian Gulch.

The park also offers sea kayaking, tide pool exploring, rock fishing, abalone diving, bicycling on a paved 3-mile trail; and lots of hiking. The **Fern Canyon Trail** is particularly good. The first part follows the creek (paved for bicycles); finish with a loop on fern-lined **Falls Trail** which passes beneath redwoods and by a 36-foot-high waterfall. Another good hike starts from a parking lot (GPS: 39.329057 N / -123.809438 W) on the north side of the cove and explores a rugged headland and the Devil's Punchbowl.

**Finding the park:** Drive north for 2 miles on CA 1 to a left (west) turn into the park and the entrance station. Continue to overlooks, the beach, campground, and trails. **Russian Gulch State Park** (PO Box 440, Mendocino, CA 95460; 707-937-5804).

*Evening light and surging surf break against sea stacks and wash across a sandy beach at Fort Bragg.*

# Point Cabrillo Light Station State Historic Park

This 296-acre state park preserves the old **Point Cabrillo Light Station,** 11 other buildings including 3 lighthouse keeper houses, the sunken remains of the historic ship *Frolic,* and open grassland on a promontory. The lighthouse, built in 1908, opened in 1909 to guide schooners carrying lumber to rebuild San Francisco after the big 1906 earthquake and after several shipwrecks on offshore rocks and reefs. The 47-foot-high lighthouse tower, topping a white wooden building with a red roof, houses a 6,800-pound Fresnel lens and flashes a warning every 10 seconds. The lighthouse is open every day 11 a.m. to 4 p.m., while the rest of the grounds are open for hiking from sunrise to sunset. Parking is free, and no admission is charged to visit. There's a gift shop inside the lighthouse.

On the north side of the park is famous **Frolic Cove.** In 1850 a clipper ship named *Frolic* was heading south to San Francisco with a load of Chinese goods when it struck a reef off today's Point Cabrillo (named in 1870 for Portuguese explorer João Rodriques Cabrillo). The stricken ship was secured in the cove, and the crew went south in long boats to Fort Ross. A year later, lumber dealer Harry Mieggs sent men to salvage the ship, but they found the local Pomo Indians had already done the job and the ship had sunk. They did report, however, to Mieggs that huge trees lined the coast. In 1852 he established a sawmill at Big River by Mendocino and the lucrative lumber industry that fueled coastal growth began in earnest.

The park also offers hiking along the headlands on **North Trail** and **South Trail.** It's a good place to see gray whales, humpback whales, orcas, dolphins, seals, and sea lions. Dogs must be leashed. No fishing.

**Finding the lighthouse:** From Mendocino, drive north on CA 1 for a couple miles. Make a left (west) turn toward Russian Gulch State Park onto Brest Drive. Take an immediate right (north) on Point Cabrillo Drive and follow it northwest for 1.3 miles to Lighthouse House Drive. Turn left into a large parking lot (GPS: 39.34978 N / -123.813322 W) at the park entrance. Walk 0.5 mile down the access road to the lighthouse. Handicapped parking is available near the lighthouse. **Point Cabrillo Light Station State Historic Park** (13800 Point Cabrillo Dr., Mendocino, CA 95460; 707-937-5804).

# Caspar Headlands State Beach

This small 0.2-mile-long sand beach, tucked into a bluff-lined cove just off CA 1, is part of a 75-acre park that also includes the **Caspar Headlands State Reserve** on the south side of the cove, which is open only by permit since public and private land is intermingled. The beach offers sunbathing, fishing, scuba diving, kayaking, and swimming if the water is calm. Across the road from the beach is **Caspar Beach RV Park & Campground.** The beach is open sunrise to sunset.

**Finding the beach:** Drive north on CA 1 for 2 miles from Russian Gulch. Turn left (west) on Caspar Little Lake Road and follow it to the beach. Park in a lot (GPS: 39.359758 N / -123.816304W) opposite the RV park entrance. **Caspar Headlands State Beach** (707-937-5804).

## Jug Handle State Natural Reserve

Jug Handle, like its neighbor parks to the south, is composed of two distinct segments—a spectacular beach and coastline and a dense forest lining a creek. The 776-acre parkland's best known feature is a staircase of five wave-cut marine terraces that step up east from the coast. Each level terrace is 100 feet higher and 100,000 years older than the one below and is populated by different plant communities.

The 2.5-mile self-guided **Ecological Staircase** nature trail explores the terraces and the unique ecosystems on each one, forming one of the few places in the world where complete record of ecological succession is plainly visible. The lowest and most recent terrace is grassland; the next terrace is covered with mixed conifers including redwoods; the third terrace from 300,000 years ago has a unique pygmy forest of dwarf cypress and pine, many no taller than eye-level and up to 100 years old. Pines and other conifers blanket the upper oldest terraces. The easy-to-follow trail is a must-do Mendocino coast hike with its giant redwoods and mature pygmy trees.

The **Jug Handle Beach** and coast is also simply beautiful with a glistening sand beach at the head of a placid cove and a mile-long coastline of bluffs, cliffs, and sea stacks amid crashing surf. It's a great beach for sitting and watching waves, chilling in the sun, wading, and fishing. Hike on the bluff top trail west of the parking area for good views of the beach and the cove's sparkling clear water.

**Finding the reserve:** From Mendocino and Fort Bragg, drive north or south respectively for about 2.5 miles. On the south end of a bridge spanning the creek, look for signs to the park. Turn west into a large parking lot (GPS: 39.375251 N / -123.816515W). Trails to the beach and bluff begin here. **Jug Handle State Natural Reserve** (707-937-5804).

## Mendocino Coast Botanical Gardens

The 17-acre **Mendocino Coast Botanical Gardens,** off CA 1 just south of Fort Bragg, is a small but interesting privately owned botanical gardens squeezed between the highway and the coast. The seaside location and moist, mild climate allow for a diversity of plants. The area, divided into a formal manicured garden and a wilder sector by the shoreline, is known for its fragrant rhododendron species and heritage roses brought by early pioneers.

The gardens are accessed by trails; many are handicapped accessible. There is also a cafe, gift shop, and nursery. You're also welcome to bring a picnic lunch to enjoy on the wildflower-festooned slopes above the ocean. Although there are blooming plants all year, it's best to come in spring and summer (rhododendrons best in April and May). Also plan on spending plenty of time since the admission is a bit pricey. Allow 2 hours to see the gardens. **Mendocino Coast Botanical Gardens** (707-964-4352; gardenbythesea.org).

## Fort Bragg

**Fort Bragg,** with a 2010 population of 7,273, is the coast's largest town between San Francisco and Eureka. Fort Bragg has long been a gritty working town, unlike its sister city Mendocino to the south. Loggers, mill workers, and fishermen live here. The town was founded in 1855 as a military fort to keep Native Americans on the Mendocino Reservation. In 1867 the area was opened to settlers, and Fort Bragg became a lumber town.

It still retains its working-class roots, but after the local lumber mill closed in 2002 and was torn down, the town, using its irresistible location, has shed its logging past and reinvented itself as a tourist destination. An example is the old Pudding Creek Trestle, built in 1916 from redwood and used to haul lumber to the mill, which is now a bridge to the coast for pedestrians and bicyclists.

The town, boasting the only traffic lights along the drive, offers lots of visitor services, including restaurants, shops, and lodging. It's a cheaper alternative for accommodations that other coastal towns with its greater choice of chain motels along CA 1 on the south side of town rather than quaint inns and B&Bs.

Downtown, centered along Main Street (CA 1), is where it's happening now in Fort Bragg. The old company store that once sold goods to mill workers is now reimagined as the **Company Store,** a mini-mall with upscale restaurants and galleries. Walk the streets and you'll find lots of galleries, boutiques, coffeehouses, and a slew of restaurants and pubs, like the **North Coast Brewing Company Taproom** (mainly for its great microbrews; try the 12-beer sampler) and standout **Piaci Pub and Pizzeria.**

**Finding the town:** Fort Bragg is 8 miles north of Mendocino on CA 1 (Shoreline Highway). The highway is Main Street through town. To fastest route to reach Fort Bragg from San Francisco is 160 miles and takes 3 hours. From the Golden Gate Bridge, drive north on US 101 to Willits. Exit west on CA 20 and drive 35 miles to Fort Bragg. **Mendocino Chamber of Commerce and Visitor Center** (217 S. Main St., Fort Bragg, CA 95437; 707-961-6300; mendocinocoast.com; fortbragg.com).

*Fort Bragg Climate*

Fort Bragg, like the rest of the California coast, offers mild weather year-round, although it is often foggy or overcast at night and in the morning. The summer is generally dry with only drizzle and light showers. September is the warmest month with daily high temperatures averaging 66°F and average lows at 49°F. The temperature rarely climbs to 90°F here on the coast. January is the coolest month with daily highs averaging 55°F and lows of 40°F. The town's average precipitation is 41 inches a year.

## Skunk Train

The California Western Railroad, affectionately called the **"Skunk Train,"** is Fort Bragg's biggest tourist attraction. The vintage logging train, named for the original smelly 1920s steam engines (it's now odorless), snakes inland through redwood forests, mountains, two tunnels, and over 30 trestles and bridges along the twisting Noyo River. Most travelers ride to a halfway point called Northspur between Fort Bragg and Willits. Most travelers turn around here and ride back although you can continue on to Willits. The trains run daily in summer from a downtown depot at West Laurel Street just west of North Main Street. (707) 964-6471; (866) 866-1690; skunktrain.com.

## Glass Beach

Where does trash become treasure? At **Glass Beach** on the north side of Fort Bragg. During the first half of the 20th century, Fort Bragg locals took their trash and shoved it over the bluffs above the coast on the northern end of the mill property at a place they simply called "The Dumps." All kinds of junk went over the edge—old automobiles, appliances, garbage, tin cans, and lots of bottles. The dump closed in the mid-1960s, and the trashed beaches were slowly cleaned up with all the big stuff hauled off to a proper refuse site. All that remained were all those bottles, which relentless Pacific waves pummeled into broken bits and then polished into glistening multicolored glass gems. Now the beach is a bit like an archaeological site with all its rounded shards remaining underfoot as artistic remnants of the town's mill history.

In 2002, before tourists and beachcombers carried all the glass chips away, the California Department of Parks & Recreation acquired the 38-acre site and put it into **MacKerricher State Park** for preservation. Now visitors can crunch around on the glass-covered beach and admire the rainbow of colors since it is against the law to pilfer the glass gems. Still, every day, there are hordes of bent-over people scavenging the beach and hauling off buckets of specimens. Come and enjoy

Glass Beach, but don't be one of the stealers! It's best to visit at low tide. Oh, and remember to wear shoes since it is still a dump with rusted hunks of metal and freshly broken bottles on the beach.

**Finding the beach:** From downtown Fort Bragg, drive north on Main Street/ CA 1 to West Elm Street. Turn left (west) on Elm and drive to a parking area at its end (GPS: 39.452146 N / -123.809672W). Walk west on an old road to the bluff top above the ocean. Scramble down steep trails to several pocket beaches.

## MacKerricher State Park

**MacKerricher State Park,** with almost 9 miles of beachfront, is one of the longest coastal parks on the drive. The park, beginning at Fort Bragg and running north to the Ten Mile River, is a superlative natural and recreation area, with sharp cliffs, rocky headlands, one of northern California's longest beaches, windswept sand dunes, rocky islands, tide pools, fields of wildflowers, and a freshwater lagoon.

The main park area centers around **Lake Cleone** 3 miles north of Fort Bragg. On the entrance road is a visitor center with interpretive displays and books. The area features 114 sites in four secluded **campgrounds**—Surfwood, Cleone, East Pinewood, and West Pinewood—with restrooms, showers, and easy beach access. Make reservations by calling (800) 444-7275 or at parks.ca.gov. Nearby is 30-acre **Lake Cleone,** a former saltwater lagoon now filled with freshwater, with a picnic area, fishing, and a 1.3-mile trail around the lake. From a parking area (GPS: 39.489056 N / -123.799374W) west of the lake, a short boardwalk trail leads out to **Laguna Point,** a good spot to sight gray whales December through April during their migration. Harbor seals are often seen here frolicking in the surf and sunning on rocks. During whale-migration season, docent-led groups meet at the visitor center and come out here to watch the gray whales spouting past. North of the parking area is a long stretch of beach, perfect for walking and sunbathing.

North of the lake, the narrow park includes a long stretch of sand dunes pushed eastward from the beach by persistent westerly winds. The park ends where Ten Mile River empties into the ocean. This 5-mile section of coast is best accessed by **Ten Mile Beach Trail,** also called Log Haul Road, which begins at Laguna Point and runs to the river. The foot trail follows an historic road that once hauled redwood logs from Ten Mile River to the Fort Bragg harbor on the Noyo River, a distance of 10 miles. Some sections of the road are washed away.

*Wave-polished pieces of glass from Fort Bragg's dump glisten among rocky sea stacks at Glass Beach.*

**Pudding Creek Beach** is a pocket beach at the mouth of Pudding Creek just north of Glass Beach and Fort Bragg. Pudding Creek backs up from shoreline sand into a long estuary. The beach's broad sandy expanse, hemmed in by bluffs on both sides, is easily accessed from CA 1. **Finding the beach:** Drive north from Fort Bragg on CA 1 to a turnoff on the left (west) side of the highway just before the Pudding Creek Trestle bike and hike trail that spans the creek. Follow a road with parking on its west side that parallels the highway (GPS: 39.457666 N / -123.806479 W); a restroom is at road's end.

**Virgin Creek Beach** is a wave-washed beach that stretches north from Virgin Creek's lagoon. The area, with a variety of habitats, offers great bird watching. Keep an eye out for shorebirds, including the endangered snowy plover. There are good tide pools to explore at low tide and surfers find good waves here. **Finding the beach:** Drive north from Fort Bragg on CA 1. About a half-mile north of Pudding Creek Beach, just past Airport Road, park in an unmarked dirt roadside lot on the right (east) side of the highway (GPS: 39.468603 N / -123.802477 W). Cross the highway, pass through a fence, and walk west for 100 yards on a trail to 10 Mile Beach Trail/Log Haul Road. Go right on the trail and walk another 100 yards. Cross a bridge over the creek to the beach.

**Ten Mile River Beach** is at the north end of the park at the mouth of the Ten Mile River. The beach offers the usual sand activities as well as excellent birding along the river estuary. No dogs allowed. **Finding the beach:** Drive north from Fort Bragg and park on the west side of the highway in a paved lot (GPS: 39.545016 N / -123.760654 W) just before CA 1 crosses a bridge over the river.

**Finding the park:** To find the Cleone Lake area and campgrounds, drive north on CA 1 from Fort Bragg for 3 miles. Turn left (west) on signed MacKerricher State Park, which leads to the visitor center, lake, campgrounds, and beach. Other access points to the long strip park are along CA 1. (707) 964-9112.

## Seaside Creek Beach

The beach, at the mouth of Seaside Creek, is a small but good pocket beach with flank cliffs and a couple sea stacks, one rising from the sand. Since it's out of the state park, it's a great beach to bring your dog to romp. It is also good for surf fishing. **Finding the beach:** Drive north on CA 1 for 0.7 mile from the Ten Mile River Bridge. Park on the west side of the road in a lot (GPS: 39.558798 / -123.765557W).

## South Kibesallah Gulch Viewpoint, Pacific Star Winery & Bruhel Point Bluff

The Shoreline Highway runs north across a marine terrace above the rocky coastline from Seaside Creek, passing **South Kibesallah Gulch Viewpoint** (GPS: 39.599193 N / -123.784866 W) on the west. A short trail leads to marvelous coast overlooks.

The highway reaches **Pacific Star Winery,** the farthest west winery in the US (GPS: 39.591976 N / -123.783611 W), 12 miles north of Fort Bragg. The winery is well worth a stop, with fine wines made with local grapes; a $5 tasting fee for 6 to 10 wines; and spectacular coastal views. (707) 964-1155; pacificstarwinery.com.

**Bruhel Point,** a 145-acre scenic area in California Coastal National Monument, is farther up the road from the winery. From the parking on the highway edge, hike about a half-mile along a trail to the cliffed point. From the cliff edge, other trails follow the bluff top to more viewpoints. The large rocky reef below is home to a large colony of harbor seals. A pocket beach is on the north side of the point. **Finding the point:** Drive north from Ten Mile River Bridge on CA 1 for 4.5 miles to mile marker 74.09. Park on the wide gravel shoulder on the west side of the highway (GPS: 39.605837 N / -123.784517 W).

## Chadbourne Gulch Beach

The highway reaches the mile-long stretch of **Chadbourne Gulch Beach** a couple miles south of Westport and just north of Bruhel Point. This remote beach, lying below the highway, is never busy. It's great for walking, surf fishing, picnicking, and surfing. It's a narrow beach so make sure you get above before the tide comes in or you may get trapped. **Finding the beach:** Drive north on CA 1 past Bruhel Point to the beach, or south 2 miles from Westport. The main parking area is at the end of a spur road in Chadbourne Gulch. Where the highway makes a big hairpin turn through the gulch, take a road on the west (marked by an "adopt a highway sign") to the beach parking lot (GPS: 39.613507 N / -123.781508W). Many roadside pullouts are along the highway above the beach. They're great viewpoints but it's difficult to access the beach from them.

## Westport

**Westport,** a supply center for mills and timber camps as well as a lumber shipping point for the area north of the Ten Mile River in the 1880s, is a compact town with about 50 buildings. It was originally dubbed Beall's Landing for its first resident Samuel Beall, but lumberman James Rodgers renamed it as a counterpoint to his hometown of Eastport, Maine. Westport was once the largest seaport between

San Francisco and Eureka and was, in the 1880s, the center of a massive freight operation that supplied inland cities. The completion of the railroad to Fort Bragg, however, spelled the beginning of the end for Westport. The town, sitting atop bluffs 13 miles north of Fort Bragg, offers basic visitor services including a general store, post office, a couple inns including the **Westport Hotel** with a restaurant and pub. Just north of town is a **KOA campground** opposite Wages Creek Road. Next to the campground is crescent-shaped **Wages Creek Beach;** park in a pull-off along CA 1 to access the beach.

## Westport-Union Landing State Beach

**Westport-Union Landing State Beach,** a 58-acre park, spreads along 3 miles of coastline alongside the Shoreline Highway 19 miles north of Fort Bragg and 3 miles north of Westport. The narrow park, part of the ancestral lands of the Cahto tribe, is a great place to get away from crowds and spend some quality coast time.

Most of the coastline is a ribbon of coarse sand and rock backed by tall bluffs. Several larger pocket beaches are found where creeks empty into the ocean, including **Pete's Beach** at the mouth of DeHaven Creek (parking lot GPS: 39.660444 N / -123.785516 W) and **Howard Creek Beach** (parking lot GPS: 39.678168 N / -123.791051 W). Several viewpoints are found along the highway; look for pullouts on the west side of the road.

Park activities are fishing for smelt and rockfish, beachcombing in tide pools, bird watching, picnicking, hiking, and camping. The park has 3 campgrounds with 86 sites (first-come first-served) scattered along the top of a bluff with ocean views at **Howard Creek.** It can be windy and cold at the open campsites, especially in winter. Swimming is not recommended because of cold water and unpredictable currents. (707) 937-5804.

## Rockport

The Shoreline Highway bends away from the coast north of Westport-Union Landing State Beach and twists up a steep wooded mountainside before dropping down to the small hamlet of **Rockport** 7 miles north of Westport. Like other North Coast towns, Rockport flourished as a logging center with a big sawmill, schools, post office, houses, and hotels before fading away in the mid-20th century until virtually nothing remains now.

**Rockport Beach** is reached by turning west (GPS: 39.73819 N / -123.8168 W) and driving down a narrow dirt road to the shore at the canyon mouth. The picturesque off-the-beaten-track beach sprawls across the head of Rockport Cove with rocky bluffs and sea stacks framing each side of it.

# Usal Road & Usal Beach Camp

The **Usal Road** is a great backcountry driving adventure on the southern edge of the Lost Coast north of CA 1. The road accesses the wildest part of California's Pacific coast on the edge of the King Range. Much of the area is in 7,500-acre **Sinkyone Wilderness State Park,** a remote and untrammeled coastal region once inhabited by the Sinkyone native people. The park has high rugged mountains cloaked in redwoods and Douglas firs, and an abrupt coastline with narrow strips of black and gray sand beaches forming the transition zone between sea and shore. The Usal Road traverses the park from south to north. The north side of the park, accessed from US 101 on the Briceland Thorn Road has a visitor center at **Needle Rock** and a couple primitive campgrounds.

Usal Road twists north for 5.3 miles to the Sinkyone Wilderness State Park boundary, then descends down to a bridge across Usal Creek. Past the bridge, take a left turn to the beach and **Usal Beach Camp,** which is 5.8 miles from CA 1. Park by the beach in a large lot (GPS: 39.832013 N / -123.850014 W). The gray-sand beach was the site of a dog hole lumber port that operated from about 1890 to 1960, shipping logs south to California's cities.

The road continues past Usal Beach for 21 more winding scenic miles to **Four Corners** on Briceland Road. This road section is harrowing with deep ruts, mud, and fallen trees—a full-value off-road trek. Travel in pairs; drive a high-clearance 4-wheel-drive vehicle; and bring cable, rope, and shovels.

The trailhead for the 16.7-mile **Lost Coast Trail** begins on the left just past the Usal Creek bridge. This fabulous trail heads north to **Bear Harbor Cove,** passing trailside campsites and gorgeous views of the rugged coast. You need a wilderness permit to hike the trail.

Usal Road is narrow, steep, and winding. There are few places to pass, to back up, or to turn around. In summer and good conditions, passenger cars can make it to Usal Beach, but it's better to have a truck, 4-wheel-drive rig, or small SUV. The road is seasonally passable. In winter it may be washed out, covered in downed timber, and muddy or impassable in heavy rain. The area receives in excess of 80 inches of rain a year, most falling November through April. RVs and trailers are not allowed.

**Usal Beach Camp,** run by the California State Parks, is a first-come first-served primitive camping area (fee area) with pit toilets almost 6 miles north of CA 1. No water. Bring your own or use creek water; remember to purify it first. The campsite can be busy and noisy on weekends. Store your food properly since this is bear country. The beach is lovely and remote—a perfect spot for a getaway.

**Finding the road:** Usal Road (Mendocino County Road 431) starts 3 miles north of Rockport, 13 miles north of Westport on CA 1 or 14.7 miles west of

Leggett and US 101 (GPS: 39.780399 N / -123.831551 W) at mile marker 90.88. The turn is not marked. For more information, contact Sinkyone Wilderness State Park (707-986-7711).

## The Lost Coast

Past Rockport, CA 1 travels across a remote landscape as it continues north, running through dense forest with almost no views and no access to the coastline. The highway turns inland 10 miles north of Westport and leaves the Mendocino coast behind. The shoreline north of here, called the **Lost Coast,** is a ragged vastness of wild mountains, stormy beaches, and few people and roads. The range and coast is so rugged that highway builders didn't attempt to traverse the area but instead turned CA 1 inland and away from the shoreline, making roads that appear to be scribbles on a map.

The King Range lifts precipitously from the rocky Lost Coast, rising 4,087 feet from the shoreline to the summit of King Peak, its high point, in a mere 3 miles. The range is geologically active with the North American crustal plate pushing over the Pacific Plate and rising some 60 feet in the last 6,000 years. The 68,000-acre **King Range National Conservation Area,** administered by the BLM, includes the range as well as 35 miles of undeveloped coastline. The area includes 42,585 acres of designated wilderness. For more information call (707) 986-5400 or (707) 825-2300.

One of the coast's best beach backpacking trips is from the mouth of the **Mattole River** north to **Shelter Cove.** Another good trek is a 3-mile hike up the **Lost Coast Trail** to the old lighthouse at **Punta Gorda.**

The last 15 miles of CA 1 heads inland, following a winding, old logging road that's now paved. Obey the numerous caution signs and drive slowly. The road corkscrews up steep canyons past lush woodlands before emerging atop lofty ridges. Several pullouts yield excellent viewpoints. Eventually, the road spirals down and across ridge lines before spanning the South Fork of the Eel River and entering Leggett.

US 101, the drive's end, lies just outside Leggett. A northward turn leads to Eureka and the Redwood Country. A south turn heads to Ukiah, Santa Rosa, and back to San Francisco.

# Eureka to Crescent City

**General description:** This 78-mile section of US 101 parallels the rugged Pacific coast, passing redwood groves and a wave-carved shoreline of beaches, cliffs, and sea stacks.

**Special attractions:** Redwood National Park, Del Norte Coast Redwoods State Park, Prairie Creek Redwoods State Park, Humboldt Lagoons State Park, Patrick's Point State Park, Humboldt Bay National Wildlife Refuge, Eureka, Fort Humboldt State Historic Park, Crescent City, hiking, backpacking, fishing, world's tallest tree, redwood forests.

**Location:** Northwestern California, from Eureka to Crescent City, 20 miles south of the Oregon border.

**Drive route number and name:** US 101 (Redwood Highway).

**Travel season:** Year-round. Fog often envelops the road in summer, while heavy winter rains make hazardous driving conditions.

**Camping:** Hundreds of campsites, including primitive ones on the beach, are in state parks, nearby Six Rivers National Forest, and private RV campgrounds.

**Services:** All services in Eureka, Arcata, McKinleyville, Trinidad, and Crescent City. Limited services in Orick and Klamath.

## The Route

The empire of the redwood stretches almost 500 miles from south of Monterey along California's coastal ranges to a small pocket in southwestern Oregon to the north. This immense span of land, wreathed in summer fog and bounded by winter storms, is home to *Sequoia sempervirens,* the coast redwood.

The Redwood Highway, US 101, traverses 78 miles of the empire's best redwood country between Eureka and Crescent City in northwestern California. This long strip of land is northern California's frontier with the ocean and boasts an almost unsurpassed natural beauty with craggy headlands jutting boldly into frothy surf, majestic stands of pristine redwood trees, broad bays and estuaries that teem with birds, and glistening sweeps of sand that form the tenuous boundary between land and sea. The land along the drive is truly unique, one of California's greatest and most memorable scenic attractions.

### Weather

California's North Coast is a land of heavy rain. As much as 100 inches falls on parts of the Redwood Coast, making lush forests and thick meadowlands. Most of the rain falls in winter when Pacific storms lash against the coastal mountains. Temperatures are also cool. January's average high in both Eureka and Crescent

# Eureka to Crescent City

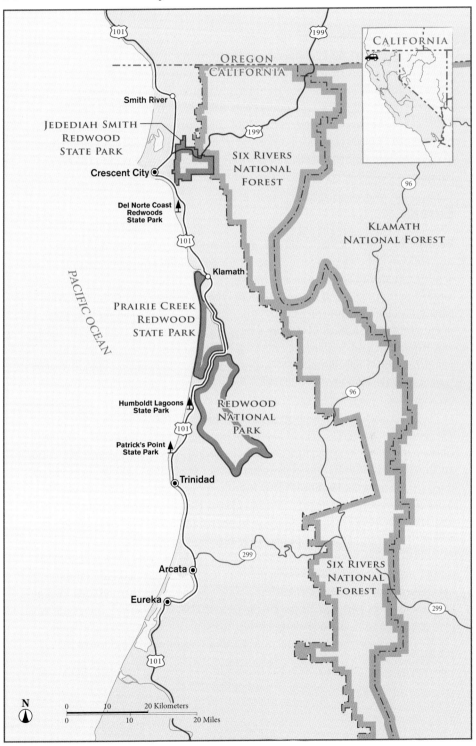

City is 53 degrees. Summer hardly warms up, with average July temperatures in Eureka only a paltry 60°F; temperatures in Crescent City climb to a 69°F average. Eureka is the usual winner of the coolest city year-round in the continental US, with little variation between summer and winter. Expect thick fog in summer along the coast and in the redwood forests. Sometimes it burns off by midday, but the mist usually hangs around all day. Biologists estimate as much as 12 percent of the moisture redwoods need is derived from the summer fogs. A good raincoat and hat are needed for hikers, campers, and beachcombers. Needless to say, sunbathing on the beach is usually not an option on the North Coast.

## Eureka

**Eureka,** the largest city on California's northern coast, is a charming, historic town that started as a prosperous seaport for the Trinity mining boom to the east. San Francisco land speculators and merchants saw beckoning opportunity on the North Coast in 1850, and several different companies raced northward to grab land and potential profits. Irishman James Ryan's group claimed the east shore of Humboldt Bay, a long inland bay named for famed naturalist Baron Alexander von Humboldt, and established a new town dubbed Eureka. Eureka is a Greek word meaning "I have found it!" It's also California's state motto. Within 3 years Eureka housed a population of 3,000. After the mining boom busted, the port became a major logging center. The harvested timber was, of course, redwood. By 1855, nine mills operated around Humboldt Bay.

The city, 284 miles north of San Francisco, has a population of 27,191 (2010 census) and offers many restored houses, including the elegant **Carson Mansion,** an Old Town area, and numerous sights and services. Eureka also has several fine museums such as the **Humboldt Bay Maritime Museum,** which interprets the North Coast's seafaring history, and the **Clarke Historical Museum,** located in Old Town, with an excellent collection of Native American basketry and other objects from regional Native American groups.

Eureka's **Old Town** is worth a stroll. This "skid row" collection of brothels, sailors' taverns, card houses, and flophouses has been renovated into a trendy area with art galleries, cafes, and shops. "Skid row" itself is a North Coast logging expression. Logs were laid crossways on steep slopes or marshes and logs pulled by oxen teams were skidded along the improvised road to railheads and mills.

For more information, contact the **Eureka Chamber of Commerce** (707-442-3738).

# Fort Humboldt State Historic Park

**Fort Humboldt State Historic Park** preserves the site of a military garrison that maintained order between settlers and gold miners who moved here after the discovery of gold and Native Americans tribes including the Yurok, Hoopa, and Wiyot. The fort, on a low hill overlooking Eureka and Humboldt Bay, operated from 1853 to 1870 before being decommissioned and falling into ruins. Today the hospital is the only original structure that remains. The park also has a logging museum with historic logging equipment.

Captain Ulysses S. Grant, later a Civil War hero and president, was stationed here before being drummed out of the service for drunkenness in 1854. On leaving Eureka, Grant prophesied to his friend Post Surgeon Jonathon Clark, "My day will come, they will hear from me yet." Grant was not sad to leave, writing, "You do not know how forsaken I feel here!"

**Finding the park:** Follow US 101 into Eureka. Go east on Highlands Avenue 1 block. Turn left (north) into the park and drive to a parking area (GPS: 40.777288 N / -124.18749 W). (707) 445-6567.

# Carson Mansion

The Carson Mansion, one of the most famous and most photographed houses in the US, has been called "the most grand Victorian home in America." The house, designed by respected San Francisco architects Samuel and Joseph Newsom, was built for lumber baron William Carson by over 100 carpenters and craftsmen between 1884 and 1886 at a cost of $84,000. The 3-floor, 18-room, 16,200-square-foot mansion was built in American Queen Anne style architecture. The house is primarily built of redwood, along with many other imported woods including primavera or "white mahogany" from Central America and other woods from Mexico, the Philippines, and East India.

Carson moved to California from eastern Canada in 1849 and failed at mining in the Trinity Mountains but discovered by 1853 that felling redwoods was almost as profitable as digging gold. By the time the house was built, his operation was producing over 15 million board feet of lumber annually. The private Ingomar Club bought the house from the Carson family in 1950 after it was slated for demolition. It's not open to the public but can easily be admired and photographed from the street.

The garish Carson Mansion is, of course, now the archetypal haunted house that's regularly used for spooky illustrations and attractions worldwide. The main tower is also duplicated as the clock tower at Disneyland's train station. **Carson Mansion** (143 M St., Eureka, CA; ingomar.org).

## Blue Ox Millworks & Historic Park

The millworks is a working custom woodworking shop that produces authentic millwork used in buildings and homes throughout the US. Using 19th-century Victorian machinery and tools, they make redwood gutters, doors, windows, molding, balusters, and Victorian gingerbread patterns. You can visit the mill as well as historic buildings including a blacksmith shop where ornamental ironwork is made, a boatbuilding shop, and a skid camp on either a guided or self-guided tour. A big hit are a pair of Belgian blue oxen named Baby and Blue. It's located just north of US 101 as it leaves Eureka on the north. **Blue Ox Millworks & Historic Park** (One X Street, Eureka, CA 95501; 707-444-3437; 800-248-4259).

## Sequoia Park Zoo

The Sequoia Park Zoo, in the heart of Eureka, is a small intimate zoo spread over 7 acres in a 60-acre parkland of towering second-growth redwood trees. The zoo, the oldest in California (founded in 1907) and the smallest accredited zoo in the US, offers over 250 animals and 75 species including primates, a petting zoo for kids, an aviary, flamingos, and 2 popular red pandas Sumo and Shifo. The zoo, which began charging admission in 2008, is affordable and easy to see in a couple hours. It's a perfect outing for children. The zoo is open daily in summer but closed on Mon in winter. **Sequoia Park Zoo** (3414 W St. Eureka, CA 95503; 707-441-4263; sequoiaparkzoo.net).

## Morris Graves Museum of Art

This compact but fine art museum, housed in the historic 1904 Carnegie Library, is named for Morris Graves (1910–2001), the founder of the Northwest School of Art and an abstract painter. He donated over 100 paintings from his personal collection to the museum, which opened in 2000. The museum, dedicated to art of the Pacific Northwest, offers rotating exhibits. **Morris Graves Museum of Art** (636 F St. Eureka, CA 95501; 707-442-0278; humboldtarts.org).

*The garish Carson Mansion, America's most famous Victorian house, was built between 1884 and 1886 for $84,000.*

# Humboldt Bay

The scenic route, following 4-lane US 101, leaves Eureka and swings around broad Humboldt Bay. The bay is California's second largest and is enclosed on the west by long sand spits with a narrow, treacherous channel that has grounded many ships. The bay, despite being the only protected harbor between San Francisco and Coos Bay, Oregon, a distance of 500 miles, was not discovered until 1806 since it is hard to see from the open ocean. Many early explorers, including Sir Francis Drake and George Vancouver, sailed by the big bay until Captain Jonathan Winship, employed by Russian-American Fur Company traders, made the first recorded entry by Europeans in June, 1906.

**Humboldt Bay,** covering 13 square miles, averages 11 feet deep with a dredged 40-foot-deep channel for big ships. Besides being an important sea port, the bay also supports over 100 fish species, over 100,000 wintering birds, and produces over half of California's oysters in the largest oyster operation on the West Coast.

# Humboldt Bay National Wildlife Refuge

The almost 4,000-acre **Humboldt Bay National Wildlife Refuge** covers the southeast side of Humboldt Bay, an area that includes Hookton Slough. This fertile wetland of tidal flats and marsh is a crucial stopover for birds on the **Pacific Flyway.** The bay supports 316 bird species, including as many as 100,000 migratory birds that feed and nest here during the winter, and over 100 fish species like coho and chinook salmon, steelhead, and sturgeon. The refuge is important habitat for the black brant and also protects the Lanphere and Ma-le'l sand dunes, a pristine coastal dune system with rare plant species, at the upper end of the west spit of Humboldt Bay.

A half-mile offshore is **Castle Rock National Wildlife Refuge.** Castle Rock, a 335-foot-high, 14-acre island thrust above the ocean, provides critical nesting and roosting habitat for seabirds including as many as 20,000 Aleutian cackling geese in winter and spring and over 100,000 common murres in summer. Harbor seals, elephant seals, and sea lions also rest on the island's surf-ravaged shore. It's closed to visitation.

The refuge offers excellent bird watching, photography, and wildlife viewing. At the **Salmon Creek** unit on the east side of the refuge off US 101 is a visitor center (open daily 8 a.m. to 5 p.m.), an observation kiosk, and photo blind. Lists of plants, animals, and birds are available at the center. A good hike is the 1.7-mile **Shorebird Loop Trail** past wetlands to Hookton Slough. The **Hookton Slough Trail** is a 1.5-mile out-and-back interpretive trail; good fishing is along the trail.

A nonmotorized boat launch at Hookton Slough parking area is the put-in for a fun paddle around **Teal Island.** Dogs, jogging, and biking are prohibited.

**Finding the refuge:** From Eureka, drive south on US 101 to exit 696 for Hookton. On the west side of the highway, go north on Eel River Drive to the visitor center and Salmon Creek unit. For the Hookton Slough unit, go straight on Hookton Road. **Humboldt Bay National Wildlife Refuge** (PO Box 576, 1020 Ranch Rd., Loleta, CA 95551; 707-733-5406; fws.gov/humboldtbay).

## Arcata

**Arcata,** 8 miles north of Eureka on the northeast side of Arcata Bay, is the second largest town in Humboldt County with a 2010 population of 17,231. It's the home of **Humboldt State University** and the **Humboldt Crabs** baseball team, a semipro team that's operated since 1945. Arcata is known for its laid-back counterculture scene and progressive politics, including at one point a majority on its city council from the Green Party. Arcata is also known as "Pot City" for its tolerant stance on marijuana. In 2012, however, citizens became fed up with the proliferation of indoor pot farms—one in seven houses is used as a grow house—and the criminal element bringing with it guard dogs, firearms, illegal pesticides, and unsavory visitors. Voters approved a 45 percent utility tax on residents and businesses that used abnormally high amounts of electricity to cut into growers' profits.

Arcata offers a pleasant downtown plaza, the 600-acre **Arcata Community Forest,** and the nearby 213-acre **Lanphere Christensen Dunes Preserve** on the Samoa Peninsula to the southwest. Here, dune plant communities from both the South and North Coasts overlap in a unique transition zone.

## Arcata Marsh & Wildlife Sanctuary

The **Arcata Marsh and Wildlife Sanctuary,** on the north end of the bay and south of Arcata, not only provides 307 acres of habitat for birds and wildlife but is also the site of Arcata's unique wastewater treatment facility. The plant transforms treated wastewater into a wetlands and sanctuary of freshwater marshes, saltwater marshes, tidal mudflats for over 270 bird species and offers 5.4 miles of trails for hikers and bikers. The best place to start is at an interpretative center with educational displays and a bookstore. There are also guided nature walks.

**Finding the refuge:** On the south side of Arcata, take exit 713 onto Samoa Boulevard West. Drive a short distance to G Street and turn left (south) and follow to the visitor center on the west. **Arcata Marsh and Wildlife Sanctuary** (569 S. G St., Arcata, CA 95521; 707-826-2359; arcatamarshfriends.org).

## McKinleyville

From Arcata the scenic highway (US 101) runs north across low farmland, crosses the Mad River, and enters McKinleyville, a town renamed in 1901 for assassinated President William McKinley. McKinleyville, with a 2010 population of 15,177, is the third largest town on the North Coast. The area's industry includes bulb and tree farms, cheese, dairies, and truck farming. The Arcata-Eureka Airport is also here at exit 722 on US 101. A popular stop is the **Six Rivers Brewery,** which offers about a dozen award-winning microbrews.

## Azalea State Natural Reserve

The 30-acre **Azalea State Reserve,** lying east of US 101 north of the Mad River, is spectacular in April and May when the aromatic white and pink-flowered western azaleas *Rhododendron occidentale* bloom on the forest floor. The parkland has restrooms, a picnic area, and a short self-guided nature trail to explore the reserve. It's often foggy in the morning and evening. Winter days can be cool and rainy so bring a raincoat.

**Finding the reserve:** Drive north from McKinleyville and Arcata on US 101. After crossing the Mad River, take exit 718 and go east on North Bank Road for 2 miles. Turn left (north) on Azalea Avenue and park on the left in a lot (GPS: 40.9176 N / -124.079228 W). (707) 488-2041.

## Mad River Beach County Park

This lonesome county park is a long stretch of sand beach sandwiched between the Pacific Ocean and the Mad River, which bends north and runs parallel to the ocean, beach, and dunes before emptying into the Pacific opposite the airport. The mile-long beach offers good walking, horseback riding, bonfires, and is dog-friendly. Harbor seals and sea lions often hang around the river's mouth. The park, open 5 a.m. to midnight, is often windy and foggy.

**Finding the beach:** The park and beach, 5 miles northwest of Arcata, are easily reached from US 101. Take exit 716 on the north side of Arcata and drive west on Guintoli Lane. Following signs to the park, turn right (north) on Heindon Road, then left (west) on Miller Lane, the right (north) on Mad River Road, which leads to the beach parking area (GPS: 40.929726 N / -124.133623 W). **Humboldt County Parks** (707- 445-7651).

# Clam Beach County Park

**Clam Beach,** a Humboldt County Park, is a long stretch of sand and dunes that runs north from the Mad River outlet and the Arcata-Eureka Airport. The beach is a local favorite for walking, horseback riding, camping, fishing, kite flying, and clamming. Clam Beach, named of course for its namesake, is a hot spot to dig California razor clams from offshore beds. The adult clams live in the surf and as far as a half-mile out from the beach, so it's best to come at low tide to dig them for your clam chowder. On low-tide days as many as 250 clammers will be out there elbow to elbow to dig the maximum of 20 clams allowed per person. Clamming season is year-round from a half hour before sunrise to a half-hour after sunset. All clams dug up count toward your day's catch. A fishing license is required.

Clam Beach also has a great ocean-side campground with 18 sites that offer great surf views. The park is dog-friendly, allows beach fires, has minimal facilities, and is free for day use.

**Finding the beach:** The park and beach, 7.5 miles north of Arcata and just north of McKinleyville, are beside US 101. From McKinleyville, drive north on US 101 and look for signed exit 723 just past the airport. Go west at the exit into the park and the parking area (GPS: 40.995075 N / -124.114417 W). **Humboldt County Parks** (707-445-7651).

# Little River State Beach

This state beach is a long sandy beach between Clam Beach County Park and the mouth of the Little River to the north. The 132-acre park includes a wide beach bordered by sand dunes covered with dune grass and brush alongside US 101 between McKinleyville and Trinidad. The day-use park offers walking, surf fishing, and surfing at the quiet beach, and kayaking and fishing in the Little River.

**Finding the beach:** Drive north on US 101 for 13 miles from Eureka or 5 miles south of Trinidad to exit 725. For beach access, go left from the highway onto Clam Beach Drive and park on the east side of the road (GPS: 41.013228 N -124.109089 W). Another parking area is to the south. To access the river part of the park, go north from the exit on Little River road, paralleling US 101 to parking. (707) 488-2041.

# Moonstone Beach County Park

**Moonstone Beach,** lying at the mouth of the Little River south of Trinidad, is a small beautiful beach flanked by rocky cliffs on the north and the long stretch of Little River State Beach south of the river. It's a fun family beach that offers sand strolling, sunbathing (on the occasional sunny day), surfing, fishing, and beachcombing. The Little River is perfect for kayaking and fishing, but it can be swift, cold, and deep in places so use caution.

The beach is popular so parking can be a problem on weekends; be prepared to park and walk to the park. Moonstone is also a great place for bouldering with lots of fun climbing problems on large blocks; across the highway to the east is another good boulder called **Elephant Rock.** In the cliffs north of the beach is a band of fine-grained sandstone filled with fossils of sand dollars, barnacles, clamshells, and mussel shells. The beach is also dog-friendly. Just remember to bring your pooper scooper and plastic bag. **Moonstone Grill** is on the bluff overlooking the beach.

**Finding the beach:** Drive north from Arcata on US 101 and take the Westhaven exit or drive south from Trinidad on Scenic Drive to Moonstone Beach Road. Follow it down to the parking lot (GPS: 41.029331 N / -124.111198 W).

## Luffenholtz Beach County Park

**Luffenholtz Beach,** sheltered by Trinidad Point to the north, is a simply spectacular cove beach with a gleaming stretch of gray sand backed by a steep bluff. Rock stacks, washed by surging waves, stud the water, giving the seascape an eternal quality. Before visiting the beach, take in the view from **Tepona Point** at the south end of the beach. The big rock block topped with grass below is **Tepona Rock.** Beyond stretches the rocky coast to the bulging promontory of Trinidad Point.

The beach is family-friendly with not only great walking but also lots of tide pools to explore. If you venture out at low tide to explore the pools in exposed reefs, pay attention to the incoming tide to avoid getting trapped by rising water. Luffenholtz Creek, dashing over boulders to the sandy shore, divides the beach in half. A small parking area with a stairway down to the beach is above the creek. Some bouldering and climbing routes are found at the south end of the beach.

**Finding the beach:** From Arcata to the south, drive north on US 101 and take exit 726 for Westhaven Drive. Go left across the highway and turn north on Scenic Drive. Follow this narrow winding road for several miles, passing Houda Cove, to Tepona Point (GPS: 41.040019 N / -124.119684 W) and a great overlook. Continue north on the road to a second parking area on the left (GPS: 41.041538 N / -124.119249 W). A long set of stairs descends from the north end of the parking lot to the beach.

# Trinidad

The town of **Trinidad** sits on a flat headland northeast of Trinidad Head, a rocky promontory that juts into the Pacific Ocean. This headland was discovered and christened Trinidad by Spanish explorer Don Bruno Hecata on June 11, 1775, Trinity Sunday. A large pine cross erected on the site marked the territory as a Spanish possession. The wooden cross was replaced by a stone one in 1913. Prior to 1700, a Yurok Indian village called Tsurai was located on today's town site. Trinidad, like Eureka, grew out of the mining boom in the nearby mountains, serving as a supply and whaling port and later as a shipping center for lumber bound for world markets.

Trinidad, with a 2010 population of 367, has a spectacular setting above the wild coastline which offers 10 public beaches, rocky bluffs backed by towering coastal redwood trees, and numerous sea stacks swept by offshore waves. The town, a state historic landmark, makes a great stop for walking its quiet streets, hiking out to **Trinidad Head,** and visiting **Trinidad Museum, Trinidad Memorial Lighthouse, Trinidad Head Lighthouse,** and the site of the old Yurok village **Tsurai.** Anglers enjoy fishing from the 500-foot-long **Trinidad Pier,** catching salmon and cod.

The town offers all visitor services, including hotels, bed-and-breakfast inns, and restaurants. A good stop is at the **Moonstone Crossing Winery** (707-677-3832) at 529 Trinity St. where you can savor fine local varietal wines in a small welcoming tasting room; especially fun after a day of hiking and beachcombing. For restaurants, try the **Lighthouse Grill** with its great veggie burgers, Beachcomber Cafe, and **Larrupin Cafe.**

**Trinidad Museum** preserves and interprets the natural history and human heritage of California's Redwood Coast in an 1899 Victorian cottage. The museum displays collections of local Native American art and artifacts, photographs, paintings, and a native plant garden. 400 Janis Ct., Trinidad, CA 95570; (707) 677-3883; moonstonecrossing.com.

The **Trinidad Memorial Lighthouse** is a 25-foot-high replica of the nearby original lighthouse on Trinidad Head. The building, overlooking Trinidad Bay, was built by the Trinidad Civic Club in 1949 as a memorial to sailors lost at sea. It houses a lens from the "real" lighthouse as well as its 1898 fog bell. **Finding the lighthouse:** From US 101 in Trinidad, take exit 728 and drive west on Main Street to Trinity Street. Turn left on Trinity and drive until it ends at Edwards Street. Park in a small lot above the lighthouse (GPS: 41.058393 N / -124.143483 W). A short trail leads to the site.

**Tsurai** or Tsurau, meaning "mountain," was the aboriginal Yurok settlement at Trinidad. A large stone marker with a bronze plaque, at the junction of

Edwards Street and Ocean Avenue just east of Trinidad Head Lighthouse, commemorates the village. The **Cher-Ae Heights Indian Community** of Trinidad Rancheria, a recognized Native American tribe of the Chetco, Hupa, Karuk, Tolowa, Wiyot, and Yurok peoples, is an 80-acre reservation along the coast just south of Trinidad. Famed for exquisite basketry, the community operates the **Cher-Ae Heights Casino** off Scenic Drive.

**Finding the town:** Trinidad, lying 15 miles north of Arcata, is just west of exit 728 off US 101 about 15 miles north of Arcata. **Greater Trinidad Chamber of Commerce** (PO Box 356, Trinidad, CA 95570; 707-677-1610).

## Trinidad Head

**Trinidad Head** is a cliff-lined promontory that juts into the Pacific Ocean immediately southwest of Trinidad. A low narrow sand spit connects the head to the mainland. Trinidad Head is composed of hard, erosion-resistant gabbro, an igneous rock that was later metamorphosed. A layer of Pleistocene age gravels sits atop the bedrock.

The fine 1.2-mile, open-loop **Trinidad Head Trail** gaining 350 feet, explores the promontory, passing through thick forests with scenic ocean views to **Patrick's Point,** including **Flatiron Rock** and **Pewetole Island.** Look for sea lions on the rocks below and migrating whales offshore. On the summit are benches and a cross labeled 1775 that commemorates the area's discovery by Spanish sailors.

**Finding Trinidad Head:** From US 101 in Trinidad, take exit 728 and drive west on Main Street to Trinity Street. Turn left on Trinity and drive until it ends at Edwards Street. Go left (west) on Edwards and drive to a T-junction. Go left on Lighthouse Road and drive down to a couple parking areas (GPS: 41.057014 N / -124.147941W). This is also the parking for the south end of Trinidad State Beach. The trailhead is on the south side of the parking lot.

## Trinidad Head Lighthouse

**Trinidad Head Lighthouse,** on the National Register of Historic Places, overlooks Trinidad Bay from the southern edge of a 196-foot-high cliff that plunges into the ocean on the south side of Trinidad Head. The compact 25-foot-high lighthouse, built in 1871, warned lumber ships of rocky disaster with its light and 4,000-pound fog bell. The light station, owned and operated by the US Coast Guard, was automated in 1974. The active lighthouse is closed to the public.

*The Trinidad Memorial Lighthouse, a replica of an earlier lighthouse, overlooks sunny Trinidad Bay.*

*Trinidad Head is a low wooded promontory that juts into the Pacific Ocean on the town of Trinidad's west side.*

Interestingly, the lighthouse, despite being high above the ocean, was swamped by a towering 200-foot wave, one of the largest ever recorded in California, during a fierce storm on December 31, 1914. The lighthouse keeper F. L. Harrington wrote, "At 4:40 p.m., I was in the tower and had just set the lens in operation and turned to wipe the lantern room windows when I observed a sea of unusual height . . . approaching. I watched it as it came in. When it struck the bluff . . . the sea shot up to the face of the bluff and over it, until the solid sea seemed to me to be on a level with where I stood in the lantern. Then it commenced to recede and the spray went 25 feet or more higher. The sea itself fell over onto the top of the bluff and struck the tower on about a level with the balcony, making a terrible jar. The whole point between the tower and the bluff was buried in water. The lens immediately stopped revolving and the tower was shivering from the impact for several seconds."

**Finding the lighthouse:** From US 101 in Trinidad, take exit 728 and drive west on Main Street to Trinity Street. Turn left on Trinity and drive until it ends at Edwards Street. Go left (west) on Edwards and drive to a T-junction. Go left on Lighthouse Road and drive down to a couple parking areas (GPS: 41.057014 N / -124.147941W).

# Trinidad State Beach

This sweep of beach, backed by a high bluff and divided by a small promontory, is simply one of northern California's most beautiful beaches. The rocky prominence of **Elk Head** and **Megwil Point** hems in the northern end of the park. Numerous offshore sea stacks and rocks, including rocky **Pewetole Island** with a forest-fringed cap, dot the coast. Bulky Trinidad Head marks the southern end of the beach.

**Trinidad Beach,** the southern section, is a wide gray-sand beach below the town. It's easily accessed from a large parking area on the isthmus between the mainland and Trinidad Head. It's a perfect spot for walking, tide pool exploring, surf fishing, and watching the waves. Swimming is, of course, not recommended because of cold water and rip currents.

The northern section of the state beach is **College Cove,** a gorgeous crescent-shaped cove and beach flanked by rocky outcrops. The sheltered beach, reached by a trail that drops 120 feet, offers colorful tide pools, beachcombing, driftwood, walking, and romantic sunsets. Look for a small arch in rock on the south end.

Several trails explore the bluff above the beach. The best leaves the parking lot and treads northwest through spruce forest to Elk Head and **Omenoku View-point,** which looks south to **Trinidad Head.** Below the overlook is a blowhole in the rocks. At the parking area and trailhead are restrooms and a small picnic area. It's best to visit the beach at low tide. Check tide tables beforehand and keep an eye on the rising tide. It comes in quickly here and can trap hikers on the rocks.

**Finding the beach:** From US 101, take exit 728 and drive west into Trinidad on Main Street. Turn right (north) on Stagecoach Road after 0.2 mile and drive 0.5 mile north to the parking area (GPS: 41.068521 N / -124.149351 W) on the left. (707) 677-3570.

# Patrick's Point State Park

Patrick's Point is a spectacular headland that juts into the Pacific Ocean north of Trinidad. The 640-acre **Patrick's Point State Park** is covered with grassy meadows sprinkled with spring wildflowers and a fringe of forest that includes Sitka spruce, Port Orford cedar, red alder, and hemlock. Sand beaches, abrupt cliffs, and promontories chiseled by the relentless Pacific surf compose the park's landscape.

The area's rich game, vegetation, and sea life attracted the indigenous Yurok Indians, who lived here seasonally. They ate sea lions as well as plentiful mussels, leaving huge shell middens or heaps of shells at their ancient campsites. To learn more about these Native Americans, visit **Sumêg** (meaning "forever"), a reconstructed Yurok village with traditional houses, sweat house and dance house, along with a native garden with plants used for medicine, food, and baskets.

**Agate Beach,** a long gray-sand beach below a tall bluff, extends north from Patrick's Point to Big Lagoon. The beach is perfect for walking. A good hike goes north 3 miles from Agate Point to Big Lagoon Spit. Look for shiny scraps of jade and agate on the beach.

The park is one of the best whale-watching spots on the Redwood Coast. The gray whales follow a 12,000-mile, 8-month migration from Arctic feeding grounds to winter calving lagoons off Baja California. November to January and March through May are the best times for whale-watching from **Patrick's Point, Wedding Rock,** and **Palmer's Point.** Binoculars are helpful in spotting the whales.

Six miles of hiking trails lace the promontory. Two-mile **Rim Trail,** following an old Yurok path from Agate Beach to Palmer's Point, is one of the best with coastal views and wildlife including sea lions, seals, and birds. The **Octopus Tree Trail** threads through an ancient grove of Sitka spruce. **Ceremonial Rock,** an ancient sea stack isolated on land, is another interesting spot reached by the **Ceremonial Rock Trail.** Ceremonial Rock is also one of the best rock climbing sites in the park. Other climbing venues are **Pacific Ocean Cliff, Mussel Rock,** and **Wedding Rock.**

The park has a visitor center, interpretative programs and walks, and a Junior Ranger program. Three excellent campgrounds—**Agate Beach, Abalone,** and **Penn Creek**—provide 124 sites with water, restrooms, and showers. Reserve campsites by calling (800) 444-7275 or visiting reserveamerica.com.

**Finding the park:** The park is 25 miles north of Eureka and 57 miles south of Crescent City. From US 101, take exit 734 and go west on Patrick Point Drive a short distance. Turn right (west) into the park and drive to the park entrance and visitor center. (GPS: 41.13519 N / -124.154686 W). The road continues to campgrounds, overlooks, and trails. (707) 677-3570.

## Big Lagoon County Park

**Big Lagoon,** a Humboldt County Park, is 7 miles north of Trinidad and just north of Patrick's Point State Park. The park anchors the southern side of **Big Lagoon,** a triangular-shaped lagoon separated from the ocean by a long thin sand spit. The placid lagoon is perfect for sailing, boardsailing, stand-up paddling, kayaking, and boating as well as fishing and wildlife study. Kayak rentals are at the boat ramp during the summer. It's also great for swimming in the warm shallow water while the surf pounds the sand spit. There's a 25-site campground among Sitka spruce with some sites next to the lagoon. You can also walk on the sand beach; looking for agates, jade, moonstones, shells, and wave-polished driftwood.

**Finding the park:** The park is 7 miles north of Trinidad. From US 101, turn west on Big Lagoon Park Road, then, following signs, go left on Lynda Road then right on Big Lagoon Park Road and drive to a parking area (GPS: 41.163622 N / -124.131096 W) by the boat ramp.

# Humboldt Lagoons State Park

Past Patrick's Point State Park, the Redwood Highway (US 101) curves around four lagoons—**Big, Dry, Stone, and Freshwater Lagoons**—along the coast. This 8-mile-long quartet of shallow bays, part of the largest lagoon system in the US, forms 2,256-acre **Humboldt Lagoons State Park,** a large area of open water, salt and freshwater marshes, and dense woods that shelter numerous migrating birds on the **Pacific Flyway** including ducks, herons, egrets, and pelicans. Long sand spits front the ocean on the west, separating the lagoons from the Pacific, and densely forested mountains rise steeply over the wetlands. Trees found here include coast redwoods, Sitka spruce, western hemlock, and Douglas fir. The park offers swimming, boating, kayaking, camping, and fishing for trout, salmon, and steelhead, as well as picnicking and walking along the mostly deserted strand. The **California Coastal Trail** follows the coast through the park.

The lagoons are part of the ancestral homeland of the Yurok tribe, California's largest Native American group with over 5,500 members, who live mostly in Del Norte and Humboldt Counties. The Yurok once inhabited both permanent and seasonal villages here, finding plentiful game, fish, and edible plants.

**Big Lagoon,** the farthest south and largest bay, is only partially within the state park, with the rest protected in **Big Lagoon County Park** with a campground and **Harry A. Merlo State Recreation Area** (707-677-3570). The lagoon offers boating, fishing, and windsurfing.

**Dry Lagoon** is exactly that—a mostly dry and swampy wetland filled with reeds and tall grass. This small lagoon was drained by farmers in the 1900s. A walk-in campground with 6 sites and small picnic area are at the south end of the lagoon.

**Stone Lagoon,** with lots of recreational opportunities, is bordered on the east by US 101 and steep forest-clad slopes. A high hill and sand spit form the western edge of the lagoon. Near the south end of the lake next to the highway is the park visitor center, with exhibits, a museum, and bookstore housed in an old motel and restaurant (GPS: 41.163622 N / -124.131096 W). The lagoon offers kayaking, fishing, and scenic views. **Stone Lagoon Boat-In Campground,** accessible by canoe or kayak, offers 6 primitive sites that overlook Ryan's Cove on the west side of the lagoon.

**Freshwater Lagoon,** located in both **Redwood National Park** and the state park, is a gorgeous aqua lake nestled between the highway and sandy strand on the west and high forested hills on the east. **Freshwater Beach** on the west side of the lagoon is in Redwood National Park. This long, popular beach, beginning at Freshwater Rocks on the south, is easy to access and often busy on weekends. You can park along the west side of the highway above the beach or plop down a lounge chair by your vehicle and wave watch.

Just north of Freshwater Lagoon is Redwood National Park's **Thomas H. Kuchel Visitor Center** (707-465-7765) off the scenic drive (GPS: 41.163622 N / -124.131096 W). The center, offering exhibits, patio talks, nature walks, a Junior Ranger program, bookstore, and lots of information, makes a great stop to learn more about the Redwood Coast. Next to the center is **Redwood Creek Beach County Park,** which includes a sand beach that runs north to Redwood Creek.

**Finding the park:** The park is 13 miles north of Trinidad, 40 miles north of Eureka, and 55 miles south of Crescent City. Access all park areas from US 101. (707) 677-3570.

## Redwood National Park

At the northern end of Freshwater Lagoon, scenic US 101 bends inland along Redwood Creek. Here among the sand dunes is the **Thomas H. Kuchel Visitor Center** (707-465-7765), the southern gateway to **Redwood National Park** and a good stop for information on camping and hiking, and to view exhibits detailing the park's unusual natural history, coastline, and human history. The park is a unique 131,983-acre national and state parkland jointly managed by the National Park Service and California State Parks to protect the best redwood groves in the world, including 38,982 acres of old-growth redwoods or 45 percent of the remaining old-growth forest.

The park scatters along the coast from here to Crescent City like a string of woody pearls. East of US 101 stretches the **Redwood Creek** section with its tall trees, while to the north are **Prairie Creek Redwoods State Park, Del Norte Coast Redwoods State Park,** and **Jedediah Smith Redwoods State Park.**

Logging over the last 150 years decimated 85 percent of California's old-growth coast redwoods, leaving huge stumps where massive giants once stood. Redwood National Park, incorporating the state parks, preserves some of the best remaining redwood forest, including the world's tallest living thing. The park was declared a World Heritage Site for its unique forests in 1982. **Redwood Information Center,** the national park visitor center, is a good place to stop for information on camping and hiking, and to view exhibits detailing the park's unusual natural history, coastline, and human history.

For more information, contact **Redwood National and State Parks** (1111 2nd St., Crescent City, CA 95531; 707-464-6101; nps.gov/redw).

# Orick

Past the Kuchel Visitor Center, the road enters **Orick.** This small town nestles in a broad pastoral valley flanked by redwood-studded mountains. Dairy farms and small ranches scatter alongside the scenic Redwood Highway. The Yuroks inhabited the area seasonally, and the town's name is derived from their word *Ore'q* meaning "mouth of the river." The town offers all services to travelers including gas, lodging, restaurants, and RV parks.

## Lady Bird Johnson Grove & Tall Trees Trail

The Lady Bird Johnson Grove, named for the former first lady and wife of President Lyndon B. Johnson, and the Tall Trees Trail in Redwood National Park are accessed from the **Bald Hills Road,** which goes east from the highway just north of Orick. This narrow 17-mile road (mileage to Lyons Ranch Trail), with grades as steep as 15 percent, twists into the Bald Hills above Redwood Creek to the heart of some of the world's tallest redwood trees. The first 13 miles of the road are paved, while the last 4 are dirt. Allow 45 minutes to drive to the end of the road and the Lyons Ranch Trailhead. Motor homes and trailers are not advised.

The Bald Hills Road passes through ancient redwood groves as well as open meadows filled with spring wildflowers and herds of Roosevelt elk. A good stop is **Redwood Creek Overlook** with spectacular views of the valley below and the blue ocean beyond. The road passes by the trailheads for **Dolason Prairie Trail** and **Lyons Ranch Trail. Schoolhouse Peak,** the park's 3,097-foot-high point, rises above Lyons Ranch.

The **Lady Bird Johnson Grove,** one of the park's most popular sites to view old-growth redwoods, lies atop a high rounded ridge at an elevation of 1,200 feet. The grove is accessed by a 1.4-mile, lollipop-loop trail that is wide, has gentle grades, and is sometimes very busy since it is the easiest place in the park to see big redwoods. It's usually hiked in a clockwise direction. **Finding the trail:** From US 101, drive 2.5 miles up a steep hill to a parking area on the right (GPS: 41.303347 N / -124.018124 W). Cross a pedestrian bridge over the road to the trailhead.

The **Tall Trees Trail** is a spectacular hike around some of the world's tallest trees, including the skyscraping **Howard A. Libbey Tree,** a spire-like redwood that towers 367.8 feet above its massive base. Discovered by *National Geographic* naturalist Paul Zahl in 1964, it was thought to be the tallest in the world until Hyperion was discovered in 2011 to be 11 feet taller. The tree, along with other 300-footers, grows on a moist gravel bench above a Redwood Creek meander. The discovery of the tree on privately owned timberland helped ensure the establishment of the national park in 1968. Prior to that, environmental organizations, including the Save-the-Redwoods League and Sierra Club, had urged the

# What is the Tallest Tree in the World?

The coast redwoods of California are the tallest trees in the world, growing in remote areas on moist gravel benches along creeks and rivers where they were saved from logging by isolation. Beginning in 1964 when a *National Geographic* team identified the almost 368-foot Howard A. Libbey Tree as the world's tallest, the discovery of other tall trees has slowly pushed the record higher. There are 8 known redwoods that are taller than 370 feet high, all of them in northern California.

The current tallest tree in the world is called Hyperion, a massive redwood that reaches 379.46 feet into the fog-filled sky of Redwood National Park. To save the tree as well as its other giant relatives, the location of Hyperion is undisclosed by the National Park Service to protect its fragile environment from human damage.

Naturalists Chris Atkins and Michael Taylor discovered the 800-year-old tree on August 25, 2006, and returned later with tree expert Steve Sillet from Humboldt State University. Sillet measured the tree from top to bottom by using a crossbow to shoot a line over a branch 250 up, then pulled and fixed a rope by which he ascended into the tree's canopy. From the top he dropped a measuring tape to the ground.

The tallest living tree that's been verifiably measured was a 414-foot Douglas fir in the Lynn Valley in British Columbia in the late 19th century.

protection of California's remaining big trees, but much of the land that was purchased for the park had already been clear-cut and in dire need of rehabilitation.

To hike to the **Tall Trees Grove,** steeply descend a trail through small redwoods to a loop through the grove. There are 2 trails to access the grove. The long way is to follow the **Dolason Prairie Trail** to the Tall Trees Trail. The best way is to obtain a free permit from **Kuchel Visitor Center,** which allows you to drive down the narrow, dirt, 6-mile-long C-Line Road to the trailhead. The trail descends 1.4 miles and 700 feet to the grove, then follows a loop for 0.9 miles before climbing the 1.4 miles back to the parking lot.

**Finding the trail:** Drive a mile east from Orick on US 101 and turn east on Bald Hills Road. Drive 7 miles and turn right to a locked gate. Use the lock combination obtained with the permit and follow the dirt road down for 6 miles to a parking lot and the trailhead (GPS: 41.208126 N / -123.993113 W).

*Hikers can mosey through a magical forest of towering redwoods at the Lady Bird Johnson Grove in Redwood National Park.*

# Trillium Falls Trail

The 2.8-mile **Trillium Falls Trail** is, besides the Lady Bird Johnson Grove Trail, one of the best easy hikes to see undisturbed old-growth redwood trees in Redwood National Park. The loop trail reaches a small falls after 0.3 mile, the turnaround point for many visitors. It's an idyllic spot with ferns, moss-covered boulders, and the brilliant white flowers of western trillium in spring. The trail continues deep into the silent forest, with the muted sounds of distant highway traffic and the wind in the treetops.

    **Finding the trailhead:** At Elk Meadow Day-Use Area about 1.5 miles north of Orick, turn west from US 101 on Davison Road and drive a short distance to a left to the trailhead and parking lot (GPS: 41.32305 N / -124.045392 W).

# Prairie Creek Redwoods State Park

The scenic drive, following US 101, runs north along Prairie Creek from Orick and quickly reaches **Prairie Creek Redwoods State Park,** a spectacular 14,000-acre sanctuary of pristine redwood forests between the highway and the shoreline. The state park is popular with its diversity of scenery, including old-growth redwood groves, open meadows, a fern-walled canyon, waterfalls, a long stretch of sandy beach, wildlife, over 75 miles of hiking trails, and 2 campgrounds. **Illuvatar,** the third largest redwood with a 20.5-foot diameter and 320-foot height, is in the park's **Atlas Grove,** an unpublished area to protect the fragile forest. It took 5 climbers 20 days to carefully measure the giant tree after its 1991 discovery.

    If you can't linger at the park, take the 8-mile-long **Newton B. Drury Scenic Parkway,** a bypass west of US 101 that wends through the park, passing silent redwood groves that reach skyward. A 4-lane, 12-mile-long stretch of US 101 skirts the eastern boundary of the park for those in a hurry.

    The park's main developed area is just north on the parkway from its southern junction with US 101. The park visitor center (GPS: 41.363912 N / -124.022904 W), with exhibits, maps, and a bookstore, is a good stop to get acquainted with the area's unique natural history. Alongside Prairie Creek are 76-site **Elk Prairie Campground** and a campfire circle. Numerous trails, including 4.3-mile **Prairie Creek,** 6.8-mile **West Ridge,** 4.5-mile **James Irvine,** and 2.8-mile **Davison,** begin by the visitor center and campground. The main attraction on the parkway here is **Elk Prairie,** a broad meadow often filled with grazing Roosevelt elk. Park on the road to view the elk.

    The parkway follows Prairie Creek north from the visitor center, passing several trailheads and redwood groves. The towering trees at times border the asphalt, blocking the sky and forming a wooden wall. **Big Tree Wayside** offers

*Roosevelt elk, the largest subspecies of North American elk, are often seen grazing at Elk Prairie.*

exactly that—the solitary **Big Tree,** a huge redwood. The **Cathedral Trees Trail** also starts here, winding 1.4 miles through a magical Ewok forest. Farther north is 7.8-mile **Rhododendron Trail** at parkway mile marker 130.54; expect spectacular flower displays in May and June. The short 0.3-mile **Ah-Pah Interpretative Trail** is a good kid hike that explains the rejuvenation of logged land at mile marker 133.50.

The park features several dirt side roads that make good excursions. **Cal Barrel Road,** beginning off the Drury Parkway, runs 3 miles through a mature redwood forest. The spectacular **Coastal Drive** turns west at the north end of the park and runs through redwoods to an unimpeded view of **Gold Bluffs Beach** and the Pacific Ocean, before turning north to US 101 on the south side of the Klamath River. **Davison Road** is a favorite back roads drive; it begins 3 miles south of the park boundary and uncoils 4 miles through second-growth forest to **Gold Bluffs Beach.** The dirt road then runs north below the bluff alongside the crashing Pacific surf for another 4 miles to the secluded trailhead for **Fern Canyon.**

Near the park's 75-site **Elk Prairie Campground,** nestled among redwoods 6 miles north of Orick, is its "prairie," a large open meadow. Elk Prairie and Gold

Bluffs Beach are home to the park's two herds of endangered **Roosevelt elk.** These elk, members of the deer family, are larger than their Rocky Mountain cousins. An adult Roosevelt bull weighs 1,000 pounds and boasts a spectacular rack of antlers 3 feet high. Remember that, despite their docile appearance, these are wild animals and particularly aggressive during the fall rut. A long pull-off lane on the road shoulder near the visitor center allows visitors to safely pull off the highway and view grazing elk. Other animals found in the redwood forest include black bear, rabbit, squirrel, mountain lion, bobcat, coyote, and fox. More than 250 species of birds have been identified in the park's wide variety of habitats. Notable birds are the spotted owl and marbled murrelet, both dependent on old-growth forests.

**Finding the park:** Prairie Creek Redwoods State Park is 50 miles north of Eureka and 25 miles south of Crescent City along US 101. All park features are easily reached from US 101 and Newton B. Drury Scenic Parkway. The park visitor center is just north of the southern junction of US 101 and the parkway. **Prairie Creek Redwoods State Park** (127011 Newton B. Drury Pkwy., Orick, CA 95555; 707-465-7335; parks.ca.gov).

# Fern Canyon

Fern Canyon in Prairie Creek Redwoods State Park is simply one of the most beautiful spots imaginable on the California coast. **Fern Canyon** is reached by dirt Davison Road, which edges north alongside long Gold Bluffs Beach to a remote parking lot. An easy 0.5-mile loop trail leaves the parking area, crisscrosses Home Creek, and enters Fern Canyon, a 50-foot-deep gorge etched into soft layers of sandstone. Above the pebbled canyon floor, 5 fern species—deer, lady, sword, chain, and five-finger ferns—blanket the walls with a hanging verdant garden. Silence reigns in this green fern kingdom, broken only by occasional birdsongs, wind rippling through the lofty treetops, and the distant roar of waves breaking on the strand. Coast redwoods, Sitka spruce, and Douglas fir loom above the canyon, blocking sunlight on rare clear days. The excellent primitive 26-site **Gold Bluffs Beach Campground** sits on the dunes a couple of miles south of Fern Canyon.

**Finding Fern Canyon:** At Elk Meadow Day-Use Area about 1.5 miles north of Orick, turn west from US 101 on Davison Road. Follow the unpaved road for 7 miles to the Fern Canyon Trailhead (GPS: 41.400638 N / -124.065768 W).

*Five fern species cover the vertical cliffs of Fern Canyon, one of the most beautiful spots on the Redwood Coast.*

# The Redwood Forest

Stop along the scenic drive in either Prairie Creek Redwoods or Del Norte Coast Redwoods State Parks and hike into the towering coast redwood forest. It's an unforgettable experience. Standing among the silent giant trees is to find yourself in the forest primeval and among what seem to be serene living gods. The redwood trees soar overhead, caring nothing for

*Dense fog envelops towering redwood trees lining US 101 in Del Norte Coast Redwoods State Park.*

their great antiquity and offering a calm aloofness in relation to our own scattered lives.

The oldest trees have witnessed as many as 50 human generations that have come and gone. No wonder that author John Steinbeck called redwoods "ambassadors from another time." The redwoods do, indeed, come from a distant time in the past when their ancestors grew in ancient forests during the Jurassic era some 160 million years ago.

These impressive trees, the tallest in the world, soar over 370 feet tall, weigh more than 2 million pounds, live as long as 2,000 years, and supply enough wood to build several houses. Yet these forest titans grow from seeds hardly larger than a pinhead; the seeds come from a cone that is smaller than most western evergreens produce, less than an inch long.

The coast redwood once spread over much of the Northern Hemisphere, growing in diverse locales including Alaska, Siberia, Greenland, Europe, and North Dakota. Subsequent changes in climate and topography reduced those great redwood forests to their present small range on California's foggy coast. Their closest relatives are the giant sequoia atop the crest of the Sierra Nevada and the rare dawn redwood found only in a secluded Chinese valley and a transplanted stand in Jedediah Smith Redwoods State Park. Today only 118,000 acres of old-growth redwoods remain, far less than the 2 million acres in 1850, and 95 percent of them are in California.

## High Bluff Beach

**High Bluff Beach,** a hidden scenic gem on the Redwood Coast, is a long stretch of narrow sand backed by a rocky bluff on the ragged coast south of the Klamath River. The beach has a remote wilderness feel and you will probably not see anyone else here except on the occasional nice weekend day. Visit the beach only at low tide since the tide quickly rises and could trap you on the rocks above surging surf; check tide tables before going.

To reach the beach from the parking area and a small picnic ground with tables (no restrooms) on the bluff top, hike north above the bluff along the edge of the forest on a trail for about a half-mile. Descend switchbacks to the southern end of the beach. Walk north on the brown sand strand to a choke of large boulders (climbers, check them out!). Scramble around them on the right to reach the wider northern section of beach.

**Finding the beach:** From US 101 at the Klamath River, turn west on County Road D7 and follow it along the Klamath River to Alder Camp Road. Turn left and follow it to Coastal Drive. Turn right and drive a short distance to a left turn onto a dirt road (GPS: 41.510373 N / -124.076092 W). Drive to High Bluffs Picnic Area and a parking lot (GPS: W 41.510321 N / -124.079177 W) above the shore. Follow a trail north above cliffs, then scramble down steep slopes to the rocky southern end of the beach.

## Klamath

The Redwood Highway (US 101) descends from Prairie Creek Redwoods State Park and crosses the mouth of the 263-mile-long **Klamath River,** California's second largest river. The Klamath is famed for its huge runs of chinook salmon and steelhead that migrate upriver in autumn to spawn and die.

The town of **Klamath** (population 779 in 2010), lies on the river's north shore on the east side of the highway. Klamath's original town site was erased by a 90-foot-deep flood on the terrifying night of December 22, 1964, when the river rose to unprecedented levels after weeks of heavy rain and snow saturated the coastal ranges. Klamath is a popular stop for anglers and offers all services; be sure to sample its famous smoked salmon jerky. Over 1,000 camp and RV sites are found by the town, making it a popular vacation destination. Besides hiking and beachcombing, you can take a jet boat ride up the river or angle for salmon and steelhead with a local fishing guide. The town lies within the 84-square-mile **Yoruk Indian Reservation;** the Yuroks, with almost 5,000 members, are California's largest tribe.

*Rows of winter waves roll onto Gold Bluffs Beach at sunset in Prairie Creek Redwoods State Park.*

Just south of Klamath is the famous **Tour-Thru Tree,** a redwood you can drive your car through. North of town on US 101 is the **Trees of Mystery,** a hokey tourist attraction made famous by Ripley's Believe It Or Not! Farther north is **Requa,** a small town that was once a thriving mining and lumber camp and earlier a Yurok village. A county road runs west from the scenic drive through Requa to **Klamath River Overlook** with a great view of the mighty river emptying into the ocean.

For more information, contact **Klamath Chamber of Commerce** (800-200-2335).

## Tour-Thru Tree

If you're driving up the Redwood Highway and decide you need a photo op, then stop at the **Tour-Thru Tree** on the south side of Klamath and drive your car through a huge living redwood tree. The almost 800-year-old Tour-Thru Tree, not to be confused with the Chandelier Drive-Thru Tree in Leggett, features a 7-foot 4-inch-wide by 9-foot 6-inch-high opening, allowing passage for standard-size cars, vans, and trucks, which was chiseled through the 15-foot diameter trunk in 1976. Driving through this tree or California's other two drive-through trees

*A giant Paul Bunyan and his Babe the Blue Ox sidekick greet visitors to the kitschy Trees of Mystery.*

is one of those rite-of-passage tourist moments that you'll remember far longer than the 2 minutes it takes to squeeze through the keyhole. Don't forget to take a snapshot of your car in it! The privately owned attraction costs 5 bucks for a car of 4 people, although if you park and walk it costs nothing. Vehicles towing trailers and motor homes are not allowed beyond the parking lot by the toll station.

**Finding the tree:** Just south of Klamath on 4-lane US 101, take the Terwer Valley exit and go east on Klamath Glen Road (CA 169). Drive 0.25 mile and make a left turn at a small sign (GPS: 41.521911 N / -124.032045 W) to the tree entrance station left of house (430 Hwy. 169); this is across the road from an emu farm. (707) 482-5971.

## Trees of Mystery

If you're tired of seeing redwood groves in the national park, then consider a family stop at the **Trees of Mystery,** a forest of roadside Americana kitsch north of Klamath. The Trees of Mystery features redwood trees including the **Cathedral Tree** with 6 trunks growing from a single root (many weddings take place here), a hollow redwood trunk, the **Candelabra Tree** with trunks growing from a fallen tree, as well as a gondola ride through the forest to a high lookout. Visitors also like to gawk and have their photo taken below a 49-foot-high replica of famed axman Paul Bunyan and his 35-foot-high sidekick Babe the Blue Ox. Bunyan, wearing 10-foot-high boots, wields a 24-foot-long ax. The original Bunyan statue, erected in 1946, lasted only a year until his papier-mâché head melted.

**Finding the attraction:** Trees of Mystery is 16 miles south of Crescent City or a couple miles north of Klamath on US 101. Park in a large lot on the east side of the highway (GPS: 41.584626 N / -124.086295 W). (707) 482-2251.

## Klamath River Overlook

The **Klamath River Overlook** is a scenic viewpoint that's perches 650 feet above the confluence of the broad Klamath River and the Pacific Ocean northwest of the town of Klamath. The views south from the viewpoint on a clear day are spectacular—below the freshwater river, after journeying 263 miles from its headwaters, empties into the Pacific; a wide sand spit anchors the southern end of the river's estuary; and beyond stretches the rugged coastal hills dropping into sand and surf.

This is a great spot for bird watching, with many of Del Norte County's 422 species seen, including bald eagles, ospreys, kestrels, loons, grebes, common murre, and hummingbirds. The overlook is also one of the best accessible places on the Redwood Coast to watch migrating Pacific gray whales as well as seals and sea lions in the estuary. A trail from the overlook drops a quarter-mile down to a lower viewpoint and more great views. From there you can continue another quarter mile to **Hidden Beach.** Bring binoculars and warm clothes, it is usually cool and breezy here.

The overlook is reached on paved Requa Road, a steep, narrow road that edges across slopes above the river. Motor homes and trailers are discouraged. The road passes the **Historic Requa Inn** (707-482-1245), a white 2-story hotel that is now a classy bed-and-breakfast inn.

**Finding the overlook:** Drive north on US 101 from Klamath for 2.3 miles or south from Crescent City for 18 miles. Exit onto Requa Road and drive west on the winding road for 2.3 miles to the overlook and parking area on the left (GPS: 41.554409 N / -124.086515 W).

*The lofty view from Klamath River Overlook includes the Klamath River estuary, a long sand spit, and fog-shrouded mountains.*

# Wilson Creek Beach

This beach, tucked into crescent-shaped False Klamath Cove at the south end of **Del Norte Coast Redwoods State Park,** is a half-mile-long sand and stone strand that stretches north from a rocky point to a narrow rocky section to a wide sand beach where Wilson Creek empties into the ocean. **Wilson Creek Beach** is perhaps the most accessible beach in Del Norte County.

The best sectors of the beach are the wide southern part by a creek and the northern sector where Wilson Creek passes under a highway bridge. Wave-washed pieces of driftwood scatter along the high tide line, making great seats for sunset views. There are also good sand strolling and tide pools at low tide. Farther north the beach becomes stonier. Swimming is greatly discouraged because of the steep beach slope, rocks, rough water and big waves, and cold conditions. Several pullouts along US 101, which runs alongside the beach, allow quick access. Facilities include restrooms, picnic tables, and firepits.

**Finding the beach:** Drive 5.5 miles north from Klamath on US 101 to the beach. Parking is at a spacious lot at the southern end on the west side of the highway (GPS: 41.596546 N / -124.101195 W). This lot is best accessed only from the southbound lane of US 101. Access the northern lot by turning west from the highway just before a big bridge over Wilson Creek. Park at a large lot (GPS: 41.603295 N / -124.100575 W).

# Del Norte Coast Redwoods State Park

Scenic highway US 101 continues north from Klamath and after a few more miles reemerges on the coast at False Klamath Cove and Wilson Creek Beach. It then enters 31,261-acre **Del Norte Coast Redwoods State Park,** another division of **Redwood National Park,** with 50 percent old-growth redwood forest and 8 miles of wild Pacific shoreline. Most of the rugged coast is inaccessible with high cliffs and a range of mountains paralleling the shoreline. The highway section through the park is lined with immense redwoods, butting against the asphalt like towering wooden pillars.

An excellent hike runs 5 miles round-trip along **Damnation Creek Trail,** an old Yurok Indian path that travels from the highway to the seashore, losing 1,000 feet along the way. Splendid old redwoods loom over the trail, their spire-like tops hidden by swirling mist. A lush undergrowth of sword ferns and rhododendrons, some as tall as 30 feet, carpet the forest floor. The trail follows an old roadbed of the Redwood Highway that was abandoned in 1935. The hike ends at an overlook above **Damnation Cove,** which offers good tide pools to explore. The hike back is strenuous. **Finding the trailhead:** Drive 8 miles south from Crescent City on US

101 to a signed parking area and trailhead on the west side of the highway at mile marker 16.

The park's 129-site **Mill Creek Campground,** in second-growth redwood forest logged in the 1920s, sits a couple miles east of the drive along Mill Creek about 7 miles south of Crescent City. The campground is open May 1 to September 7; showers, restrooms, tables, and food lockers are available. Call (800) 444-7275 or visit reserveamerica.com for reservations.

**Finding the park:** The state park is south of Crescent City by the park entrance to Wilson Creek Beach on the south. The most developed park area is at Mill Creek Campground 7 miles south of Crescent City. (707) 465-7335.

## Enderts Beach

**Enderts Beach** is a small beautiful beach that offers lots of privacy, although it can occasionally be busy on summer weekends. The beach tucks between a couple rocky points. The quarter-mile-long beach is great for a solitary stroll, watching the waves roll in, or exploring tide pools at low tide.

**Finding the beach:** From Crescent City, drive south 3 miles and turn right on Enderts Beach Road. Follow it along the coast to a parking area (GPS: 41.70025 N / -124.140296 W) with picnic tables, restrooms, and an overlook. To access the beach, descend a steep 0.6-mile-long trail to the shore. **Redwood National Park** (707-464-6101).

## Crescent Beach

Crescent City is defined by **Crescent Beach,** a long sweep of sandy beach south of town. This easily accessible beach is justifiably popular with nearby parking, picnic tables, driftwood, and lots of sand for sprawling, strolling, and building sand castles. While swimming is generally not recommended, there are plenty of small- and medium-size waves for novice surfers. Dogs must be leashed, and taking driftwood is prohibited.

**Finding the beach:** From Crescent City, drive south 3 miles and turn right on Enderts Beach Road. Follow it along the coast to a beach-level parking area (GPS: 41.727127 N / -124.152154 W) with picnic tables, restrooms, and a short trail to the beach. **Redwood National Park** (707-464-6101).

# Crescent City

At the north end of Crescent Beach, US 101 bends northwest along the coast and enters **Crescent City**, an old seaport found in 1853. The city, with a 2010 population of 7,643, spreads across the southern end of St. George's Point, a triangular-shaped promontory jutting into the Pacific Ocean. The biggest business for the city, the largest in far northern California, is the Pelican Bay State Prison, a maximum security facility that houses the worst of the state's felons. The prison, opening in 1989 on a site 8 miles north of town, is its largest employer and pumps over $100 million into the local economy, allowing Crescent City and Del Norte County to flourish after long having one of the state's lowest rates of per capita income.

Crescent City and the surrounding area is the tsunami capital of the US, with at least 34 tsunamis or tidal waves occurring between 1933 and 2012. The largest and most destructive tsunami to strike the Pacific coast was on March 27, 1964, after a giant 8.8 earthquake near Anchorage, Alaska. The first wave of water reached Crescent City about 4 hours after the earthquake, but it was the fourth wave which inundated the town, destroying 289 buildings, killing 12 people, and completely erasing 30 city blocks. The last tsunami to hit Crescent City was from the 9.0 earthquake in Japan on March 11, 2011, washing 5 people out to sea, killing one, and causing severe damage to the harbor.

Crescent City, famed for its Easter lily farms, was laid out in 1852 along a crescent-shaped harbor. The town offers a rough, weatherworn look with its cool, foggy days and sea breezes.

## Crescent City Climate

Crescent City basks in a mild but wet climate. The area, one of California's wettest, is bathed in an annual rainfall of 67 inches, with rainy season from October to March. The wettest month is December with 11 inches. Summers by contrast are considerably drier, with July receiving less than a half-inch of rainfall. Temperatures are generally mild but cool with December highs averaging 54°F and August highs 66°F. Only 15 days in winter drop below 32°F, and snow virtually never occurs; the highest snowfall in a day was 6 inches in 1972. When visiting, plan on bringing a raincoat and sweater, even in summer.

## Crescent City Attractions

Attractions and points of interest in Crescent City include **Del Norte County Historical Society Main Museum, Beachfront Park, Battery Point Lighthouse, Ocean World, South Beach, Pebble Beach,** and **Crescent City Harbor**. For more information, stop by or call the **Crescent City and Del Norte County Chamber of Commerce Visitor Center (**1001 Front St., Crescent City, CA 95531; 707-464-3174 or 800-343-8300; exploredelnorte.com).

*An array of sculptures adorn an outdoor art gallery along US 101 across from South Beach.*

## South Beach

**South Beach,** immediately southeast of the Crescent City Harbor, is a popular sand beach that's generally protected from high seas. The beach offers sunbathing (when the sun is out), walking, sunset views, and good beginner surfing waves. The water is cold here though, rarely rising about 59°F so a wet suit is advisable. Nearby on Anchor Way at the pier is **South Beach Outfitters** (877-330-SURF), a surf and gift shop that offers rentals of boards and wet suits. The annual **Noll Longboard Classic Surf Contest** is held here in early October. It's open to surfers of all ages and skill levels, but all surfboards must be over 9 feet in length.

    **Finding the beach:** Park on the west side of US 101 (GPS: 41.745021 N / -124.174502 W) just before Anchor Way on the south side of Crescent City.

*Gentle waves lap onto South Beach, a perfect sand beach for an evening stroll, on the south side of Crescent City.*

## Del Norte County Historical Society Main Museum

The **Del Norte County Historical Society Main Museum** offers a look at northern California's colorful history, including a marvelous collection of Native American basketry from the local Yurok and Tolowa tribes as well as information and photographs of the great tsunami of 1964. The museum is open daily except Sun May through Sept. 577 H St., Crescent City, CA 95531; (707) 464-3922; delnorte history.com.

## Ocean World

**Ocean World,** a private aquarium, is a fun stop for the family. You take a guided tour past various aquariums filled with underwater life, including sharks, eels, rays, seals, and sea lions. Kids will especially enjoy the shark-petting area, performing sea lions, touch-and-feel tide pool exhibit, and having their photo taking in the skeletal mouth of an 8-foot-high shark jaw. 304 US 101 South, Crescent City, CA 95531; (707) 464-4900; oceanworldonline.com.

# Battery Point Lighthouse

**Battery Point Lighthouse,** one of the first lighthouses on the California coast, is a picturesque lighthouse perched atop an isolated rocky isle that juts into the ocean next to the Crescent City Harbor. The islet is connected to the mainland by a narrow rocky isthmus that is washed by high tides. The lighthouse is only accessible by walking across the isthmus at low tide.

The still-active lighthouse was built in 1855 and became operational the following year as Crescent City Light Station when the first oil lamps were lit on December 10, 1856. The lighthouse was automated in 1953 and operated by the US Coast Guard until it was decommissioned in 1965. The light was reactivated to aid navigation in 1982 and has since been open for visitation. The lighthouse and museum are now open for public tours that explore the living quarters of keepers with furniture and artifacts that date to the 1850s as well as photographs and documents and a climb up the light tower.

The classic lighthouse, perched on its windswept rock, is a popular subject for photographers and artists. It's also been used in movies, television programs, music videos, and ads and is often the site of weddings. It's also reputedly haunted by several ghosts. Caretaker Jerry Tugel reported that his slippers, carefully placed beside his bed, were turned around in the morning, which his wife Nadine denied doing. The sound of heavy boots trudging up the lighthouse stairs have also been heard with the lamp turned off afterwards, and some visitors on tours have reported a presence and were touched on the shoulder.

Extreme caution must be taken when visiting the lighthouse since the high tide comes in quickly and waves can inundate the rocky causeway. Also watch for sneaker waves which can knock you off your feet, even when the tide is low. There are no restrooms on the island. The lighthouse is open April through September on Wed to Sun 10 a.m. to 4 p.m. The area is tended by the Del Norte County Historical Society.

**Finding the lighthouse:** The lighthouse is on the Crescent City coast. Access it from US 101/Redwood Highway by turning west on Front Street near the harbor. Follow Front Street to the coast and turn left on SA Street. Drive 2 blocks and park in a lot (GPS: 41.7464 N / -124.201405 W). Walk down a fenced trail to the beach and cross the isthmus to the lighthouse. A couple picnic tables are by the parking and restrooms on the east side of the lot. For information and tours, call (707) 464-3922.

# Pebble Beach

**Pebble Beach** is a long stretch of sand and stony beach that extends northwest from the western edge of Crescent City to the southern edge of the local airport. The easily accessible beach is great for walking, hunting for agates, and sunsets on clear evenings. There are restrooms and tables. It's a popular beach for surfing with its easy access; not recommended for surfing at high tide.

Just south of Pebble Beach is a good overlook opposite **Brother Jonathan Park.** The view includes rocky sea stacks poking above the ocean and a distant view, on a clear day, of offshore **St. George's Reef Lighthouse** 6 miles in the northwest. The *Brother Jonathan,* a sidewheel ship, struck a rock 4 miles west of here in July 1865 and sank. The loss of 225 lives plus the payroll for US Army troops in the northwest make it California's worst maritime disaster. There is also a good view of 19-acre **Castle Rock National Wildlife Refuge,** a rocky uninhabited island that provides refuge for birds and a sea lion rookery.

**Finding the beach:** Access the beach from US 101/Redwood Highway by turning west on 9th Street and drive southwest to South Pebble Beach Drive. Go right on Pebble Beach Drive and drive northwest on the coastal road to several parking areas. The first one overlooks a rocky point (GPS: 41.756773 N / -124.221401 W). Others are farther up the coast on North Pebble Beach Drive.

# Point St. George

**Point St. George** is a spectacular rocky headland that juts into the Pacific Ocean west of Jack McNamara Field, the local airport. The point offers a mix of colorful cliffs, rocky reef, and beach, allowing for exploring tide pools, hiking along the bluff top, great sunsets on clear evenings, and beach walking, although it is not easy to access the beach. Swimming is not recommended due to unpredictable rogue waves, strong undertow currents, and cold water. No facilities are found. The point is a great spot for whale-watching.

**Radio Beach,** named for old radio towers here, is the long stretch of wide beach north of the point. It's lonesome, scenic, and easy to reach by following an old road north to the beach from the parking lot.

**Finding the point:** From Crescent City, follow the scenic Pebble Beach Road north from Pebble Beach or take exit 791 off US 101 and drive west on Washington Boulevard to Pebble Beach Road and turn right or north. Follow the road to a parking lot at its end (GPS: 41.783273 N / -124.25226 W) near the point.

*The historic and haunted Battery Point Lighthouse perches on a rocky isle that can be reached only at low tide.*

# Smith River Scenic Byway

The 33-mile-long **Smith River Scenic Byway** follows US 199 east from Crescent City as it weaves along the Smith River through some of northern California's most beautiful country. The three-forked Smith River, the longest National Wild and Scenic River in the US, arises high atop the Siskiyou Mountains and boasts the distinction of being California's last undammed river system with 315 miles of wild and scenic waterway. The coastal mountains bisected by the river basin are not particularly rocky and high—none reach over 7,000 feet—but they form a rugged tangle of forested ridges that march from the Siskiyou crest almost to the river's floodplain on the Pacific coast. The region is cool, foggy, and wet, with over 90 inches of rain falling a year.

The scenic drive follows the Middle Fork of the Smith River, passing towering redwoods in **Jedediah Smith Redwoods State Park** and traversing **Smith River National Recreation Area.** The 305,169-acre area, in Six Rivers National Forest, protects the region's unique scenery, pristine rivers and creeks, wildlife, fisheries, rich ecological diversity, and historical sites. The Smith River offers excellent fishing for trophy-sized chinook salmon and steelhead trout as well as great rafting. There are numerous hiking trails as well as 5 campgrounds.

**Finding the byway:** Begin near Crescent City at the junction of US 101 and US 199 near Bertsch Terrace. Drive northeast on US 199 past Gasquet and follow the Smith River to the forest boundary south of the California and Oregon border. **For more information,** contact **Six Rivers National Forest** (707-442-1721).

# Jedediah Smith Redwoods State Park

The Redwood Highway, following US 199, leaves US 101 just north of Crescent City and climbs into rounded hills that are covered with towering redwoods in **Jedediah Smith Redwoods State Park.** The 10,430-acre area, California's northernmost redwood parkland, is named for trailblazer, mountain man, and fur trader Jedediah Smith. Smith was the first white man to travel overland from the Mississippi River to the Pacific coast and in 1828 leading a small party and more than 300 horses and mules to Oregon. The party was constantly harassed by Indians who thought the horses were a new type of elk. Eventually, Smith's party reached a beach at today's Crescent City before pushing on to Oregon where Umpquas massacred all but Smith and three men. Comanches killed him 3 years later on the Santa Fe Trail at age 33.

*Tall redwood trees dwarf a leafy rhododendron
in Jedediah Smith Redwoods State Park.*

The park is breathtaking with tall coast redwoods, *Sequoia sempervirens,* rearing up along a narrow, winding road, and a dense understory of ferns, rhododendrons, and azaleas on the forest floor. The park, established in 1929, contains 46 memorial redwood groves. One of the park's largest trees, in **Stout Memorial Grove,** soars 340 feet high with a 22-foot-thick trunk. Other tall redwoods are found in the park, including the **Grove of Titans,** but their location is kept secret to avoid damage and disturbance to these forest giants. **Lost Monarch,** the third largest known redwood, measures 27 feet in diameter at chest height, rises to 320 feet, and contains 34,914 cubic feet of wood.

The park also harbors a stand of rare dawn redwoods, a tree thought to be extinct until discovered in a remote Chinese valley in 1948. A Humboldt State University professor brought these trees from China as seedlings.

The redwoods here flourish along damp riverside terraces above the Smith River, growing in almost pure stands with only shade-tolerant shrubs and trees carpeting their feet. A good stop along the drive is the 0.9-mile-long **Simpson Reed Trail** in the roadside **Simpson Reed Grove.** The path leaves a parking area and winds among the forest giants, passing fallen trunks, dense fern thickets, sprawling vine maples, western hemlocks, huckleberries, and clover-like redwood sorrel.

The drive continues through the redwood groves, and 4 miles from the highway junction, it crosses the Smith River, its placid water skimming over gravel bars. A side road, CA 197, turns north here and follows the river to US 101. A side trip worth taking is the meandering **Howland Hill Road,** a redwood-lined lane that follows Mill Creek southwest to Howland Summit and Crescent City. The road begins in Hiouchi.

The park's main facilities nestle along the Smith River almost a mile east of the highway bridge. Stop at the park **Visitor Center** to get oriented or participate in interpretative activities. Across the highway from the state park visitor center is the larger **Hiouchi Information Center** (707-458-3294) for Redwood National Park; it offers exhibits, natural history, ranger-led walks and talks, a Junior Ranger program, and campfire programs.

A short trail begins at the park visitor center and heads to a swimming beach. It's good in summer but watch for high water and strong currents. The park offers an 89-site campground with restrooms and showers; make reservations at (800) 444-7275, at parks.ca.gov, or through reserveamerica.com. Good picnicking is at an area along the Smith River before the campground. Almost 20 miles of trails stitch the park. The best redwood hikes include 0.6-mile **Stout Grove Trail,** which threads through a cathedral of redwoods, and 5.2-mile **Boy Scout Tree Trail** off Howland Hills Road. There's good fishing for salmon, steelhead, and cutthroat trout; anglers must be 16 and have a valid state license. The state's record rainbow trout was caught here, a 27-pound whopper.

**Finding the park:** The park is northeast of Crescent City. Drive north on US 101/Redwood Highway to a major junction. Go east on US 199 toward Grants Pass, Oregon, into the park. The visitor center and campground area is almost 5 miles from the junction. 1111 2nd St., Crescent City, CA 95531; (707) 458-3018 Entrance Station; (707) 458-3496 Visitor Center.

## Tolowa Dunes State Park

A broad coastal plain, split by the Smith River, spreads north from Crescent City, encompassing **Lake Earl** and smaller **Lake Tolowa.** The two lakes along with a surrounding ancient sand dune field now mostly anchored with vegetation forms 5,000-acre **Tolowa Dunes State Park.**

This diverse area offers various habitats, including beach, sand dunes, vegetated dunes, forested hills, and wetlands which support plentiful birds and wildlife. It's an important stop on the **Pacific Flyway** for migrating birds. The park also includes a 7.5-mile-long stretch of remote sand beach fronting **Pelican Bay**—perfect for solitary hikes. The park has 30 miles of trails for hikers and equestrians and two primitive campgrounds—one for horses and a 6-site walk-in one.

The area is also the ancestral home of the Tolowa Dee-ni' or "The People," a Native American tribe that still lives here at the **Smith River Rancheria** near the Oregon border. The Athapascan-speaking Tolowa were brutally massacred by Anglo-Americans in the 19th century or succumbed to diseases until by 1921 only 120 members were left. Now the tribe has over 1,000 members.

**Finding the park:** The park is 2 miles northwest of Crescent City. In Crescent City, turn off US 101 onto Northcrest Drive and head north. Drive to the north side of town and turn left or west on Old Mill Road. Drive northwest on the road, which eventually becomes dirt, until it ends on the south side of Lake Earl at a turnaround and parking (GPS: 41.838482 N / -124.205672 W). (707) 465-7335.

## Kellogg Beach Park

**Kellogg Beach** is a continuation of the beach at **Tolowa Dunes State Park,** running north a few miles to the Smith River estuary. It's a gorgeous sand beach that is rarely visited and well off-the-beaten track so you will have it to yourself. Any other visitors are usually within a couple hundred yards of the parking area. Windswept sand dunes sprinkled with tall tawny grass back up the beach. It's a great beach for walking and looking at smooth wave-tossed pieces of driftwood. There are no facilities and camping is not allowed, although folks do park their RVs out here overnight. It is often windy so be prepared for cool temperatures.

**Finding the beach:** From Crescent City, drive north on US 101 for about 8 miles. South of the town of Smith River, make a turn to the west on Kings Valley Road and follow it to Lake Earl Drive where it turns into Moorehead Road. Drive straight west on Moorehead until it dead-ends at Lower Lake Road and turn right or north. Drive a short distance and turn left or west on Kellogg Road. Follow Kellogg west until it ends at a beach parking area (GPS: 41.869283 N / -124.21193 W). The route from US 101 to the beach is signed.

## Clifford Kamph Memorial Park

The small **Clifford Kamph Memorial Park,** a Del Norte County parkland, includes a small strip of windy sand beach backed by dunes along with 12 campsites, including walk-in tent and sites at the parking area. The park has restrooms with flush toilets, water, picnic tables, trails, and beach activities. Be prepared for wind.

**Finding the park:** This area is 2 miles south of the Oregon border on the west side of US 101. From Crescent City, drive north on US 101 to the town of Smith River. Continue 4.8 miles north from Smith River through Smith River Rancheria to a marked left or west turn to the roadside area and parking lot (GPS: 41.973502 N / -124.203776 W). (707) 464-7230.

## Pelican Beach State Park

**Pelican Beach** is a remote and unspoiled beach that sprawls along the Pacific coast only a half-mile south of the Oregon border, making it the northernmost beach in California and one of its least visited. The 5-acre undeveloped park offers lots of solitude, sprawling ocean views, excellent offshore fishing, beachcombing, weathered driftwood, and great beach hiking. The beach is open from sunrise to sunset, has no facilities, and has free roadside parking. There are nearby hotels.

**Finding the beach:** Pelican Beach is 21 miles north of Crescent City and a half-mile south of the Oregon border. Drive north from Crescent City and make the last left or west turn before the agricultural inspection station. Drive a short distance to a couple parking areas above the beach (GPS: 41.992641 N / -124.208832W). (707) 465-2145.

# APPENDIX:
# FOR MORE INFORMATION

## General Information

**California Department of Parks & Recreation**
1416 9th St.
Sacramento, CA 95814
(916) 653-6995 or (800) 777-0369
parks.ca.gov

**California Tourism**
PO Box 1499
Sacramento, CA 95812-1499
(916) 444-4429 or (877) 225-4367
visitcalifornia.com

**Los Angeles Tourism & Convention Board**
Hollywood & Highland Center
6801 Hollywood Blvd.
Hollywood, CA 90028
(323) 467-6412
discoverlosangeles.com

**National Park Service**
Pacific West Region
333 Bush St., Ste. 500
San Francisco, CA 94104-2828
(415) 623-2100
nps.gov/state/ca

**San Francisco Chamber of Commerce**
235 Montgomery St., 12th Fl.
San Francisco, CA 94104
(415) 392-4520
sfchamber.com/visitor

**San Francisco Travel**
900 Market St.
San Francisco, CA 94102-2804
(415) 391-2000
sanfrancisco.travel

## Northern Central Coast

**Año Nuevo State Park**
1 New Years Creek Rd.
Pescadero, CA 94060
(650) 879-2025

**Bean Hollow State Beach**
(650) 726-8819

**Big Basin Redwoods State Park**
21600 Big Basin Way
Boulder Creek, CA 95006
(831) 338-8860

**Butano State Park**
(650) 879-2040

**Carmel Chamber of Commerce**
PO Box 4444
Carmel CA 93921
(800) 550-4333
carmelcalifornia.com

**Carmel Mission**
3080 Rio Rd.
Carmel, CA 93923
(831) 624-1271
carmelmission.org

**Fitzgerald Marine Reserve**
200 Nevada Ave.
Moss Beach, CA 94038
(650) 728-3584
fitzgeraldreserve.org

**Forest of Nisene Marks State Park**
Aptos Creek Road/Soquel Drive
Aptos, CA
(831) 763-7062

**Fort Ord Dunes State Park**
(831) 649-2836

**Half Moon Bay State Beach**
95 Kelly Ave.
Half Moon Bay, CA 94019
(650) 726-8819

**Henry Cowell Redwoods State Park**
101 N. Big Trees Park Rd.
Felton, CA 95018
(831) 335-4598

**Manresa State Beach**
(831) 761-1795

**Marina State Beach**
(831) 649-2836

**Mission Santa Cruz**
144 School St.
Santa Cruz, CA 95060
(831) 425-5849
parks.ca.gov

**Montara State Beach**
(650) 726-8819

**Monterey Bay Aquarium**
886 Cannery Row
Monterey, CA 93940
(831) 648-4888
(866) 963-9645 (tickets)
montereybayaquarium.org

**Monterey County Convention and Visitors Bureau**
PO Box 1770
Monterey, CA 93942
(877) MONTEREY
seemonterey.com

**Monterey State Historic Park**
20 Custom House Plaza
Monterey, CA 93940
(831) 649-7118

**Moss Landing State Beach**
(831) 649-2836

**Mystery Spot**
465 Mystery Spot Rd.
Santa Cruz, CA 95065
(831) 423-8897
mysteryspot.com

**Natural Bridges State Park**
Swanton Boulevard & W Cliff Drive
Santa Cruz, CA 95067
(831) 423-4609

**New Brighton State Beach**
(831) 464-6330

**Pacifica State Beach**
(650) 738-7381

**Pacific Grove Chamber of Commerce**
584 Central Ave.
Pacific Grove, CA 93950
(831) 373-3304
pacificgrove.org

**Pacific Grove Museum of Natural History**
165 Forest Ave.
Pacific Grove, CA 93950
(831) 648-5716
pgmuseum.org

**Pescadero State Beach**
(650) 879-2170

**Point Montara Hostel & Light Station**
PO Box 737
Montara, CA 94037
(650) 728-7177
norcalhostels.org/montara.

**Pomponio State Beach**
(650) 879-2170

**Salinas River National Wildlife Refuge**
1 Marshlands Rd.
Fremont, CA 94555
(510) 792-0222
fws.gov/refuge

**Salinas River State Beach**
(831) 649-2836

**San Gregorio State Beach**
(650) 726-8819

**Santa Cruz Beach Boardwalk**
400 Beach St.
Santa Cruz, CA 95060
(831) 423-5590
beachboardwalk.com

**Santa Cruz County Conference & Visitors Council**
303 Water St., Ste. 100
Santa Cruz, CA 95060
(800) 833-3494 or (831) 425-1234

**Santa Cruz County Department of Parks, Open Space and Cultural Services**
979 17th Ave.
Santa Cruz CA, 95062
(831) 454-7901

**Santa Cruz Museum of Art & History**
705 Front St.
Santa Cruz, CA 95060
(831) 429-1964
santacruzmah.org

**Santa Cruz Museum of Natural History**
1305 E. Cliff Dr.
Santa Cruz, CA 95062
(831) 420-6115
santacruzmuseums.org

**Santa Cruz Surfing Museum**
809 Center St.
Santa Cruz, CA 95060
(831) 420-6289
santacruzsurfingmuseum.org

**Seacliff State Beach**
(831) 685-6442

**Seymour Marine Discovery Center**
100 Shaffer Rd.
Santa Cruz, CA 95060
(831) 459-3800
seymourcenter.ucsc.edu

**Sunset State Beach**
(831) 763-7063

**Tor House**
26304 Ocean View Ave.
Carmel-by-the-Sea, CA 93923
(831) 624-1813
torhouse.org

**Wilder Ranch State Park**
1401 Old Coast Rd.
Santa Cruz, CA 95060
(831) 423-9703

**Zmudowski State Beach**
(831) 649-2836

## Big Sur Coast

**Andrew Molera State Park**
Big Sur Station #1
47555 CA 1
Big Sur, CA 93920
(831) 667-2315

**Cayucos State Beach**
(805) 781-5930

**Esalen Institute**
55000 CA 1
Big Sur, CA 93920
(831) 667-3000 or 888-837-2536
esalen.org

**Garrapata State Park**
(831) 624-4909

**Hearst San Simeon State Historical Monument**
750 Hearst Castle Rd.
San Simeon, CA 93452
(800) 444-4445
hearstcastle.org

**Hearst San Simeon State Park**
500 San Simeon Creek Rd.
Cambria, CA 93428
(805) 927-2020

**Julia Pfeiffer Burns State Park**
Big Sur Station #1
47555 CA 1
Big Sur, CA 93920
(831) 667-2315

**Limekiln State Park**
CA 1
Big Sur, CA 93920
(805) 434-1996

**Montaña de Oro State Park**
(805) 528-0513

**Morro Bay Chamber of Commerce & Visitor Center**
845 Embarcadero Rd., Ste. D
Morro Bay, CA 93442
(805) 225-1633
morrobay.org

**Morro Bay State Park**
Morro Bay State Park Road
Morro Bay, CA 93442
(805) 772-2560
slostateparks.com

**Morro Strand State Beach**
(805) 772-2560

**Pfeiffer Big Sur State Park**
Big Sur Station #1
47555 CA 1
Big Sur, CA 93920
(831) 667-2315

**Point Sur State Historic Park**
Big Sur Station #1
Big Sur, CA 93920
(831) 625-4419

**William R. Hearst Memorial State Beach**
750 Hearst Castle Rd.
San Simeon, CA 93452
(805) 927-2020

# South Central Coast

**The Dunes Center**
1065 Guadalupe St.
Guadalupe, CA 93434
(805) 343-2455

**El Capitan State Beach**
10 Refugio Beach Rd.
Goleta CA 93117
(805) 968-1033

**Gaviota State Park**
10 Refugio Beach Rd.
Goleta, CA 93117
(805) 968-1033

**Jalama Beach County Park**
9999 Jalama Rd.
Lompoc, CA 93436
(805) 736-3504

**Pismo Beach State Park**
555 Pier Ave.
Oceano, CA 93445
(805) 489-1869

**Refugio State Beach**
10 Refugio Beach Rd.
Goleta, CA 93117
(805) 968-1033

**Santa Barbara Conference & Visitors Bureau**
500 E. Montecito St.
Santa Barbara, CA 93103
(805) 966-9222
santabarbaraca.com

**Santa Barbara County Parks**
610 Mission Canyon Rd.
Santa Barbara, CA 93105
(805) 568-2462
countyofsb.org/parks

**Santa Barbara Parks & Recreation Department**
620 Laguna St.
Santa Barbara, CA 93101
(805) 564-5418
santabarbaraca.gov

# Marin-Sonoma-Mendocino Coast Scenic Drive

**Audubon Canyon Ranch**
4900 CA 1
Stinson Beach, CA 94970
(415) 868-9244
egret.org

**Café Aquatic**
10439 Hwy 1
Jenner, CA 95450
(707) 865-2251

**Caspar Headlands State Beach**
(707) 937-5804

**Fort Ross State Historic Park**
19005 CA 1
Jenner, CA 95450
(707) 847-3286
parks.ca.gov

**Golden Gate National Recreation Area**
Bldg. 201, Fort Mason
San Francisco, CA 94123-0022
(415) 561-4700
nps.gov/goga

**Jenner Inn**
10400 Coast Route 1
Jenner, CA, 95450, USA
707.865.2377
jennerinn.com/

Jug Handle State Natural Reserve
(707) 937-5804

Manchester State Park
(707) 882-2463

Marin Headlands Visitor Center
(GGNRA)
Fort Barry, Bldg. 948
Sausalito, CA 94965
(415) 331-1540
nps.gov/goga

Mendocino Coast Botanical Gardens
707-964-4352
gardenbythesea.org

Mendocino Coast Chamber of
Commerce & Visitor Center
217 S. Main St.
Fort Bragg, CA 95437
(707) 961-6300 or (800) 726-2780
mendocinocoast.com

Mendocino Headlands State Park
PO Box 440
Mendocino, CA 95460
(707) 937-5804

Mount Tamalpais State Park
801 Panoramic Hwy.
Mill Valley, CA 94941
(415) 388-2070

Muir Woods National Monument
Mill Valley, CA 94941
(415) 388-2595
nps.gov/muwo

Navarro River Redwoods State Park
CA 128
Albion, CA 95410
(707) 937-5804

Point Arena Lighthouse Keepers
45500 Lighthouse Rd.
Point Arena, CA 95468
(877) 725-4448 or (707) 882-2809
pointarenalighthouse.com

Point Cabrillo Light Station State
Historic Park
13800 Point Cabrillo Dr.
Mendocino, CA 95460
(707) 937-5804

Point Reyes National Seashore
1 Bear Valley Rd.
Point Reyes Station, CA 94956
(415) 464-5100
nps.gov/pore

Redwood Coast Chamber of
Commerce
39150 S. CA 1
Gualala CA 95445
(707) 884-1080 or 800-778-5252

Rivers End
11048 California 1
Jenner, CA 95450
(707) 865-2484

Russian Gulch State Park
PO Box 440
Mendocino, CA 95460
(707) 937-5804

Salt Point State Park
25050 CA 1
Jenner, CA 95450
(707) 847-3221
parks.ca.gov

Samuel P. Taylor State Park
8889 Sir Francis Drake Blvd.
Lagunitas, CA 94938
(415) 488-9897

**Schooner Gulch State Beach**
(707) 937-5804

**Sinkyone Wilderness State Park**
(707) 986-7711

**Slide Ranch**
(415) 381-6155
slideranch.org

**Sonoma Coast State Park**
3095 CA 1
Bodega Bay, CA 94923
(707) 875-3483

**Sonoma Coast Visitor Center**
850 CA 1
Bodega Bay, CA 94923
(707) 875-3866
bodegabaytravel.com

**Stinson Beach**
stinsonbeachonline.com

**Van Damme State Park**
(707) 937-5804

**West Marin County Chamber of Commerce**
PO Box 1045
Point Reyes Station, CA 94956
(415) 663-9232
pointreyes.org

## Redwood Coast

**Battery Point Lighthouse**
577 H St.
Crescent City, CA 95531
(707) 464-3089 or (707) 464-3922
lighthousefriends.com

**California Coastal National Monument**
Bureau of Land Management
2800 Cottage Way, W-1623
Sacramento, CA 95825
(916) 978-4636
blm.gov

**Crescent City and Del Norte County Chamber of Commerce Visitor Center**
1001 Front St.
Crescent City, CA 95531
(707) 464-3174 or (800) 343-8300
exploredelnorte.com

**Del Norte Coast Redwoods State Park**
1111 2nd St.
Crescent City, CA 95531
(707) 465-7335

**Del Norte County Historical Society Main Museum**
577 H St.
Crescent City, CA 9553
(707) 464-3922
delnortehistory.com

**Del Norte County Parks Department**
840 - 9 St., Ste. 11
Crescent City, CA 95531
(707) 464-7230

**Fort Humboldt State Historic Park**
3431 Fort Ave.
Eureka, CA 95503
707-445-6567

**Greater Trinidad Chamber of Commerce**
PO Box 356
Trinidad, CA 95570
(707) 677-1610
trinidadcalif.com

**Humboldt Lagoons State Park**
15336 CA 101
Trinidad, CA 95570
(707) 677-3570

**Humboldt Redwoods State Park**
PO Box 100
Weott CA 95571
(707) 946-2409 or (707) 946-2263

**Jedediah Smith Redwoods State Park**
1111 2nd St.
Crescent City, CA 95531
(707) 458-3018 Entrance Station
(707) 458-3496 Visitor Center

**Klamath Chamber of Commerce**
PO Box 476
Klamath, CA 95548
(800) 200-2335
klamathchamber.com

**Ocean World**
304 US 101 South
Crescent City, CA 95531
(707) 464-4900
oceanworldonline.com

**Patrick's Point State Park**
4150 Patrick's Point Dr.
Trinidad, CA 95570
(707) 677-3570

**Prairie Creek Redwoods State Park**
127011 Newton B. Drury Pkwy.
Orick, CA 95555
(707) 465-7335
parks.ca.gov

**Redwood Coast Chamber of Commerce**
39150 S. CA 1
Gualala CA 95445
(707) 884-1080 or (800) 778-5252
redwoodcoastchamber.com

**Redwood National Park**
1111 2nd St.
Crescent City, CA 95531
(707) 464-6101
nps.gov/redw

**Six Rivers National Forest**
1330 Bayshore Way
Eureka, CA 95501
(707) 442-1721
fs.usda.gov

**Tolowa Dunes State Park**
1111 2nd St.
Crescent City, CA 95531
(707) 465-7335

**Trinidad State Beach**
(707) 677-3570

# INDEX